Praise for

Peacebuilding in Community Colleges

"While many in the world of U.S. community colleges innovate, few have led in international innovation, and fewer still in international innovations that directly contribute to peace. David Smith has been a leader in this arena, recognizing the realities as well as the potential of community colleges and their programmatic adaptability for this critical application. *Peacebuilding in Community Colleges* is at once practical and visionary, urging the community college beyond its local mission toward global impact by displaying approaches for making a direct and literal difference in the world. Unquestionably, a useful text for campus internationalization."

—**Paul McVeigh**, associate vice president, Global Studies and Programs, Northern Virginia Community College

"*Peacebuilding in Community Colleges* is a groundbreaking volume that skillfully unites the voices of experts and emerging peacebuilding practitioners in redefining the role of education and positioning educational policy and practice at the core of peacebuilding and conflict resolution efforts. Animating peace theory with authentic and practical examples from a broad cross-country range of U.S. community colleges, Smith and the contributing authors highlight the importance of innovative curricular approaches in affirming the interconnectedness of local and global experiences and narratives and in fostering peace-driven social activism. This 17-chapter volume is a major contribution to the peace education discourse and a very rich resource for any academic program or institution interested in initiating curricular transformation to empower students and faculty to develop the dispositions, skills, and commitments necessary to further the enduring quest for peace."

—**Elavie Ndura**, professor of education and academic program coordinator of the Multilingual/Multicultural Education Program, George Mason University

"This volume conveys not only practical guidance and models for those interested in creating a place for peace studies in the community college curriculum. It also shows how courses and programs focused on peacebuilding connect students, institutions, and communities to what is happening in the rest of the world in meaningful ways. Beyond its intention to offer specific examples of curriculum development and creative pedagogy to community colleges, it shines a wider light on using peace studies as a way to effectively bring global studies to students through substantive issues."

—**Patti McGill Peterson**, presidential advisor, Internationalization and Global Engagement, American Council on Education

"Smith and the impressive group of assembled contributors make a persuasive case that community colleges can serve as frontline academic institutions in the development of globally focused peace and conflict studies programs. Each chapter tells a compelling story with practical lessons for program developers, faculty, and students of peace and conflict studies. Throughout the book one finds insightful responses to program challenges, enhanced collaborative teaching methods, powerful descriptions of experiential learning programs, and the enriched use of technology in delivering courses that engage students in new ways."

—**Brian Polkinghorn**, distinguished professor and executive director, Center for Conflict Resolution, Salisbury University

Peacebuilding in Community Colleges

Peacebuilding in Community Colleges

A Teaching Resource

DAVID J. SMITH
EDITOR

UNITED STATES INSTITUTE OF PEACE PRESS
Washington, D.C.

UNITED STATES INSTITUTE OF PEACE
2301 Constitution Avenue, NW
Washington, DC 20037
www.usip.org

First published 2013

Printed in the United States of America

The paper used in this publication meets the minimum requirements of American National Standards for Information Science—Permanence of Paper for Printed Library Materials, ANSI Z39.48-1984.

Library of Congress Cataloging-in-Publication Data

Peacebuilding in community colleges : a teaching resource / David J. Smith, editor.
    pages cm
  Includes index.
  ISBN 978-1-60127-147-1 (pbk. : alk. paper)
  eISBN 978-1-60127-167-9
  1. Conflict management—Study and teaching (Higher)   I. Smith, David J., 1960 January 3– editor of compilation.
  HD42.P43 2013
  303.6'60711—dc23
                                                        2012049699

Contents

Acknowledgments

This book would not have been possible without the help of many colleagues inside and outside the United States Institute of Peace. Most of all, I want to thank Pamela Aall for her support in recognizing the importance of working with community colleges as a means to increase peacebuilding efforts and raise awareness about the Institute. Also, many colleagues took time to review chapters. My deepest thanks to Linda Bishai, Bev Blois, Skip Cole, Ann-Louise Colgan, Nadia Gerspacher, Stephanie Hallock, Jeff Helsing, Raina Kim, Matt Levinger, Alison Milofsky, Mary Hope Schwoebel, Dominic Kiraly, Peter Weinberger, Mike Daher, Kurt Hoffman, Wade Watkins, Lexi Almy, and many others. And, of course, all the chapter authors have my eternal thanks for their tireless efforts at writing, rewriting, and dealing with my ever shorter deadlines. Finally, I want to thank my wife, Lena, and our children, Lorenzo and Sonya, for their love, support, and patience while I pursued this project.

David J. Smith

PART ONE

MAKING CONNECTIONS

1

Teaching Peace in Democracy's Colleges

DAVID J. SMITH

Education is the most powerful weapon which you can use to
change the world. —*Nelson Mandela*

This book examines the convergence of two rising phenomena that have important implications both for Americans and for internationals in promoting a future society that is stable, safe, and peaceful. The first is the emergence of community colleges as a major force in educating individuals of all ages, ethnicities, cultural groups, and personal circumstances, using approaches that promote global awareness—whether by fostering appreciation and understanding of international events and thereby increasing public engagement, or by honing aptitudes and instilling attitudes that can be used to secure employment in an increasingly globalized world. The other phenomenon in play is the increasing importance of promoting broad-based educational strategies to advance the work of peace. As communities continue to be prone to conflict and violence, education is playing an increasingly important role in promoting worldviews, teaching personal and professional skills, and supporting local capacities that foster stability and build peace. And two-year colleges, because of their open enrollment, ethnic and cultural diversity, adaptability to changing societal needs, and focus on community building, are increasingly being seen as a critical linchpin in these efforts' success.

In the United States, increasing student cultural and ethnic diversity is challenging educators to focus on personal and group conflict and violence, not only in local contexts but also in distant communities where immigrant populations originate. Thus, teaching peace today in community colleges has both local and international dimensions. A useful approach for viewing the work of peace today is through the lens of peacebuilding. Peacebuilding is broadly defined as the "full array of processes, approaches, and stages needed to transform conflict toward more sustainable, peaceful relationships" (Lederach 1997, 20). It may encompass a range of strategies, including "providing humanitarian relief, protecting human rights, ensuring security, establishing nonviolent modes of resolving conflicts, fostering reconciliation, providing trauma healing services, repatriating refugees and resettling internally displaced persons, supporting broad-based education, and aiding in economic reconstruction" (Snodderly 2011, 40). Community colleges, through their missions and strategies, can play an important role, not only in raising awareness of peacebuilding activities but also in providing students and public audiences with skills and foundational knowledge on which successful professional careers and personal engagement can be built. The next generation of community activists, conflict resolvers, peace educators, humanitarian workers, and others working to promote a better world can start their peacebuilding journey in community colleges—and many of them will.

Community colleges in the United States are often referred to as "democracy's colleges" (Boggs 2010). This moniker stems from both the objectives of community colleges and the populations they serve. Established in the early twentieth century, these institutions provide educational offerings for all but, in particular, the middle and lower socioeconomic strata of society, which are bourgeoning today because of social mobility and immigration. A successor to the populist Chautauqua educational movement, which was characterized by holistic public education, community colleges today are viewed as places where education is available to all, regardless of one's position or station in life. Today, *lifelong learning* (providing learning opportunities to all, including adult learners) and *developmental education* (promoting education to increase reading, writing, and computational abilities, frequently among marginalized and disadvantaged groups) are fully integrated into their identities and missions. Whether working in rural or urban communities, with minority populations, with women, or with immigrant groups, community colleges have been true to their original purpose: to serve the aspirations of those most in need of broad-based education and vocational training.

While community colleges have become a fixture on the American educational landscape, the concept of using education to promote peacebuilding is relatively new, though the actual work of peacebuilding has a longer history. Working within societies to promote stability and creating opportunities for citizens has long been an important goal of the international community, particularly in post-conflict environments. The first modern major global effort was an American one: the Marshall Plan after World War II, which used a primarily economic strategy aimed at bringing hope and stability to postwar Europe. The Marshall Plan had important long-term implications for building in Europe a society that enshrined respect for human rights and promoted broad-based democracy. Arguably, the political and economic integration of Europe resulting in the European Union was seeded by this large-scale effort. In the years since the Marshall Plan, the United States and the greater international community have focused on societies emerging from conflict, with the objective of creating stability and peace. United Nations Secretary-General Boutros Boutros-Ghali, in his 1992 manifesto "An Agenda for Peace," argued for peacebuilding as a critical obligation of the international community, particularly in societies emerging from internal strife (Boutros-Ghali 1992). Since then, peacebuilding has taken on a broader interpretation, meaning not only efforts in post-conflict environments but also the wide array of strategies that are employed to prevent conflict (Levinger 2010).

The role of education in teaching peace in the postsecondary environment has been carefully examined.[1] Though there is clear consensus that teaching about peace has important value, targeted efforts at the community college level were lacking in the past.[2] In community colleges today, teaching about global peace finds a close alliance with international education. Nevertheless, efforts to promote globally educated students have been uneven. Attempts to strengthen global education have been launched by an array of organizations, including the American Association of Community Colleges (AACC), Community Colleges for International Development (CCID), and the American Council on International Intercultural Education (which merged with CCID in 2007), working with such philanthropic groups as the Stanley Foundation. However, many efforts by community colleges are nascent if they exist at all. Global education has, at times, been difficult to emphasize in community colleges, where local concerns and priorities dominate.

The field of peace studies in U.S. academia is over sixty years old, and the related field of conflict resolution dates from the 1980s. Manchester College established the first undergraduate program in peace studies in 1948, while George Mason University is often thought of as having the first graduate program in conflict resolution, establishing a master's degree program in 1981 and then a doctoral program 1988. It is now estimated that there are nearly 100 graduate programs in conflict resolution, peace studies, and related fields in the United States, with another 85 in other parts of the English-speaking world (Salisbury Univ. 2007). Although Berkshire Community College (MA) established a program in 1982, until recently few established programs at the community college level focused on teaching students about peaceful approaches to conflict, and the skills of conflict resolution (see box 1.1).

---

1. See Aall, Helsing, and Tidwell 2007; McElwee et al. 2009; Harris, Fisk, and Rank 1998; Harris and Shuster 2006.
2. See Smith 2008, 63-78; but see Lincoln 2001, 37-39.

Box 1.1: Early Efforts

The current efforts at building peace and conflict initiatives at community colleges have built on the visionary work of others. Starting in 1990, the League for Innovation in the Community College supported the development of peace and global studies efforts through its "Educating for Global Responsibility" project. The effort consisted of faculty development workshops and efforts at curriculum design. Projects were started at Dallas County Community Colleges, Miami Dade Community College, Cuyahoga Community College, Kern County Community College District, and Lane Community College. These efforts were led by Barbara J. Wien and Edmund J. Gleazer Jr., president emeritus of the American Association of Community Colleges.

The programs began with local conflicts, which had broader regional, national, and global dimensions. Faculty workshops and curricula then demonstrated how these deeply rooted conflicts could be resolved using peaceful approaches and a conflict resolution lens. Many leaders and grassroots sectors were sought out and engaged in brainstorming, problem solving, and consensus building at forums and in study circles to generate creative solutions. As a result, community colleges became laboratories for fostering peacemaking skills and educating for social and global responsibility.

Programs and initiatives have started to emerge, and as of 2012, twenty-one exist across the United States. (See appendix B.) With nearly 1,200 community colleges currently enrolling nearly 8 million credit students—44 percent of all U.S. undergraduates—there is much room for growth (AACC 2012). Many of these students attend community colleges for vocational education and, hence, will likely not participate in further formal education upon completing their program. For this reason, the window of opportunity available for students pursuing vocational careers is small, and it is vitally important that faculty take advantage of it. As this book will reveal, the lack of peace and conflict programmatic efforts available for either career or transfer students does not reflect a lack of faculty and institutional motivation or innovation.

This book represents a commitment by the United States Institute of Peace (USIP) to support community colleges in giving their students the opportunity to study complex issues of global conflict and promote peacebuilding, through teaching and training as well as through example and practice. As a congressionally established national institution, USIP is charged to serve America "through the widest possible range of education and training, basic and applied research opportunities, and peace information services on the means to promote international peace and the resolution of conflicts among the nations and peoples of the world without recourse to violence."[3] To that

---

3. *U.S. Institute of Peace Act,* Title XVII of the *Defense Authorization Act of 1985,* Public Law No. 98-525 (Oct. 19, 1984), 98 Stat. 2492, 2649, 22 U.S.C. 4601-4611, as amended.

Box 1.2: USIP Collaboration

In 2010, at Henry Ford Community College in Dearborn, Michigan—a city where nearly 40 percent of the population is of Arab descent—USIP cosponsored a seminar on teaching conflict resolution and peacebuilding in an Arab-American cultural context. USIP has also sponsored seminars focused on peacebuilding in Arab and Muslim contexts at Mission College in California (2009), Madison Area Technical College in Wisconsin (2008), and Minneapolis Community and Technical College and Century College in Minnesota (2007).

At Northern Virginia Community College (2007), USIP held a seminar titled "Identity and Global Conflict: Implications for the 21st Century," which focused on the challenges facing diaspora groups. Nearly 170 ethnic and cultural groups are represented at the college.

At Richland College in Texas (2006), USIP held a seminar titled "Global Responsibility: How Educating for Peace Fosters a Better World."

Working with nine community colleges, USIP held a seminar on teaching about global conflict for the South Carolina International Education Consortium in Columbia, South Carolina (2000).

end, starting in the 1990s, the Institute sponsored faculty development opportunities designed to build capacity in community colleges for teaching and building peace. These efforts took two basic forms. The first consisted of weeklong seminars that brought faculty and administrators together to explore war and peace and approaches on how to bring these issues into the classroom. During these programs, participants were tasked with developing projects that they would implement at their colleges. More frequent than the weeklong seminars were focused workshops collaborating with community colleges and associations around the United States. These more localized approaches often resulted in the convening of local organizations and constituents that had not worked together before but now realized the great potential of collaboration with a community college in achieving important goals. These events often had a specific focus such as a regional conflict (e.g., in the Middle East or Africa), looked at that conflict through a specific ethnic, cultural, or religious lens (e.g., that of an Arab expatriate community), or examined a specific discipline or approach to promoting peace (e.g., human rights or peace studies) (e.g., box 1.2). Frequently, a seminar had elements of all three approaches. Also, the Institute has offered its expertise in helping community colleges design sustainable efforts to teach about the field. These combined efforts have resulted in Institute staff working directly with more than 200 two-year institutions across the United States. These multiple approaches have fostered a community of educators working for peace. In working closely with community colleges, USIP has been able to increase peacebuilding awareness not only in these institutions but also, more importantly, in the diverse communities they serve. These efforts continue today through the Institute's Global Peacebuilding Center and Academy for International Conflict Management and Peacebuilding.

This volume is designed to guide the community college professional, whether a junior faculty member searching for her teaching niche, a senior administrator looking to promote the college with new audiences and environments, or a trustee exploring how to set his college apart from others. The authors, for the most part, are education leaders who have participated in USIP programs and have succeeded in translating their experiences into tangible efforts at their institutions. Their writings are augmented by those of experts in the fields of peace studies and global education who know community colleges well and can speak to their potential in teaching about global peacebuilding. Each chapter endeavors to tell a story of how a community college can play an essential role in promoting peace. Together, these stories serve as a guide to community colleges in developing their own visions of teaching about peace.

Structure of the Book

This book is designed to consider a range of strategies for developing peace-building efforts in community colleges. It functions as a how-to for faculty and administrators considering practical and tested ways to transform the teaching and learning environment. With this in mind, most chapters are augmented by materials that can provide the starting point for community college professionals.

Part 1, "Making Connections," introduces the reader to different authors' notions of the field and how it intersects with international education. John Paul Lederach's chapter provides insights to his own path to peacebuilding which was first nurtured at Hesston College, a two-year school in Kansas. George A. Lopez's chapter provides a primer on the current forces in the field, and how they can be considered in a community college context. Both Lederach and Lopez are with the Kroc Institute for International Peace Studies at the University of Notre Dame. Kent A. Farnsworth, recently retired endowed professor of community college leadership at the University of Missouri St. Louis, argues for constructivism as a learning theory and as the necessary bridge between the need to find peace and the global world we live in. Farnsworth also traces the work that has been accomplished in community colleges to promote global education.

Part 2, "Building Programs and Initiatives," reviews specific programmatic ways of making peacebuilding studies a structural part of a college. Abbie Jenks, from Greenfield Community College in western Massachusetts, and Jeff Dykhuizen, from Delta College in mid-Michigan, present their models on developing academic programs in global peace studies. Both programs also look at peace through an ecological lens, thus demonstrating the ability of community colleges to develop curricula that are responsive to community and societal needs. Jennifer Batton, director of Cuyahoga Community College's Global Issues Resource Center in Cleveland, and Susan Lohwater, who teaches at the same institution, tackle the process of developing a coherent peace and conflict studies program for students. They focus on the steps that might be required to launch a program that has specific career and skills-based objectives. Kara Paige and Tu Van Trieu collaborate to look broadly at teaching peacebuilding and conflict resolution in the community college setting. They discuss the strategies of San Antonio's Northwest Vista College and Howard Community College in Columbia, Maryland, for teaching about conflict resolution. Karen Davis writes about the experiences of Pasco-Hernando Community College's community-focused Peace and Social Justice Institute and the lessons learned, particularly as they relate to the Florida college's annual Peace Week. Vasiliki Anastasakos of Northampton Community College in Pennsylvania, drawing on her experiences in Turkey and Costa Rica, shows how students and faculty can engage in peace-focused study abroad. Finally, Scott Branks del Llano, from Richland College in Dallas, shares his school's experiences in teaching English as a peacebuilding objective in Mozambique, which suffered a brutal civil war in the 1980s.

In part 3, "Educating Peacebuilders," the writers focus on pedagogical approaches they have used to create engaging and rigorous classroom experiences. Jennifer Haydel and John Brenner, faculty members at community colleges in suburban Maryland outside Washington, D.C. (Montgomery College), and rural Virginia (Southwest Virginia Community College) respectively, provide guidance to approaches for teaching in demographically different environments. Human rights and international humanitarian law are considered together in a chapter by Cindy Epperson, of St. Louis Community College, and Isabelle Daoust, formerly of the International Humanitarian Law Unit of the American Red Cross. Sarah Zale, of Shoreline Community College in Washington State, and Jane Rosecrans, of J. Sargeant Reynolds Community College in Virginia, share their approaches to teaching peace within a humanities context: Zale through English composition and Rosecrans through religious studies. Paul Forage discusses his efforts to establish at Indian River State College in Florida a humanitarian training center designed to give students hands-on experience working in conflict zones such as Haiti. An aspect of his program involves taking students to Macedonia for a two-week extended role-play immersion activity in a simulated humanitarian crisis. Whittier College's Joyce Kaufman developed the

International Negotiations Modules Project (INMP) in the 1990s to provide experience for community colleges using Web-based negotiations, and Gregory P. Rabb of Jamestown Community College in New York has been using INMP with his students for over fifteen years. Their chapter explores the benefits of the program, and opportunities for engaging students in simulation-based learning. Barbara Thorngren and Michelle Ronayne, both New Hampshire educators, examine the pedagogical approaches necessary to promote learning in a peace and conflict-themed classroom.

The final section, "Future Implications," provides a common frame for community college efforts, discusses important trends among those efforts, and presents future challenges that must be faced, and opportunities that can be leveraged. Two appendixes are included: the first is a list of resources that colleges can consider in developing peacebuilding strategies, and the second lists colleges that are supporting peace and conflict programs and initiatives, thereby showing the growth of the field, particularly in the past five years.

For the teaching of peace in community colleges to get a firm footing, more path clearing and foundation building is still needed. The contributors hope that this book will serve as an important and useful resource for professionals as they consider furthering the community college mission of globally educating students and encouraging them to see themselves as peacebuilders in their professional and personal lives.

References

Aall, Pamela, Jeffrey W. Helsing, and Alan C. Tidwell. 2007. "Addressing Conflict through Education." In *Peacemaking in International Conflict*, ed. I. William Zartman. Rev. ed. Washington, DC: United States Institute of Peace Press.

American Association of Community Colleges (AACC). 2012. "Fast Facts." www.aacc.nche.edu/AboutCC/Pages/fastfacts.aspx.

Boggs, George R. 2010. "Democracy's Colleges: The Evolution of the Community College in America." American Association of Community Colleges, Aug. 19, 2010. www.aacc.nche.edu/AboutCC/whsummit/Documents/boggs_whsummit brief.pdf.

Boutros-Ghali, Boutros. 1992. "An Agenda for Peace, Preventive Diplomacy, Peacemaking and Peace-Keeping." Report of the Secretary-General, June 17, 1992. www.unrol.org/doc.aspx?n=A_47_277.pdf.

Harris, Ian M., Larry J. Fisk, and Carol Rank, eds. 1998. "A Portrait of University Peace Studies in North America and Western Europe at the End of the Millennium." *International Journal of Peace Studies* 3 (January).

Harris, Ian M., and Amy L. Shuster, eds. 2006. *Global Directory of Peace Studies and Conflict Resolution Programs.* 7th ed. San Francisco: Peace and Justice Studies Association and International Peace Research Association Foundation.

Lederach, John Paul. 1997. *Building Peace: Sustainable Reconciliation in Divided Societies.* Washington, DC: United States Institute of Peace Press.

Levinger, Matthew. 2010. "Enhancing Security through Peacebuilding." *Great Decisions 2010* New York: Foreign Policy Association, 93-102.

Lincoln, Melinda. 2001. "Conflict Resolution Communications." *Community College Journal* 72 (3): 37-39.

McElwee, Timothy A., B. Welling Hall, Joseph Liechty, and Julie Garber, eds. 2009. *Peace, Justice, and Security Studies: A Curriculum Guide.* 7th ed. Boulder, CO: Lynne Rienner.

Salisbury Univ. 2007. "Graduate Programs in the Field of Conflict Resolution." www.conflict-resolution.org/sitebody/education/grad.htm.

Smith, David J. 2008. "Global Peace, Conflict and Security: Approaches Taken by American Community Colleges." *Journal of Peace Education* 5 (1): 63-78.

Snodderly, Dan, ed. 2011. *Peace Terms.* Washington, DC: United States Institute of Peace.

2

Launching a Career in Peacebuilding

JOHN PAUL LEDERACH

So hope for a great sea change on the far side of revenge. Believe that a further shore is reachable from here. Believe in miracles and cures and healing wells. —*Seamus Heaney,* The Cure at Troy

I attended Hesston College in the school years of 1973–75. In those days, we referred to it as a "junior college," but I don't think there was anything junior about it. At the time, it would not have occurred to me that going to Hesston was anything less or more than heading off to the next level of school. Mostly it was independence. Well, sort of—I grew up in Hesston, Kansas, a town that has mostly maintained a population of about three thousand people and whose primary industries focus on agriculture and farming in this part of the American central plains. I did not have far to go from home to my dorm room. My parents taught at Hesston College, and we lived at the edge of campus. But the journey in those first years of college-level studies opened a world of possibility I would never have imagined or expected when I first started.

Hesston College's theme, displayed prominently in brochures and banners across the campus, states, "Start here. Go everywhere." This was certainly my experience.

I have often wondered what created this opening in the formative years of my career. Having now taught extensively in universities and having done a lot of adult education in different parts of the world, I find two things to be true about learning.

First, I have come to believe that every individual learner finds her- or himself on a unique journey of awareness, something both below and beyond knowledge. Paulo Freire called this "conscientization," which translates as becoming cognizant of self in the world. This kind of awareness sparks the imagination about who I am, what I know and can learn, what is happening around me, and how I can respond. It links trust in self and critical understanding with action. For most of us, experience with this kind of insight comes in doses and moments—from elementary school, when we learn to read our first words and have this sense of empowerment, to the impact of a particular book that "opens" our eyes, to perhaps a classroom discussion when we say something we didn't even know we knew. The moment constitutes an epiphany with a life-changing quality. We emerge from these moments with eyes and hearts that see the worlds within and around us differently.

Second, I believe that this unique journey poses a challenge for education. As educators, we cannot control or predict when the epiphany moments will emerge. It is quite possible for a student to dominate the content of any topic and not have an epiphany. And it is quite possible for a student not to understand the content fully or even adequately and yet have an epiphany. This thing I call "epiphany" is not about the more visible "head" side of education. It is about the heart's way, the powerful nexus that links heart, head, and spirit.

For educators, the two ingredients that have the greatest potential to create the environment for the heart's way to open are authenticity and trust. We may teach in a thousand different ways and styles—from lectures to lab experiments—but when, as educators, we share a sense of our passion and we are present as authentic people, something transformative happens.

On the other side of this relationship, we find learners, people seeking to understand and grow. What we may forget too readily is that learning requires vulnerability. As learners, we constantly must be at the edge of what we know and have experienced. By definition, learning contains what anthropologists call a liminal experience—to live in the space between the known and the yet to be. As learners, we must venture into the place not yet known. What a good educator will provide is the encouragement to venture toward the edge and the safety net of trusting that the world does not end if you fall. Trust creates a platform. Try. If you fall short—and we all have—get up and try again. This is the core of learning. We can't do it for you, but we will be here with you.

Hesston College opened my heart's way. I had my first adult epiphanies on this campus of some five hundred students. Looking back, I can see several keys.

Keys: Why Hesston College Made a Difference

The first key had mostly to do with the accessibility, responsiveness, and passions of my professors. For the most part, classes were small and intimate. I remember quite a few of them in my freshman year that took up topics that engaged me in new ways. I found consistently that whenever I really wanted to talk more about something it was easy to find teachers and have a conversation.

To be honest, I was in a period of my development where I had lots of questions—about faith, politics, the "system," power, and ethics. I can remember questioning about half of what I was required to read or learn. While Hesston College comes from a Christian, Mennonite tradition and espouses those values (a tradition that I share and that can, of course, be quite sectarian in its view of faith and engagement of the world), I never found narrow-minded or rigid professors. But I did find people who, while they had questions, were comfortable in their own skins and who never saw the pursuit and inquiry of truth as contradictory with the expression of their faith, even if some of the inquiries radically questioned faith itself. I can, in fact, remember the class one late morning when, in a round of discussions that must have bordered on the radical, the professor asked, "What does the word 'radical' mean?" Most quick responses circled around words such as "revolution" and "extreme." One of my classmates was from Argentina, with Spanish as his native tongue. He said quite simply, "The Latin origin of the word 'radical' is 'root.' It means to go deep, to get to the root, the essence of something." I will never forget that epiphany. I wished I spoke Spanish. I wished I had some notion of Latin. And I suddenly had the whole of a different inquiry before me: how do we get to the root, the essence of things?

My professors were passionate about their topics. That passion came in many forms, but I experienced it by sensing their excitement about something they were teaching. They were not just thinking about it; they were doing it. I suppose this comes with the Mennonite ethos. Where I grew up, if you have a barn full of manure, you don't much sit around and discuss the nature and origins of manure—you get a pitchfork and clean it up. The same ethos seemed true of the topics covered in my early requirements. Most of my profs were actively engaged in doing something in the areas they taught.

I had one professor whose life was art and clay. I was so inspired by his passion for art, I almost became a potter—in fact, I may yet go back to that someday. His care for craft, his eye for form, and his engagement of art remained with me for a lifetime. I had another, much older professor who taught English and literature. She had all the features of my grandmother from Pennsylvania: hair pulled back in a tight bun and classic Mennonite dress. She loved Shakespeare. I approached the class as a requirement, with a "need to survive" and very low expectations. In our first session, she spontaneously broke into Shakespeare, a long section recited without hesitation. I was transfixed, and the room suddenly seemed filled with something transcendent. I will never forget the moment. *Epiphany*. And I will not forget, eight weeks later, reciting a page and a half of Shakespeare by memory, or what I felt seeing her bobbing, approving nod.

A second key in my development emerged around courses that engaged the theology and practice of peace. The Mennonites, considered one of the historic peace churches, come from a long tradition of pacifism. By osmosis and exposure, I would have assumed for many of my early years that our theology was good, understood, and clear. But it was never my own until I emerged from the first two formative years at Hesston College.

The curriculum did not have a specialty degree in the area of peace studies, though certainly courses and intensive seminars were offered that gave me an introduction to aspects of the wider field. But I consistently found that my required classes engaged questions related to social change, faith, and the ethics of peace and violence. For the first time, I interacted with people who felt passionate about these topics. And who disagreed! I read books that discussed the varieties of views of what is right and wrong with active nonviolence, war, and peace. And I found myself increasingly drawn to these topics, with a passion not just to study it but to do something about it, and opportunities arose. In the course of two years through the specialized intensive weekends, I met and spent time with people involved in nonviolent direct action to end the Vietnam war and in civil disobedience to end the production of nuclear weapons, and with theologians who espoused the way of traditional *nonresistance* and *separateness,* who would view contemporary nonviolence as a form of political engagement to be held at arm's length. The range of exposure required and permitted me to take my first steps in forming my own understanding.

A third key emerged around pedagogical innovation. This small campus experimented with learning methods in a variety of ways. We had access to a January term that carried us from the Midwest to parts unknown. We had intensive seminar weekends that would bring in the most unexpected visitors and lecturers. We had class assignments in the general education sequence, known at the time as Foundation Studies, that required us to read, discuss, and do. Take the topic of empathy, for example. We were asked to do something that would have us experience the reality of another person's life different from our own. Some blindfolded themselves for a day. Others spent time with people from an entirely different language or ethnic group. My roommate and I decided we would see what it was like to be broke and destitute. We agreed to take one dollar each and hitchhike to Oklahoma City and back. I don't think this is what our professors had in mind, but we thought it best not to ask permission. It took us more days than expected. We slept under bridges, panhandled for food, and generally "Jack Kerouac-ed" our way home. I think it served us well. The one thing I will not forget is a waitress on the outskirts of Oklahoma City who gave us a full breakfast out of her pocket money when she saw us devour the single order of toast we could afford. Even today when I tip, especially in small restaurants with people who look as though they may well be working their "second job," I always try to leave more than required. Generosity does pay forward.

In January 1974, I participated in a monthlong class in the Middle East, traveling through Lebanon, Egypt, Jordan, Palestine, and Israel. The exposure to refugee camps, the edges of war, and the challenges of conflict entered my life for the first time. A year later, January 1975, I spent a month in the inner city of Washington, D.C. We didn't immerse ourselves in the power politics of the Capitol. We were dropped into the life of poor communities and racial divides. My education in those experiences went from head to heart. I felt something calling and pulling. The pursuit of this call, which, at the time, I thought should carry me back to the Middle East, led to a hiatus—leaving my academic career for three years to do voluntary service abroad. I never did make it back to the Middle East, but the passion sparked in those J-term exposures led me to learn three languages and pursue a vocation dedicated to finding better ways to respond to conflict, social division, and violence. By the time I came back to finish my undergraduate degree, it was clear that I wanted to focus on peace and conflict studies. Academic degree programs on these topics were not easy to find in the 1970s. And questions abounded about what exactly you will do with a peace studies degree, but the passion sparked early on at Hesston College never left me with a doubt.

Final Reflections

I am writing this short chapter in Nepal. The peace process that ended a ten-year civil war here is reaching yet another landmark crisis as we barrel down the calendar toward May 28, 2011, the deadline set for writing a constitution and completing the integration of combatants. Neither commitment has been accomplished. It will be a week of intensive negotiations. This week again—the thirtieth visit I have made to Nepal over the past eight years—I recognize how easily I could say, "Toto, I've a feeling we're not in Kansas anymore." Yet I carry part of Kansas with me. It will soon be forty years since I entered Hesston College, but it has been present at nearly every stage. I eventually completed an undergraduate degree in peace studies and history and a PhD in sociology. I have prepared myself as a mediator and facilitator. I have written twenty-some books and manuals on peacebuilding. I now teach at the University of Notre Dame's Kroc Institute for International Peace Studies and continue to support Eastern Mennonite University's Center for Justice and Peacebuilding. I have conducted training workshops on conflict and peacebuilding in more than thirty countries. This week in

Nepal, I will sit with high-level politicians, trying to find a way through their disagreements, and I will sit with grassroots communities working on natural resource conflicts over water, forests, and land. It's my daily bread.

I think it accurate to say it all started at Hesston College. I learned simple lessons from my professors that go beyond the materials, books, and classes from those years.

Follow your passions.
Trust your questions.
Believe in the power of conversations.
Start here. Go everywhere.

3

Challenges of Building Peace Studies in the Early Twenty-First Century

GEORGE A. LOPEZ

It isn't enough to talk about peace. One must believe in it. And it isn't enough to believe in it. One must work at it.   —Eleanor Roosevelt

Academic Peace Studies: The Moment Is the Movement

The systematic studying and teaching about peace challenges faculty and students to come face-to-face with numerous puzzles and dilemmas that both engage and transcend the time we live in. Concerning teaching, the perennial questions emerge, which every peace studies program should be addressing: What causes war? What drives people to embrace systematic violence? So, too, peace studies should ask, what brings peace? Is the answer found in the hearts of people, or does it stem from the creation of large-scale mediating institutions? Can peace come only at the end of a long war?

These are worthy organizing queries for programs, whether their higher-education home is in the Ivy League; a major land-grant university; a small, church-affiliated liberal arts college; or a community college. This book concerns the last of these, with their rich diversity ranging from large and growing urban-based institutions to smaller rural and suburban campuses. While the institutional mission of each academy will lead its faculty to structure its own distinct peace studies program and courses, addressing the queries I have posed will likely be at their core.[1]

That doesn't mean the conceptual foundation for modern peace studies should be confined to only these essential puzzles. Rather, twelve years after the tragic events of September 11, 2001, the conceptual parameters of peace studies must also include the current "violence and peace *problematique*" as it unfolds in our place and time. This demands a concern not only for terrorism

---

An earlier version of these ideas was delivered in a presentation to students and faculty of the University of Bridgeport's Global Development and Peace program, March 4, 2010.

1. For a survey of trends on many campuses, see McElwee et al. 2009. For community colleges, see Smith 2008.

but also for global warming, gang or warlord-style violence, and the effects of war on civilians in far-flung locales, as well as on the armed forces members who were its combatants.

This contemporary dimension of peace studies embraces concerns about human, national, and global security in a world of diverse violence, as well as methods of conflict resolution and the study of peacebuilding that this young century has thrust on us as a nation. It is clear that the study and teaching of peace poses numerous questions related to the perennial ones but refined for the current circumstances. Thus, "What causes war?" must yield classroom and research time to "Why would some people opt to be suicide bombers?" And ultimately, "What are the effects of suicide bombings on those living close by or in service units where it occurs?"

This is a difficult and challenging time for those interested in the study of peace, justice, and the building of secure and functional relationships among people who have vast differences. Yet the difficulties can be expressed or addressed in different ways, such as through the use of violence. Also, since this is the country we are teaching and learning in, it is essential for us to grasp the importance of the American experience.

While peace studies have often been criticized for being too "present minded," the post-9/11 decade does point to something significant, troublesome, difficult, opportune, and imperative about the study and teaching of peace in an American culture that has experienced a prolonged "war on terror." And on the basis of this experience, we can and must renew and revitalize the conceptual foundations of our field. This is a moment that can indeed give way to a movement of curricular and program redefinition, where educational institutions such as community colleges are already on the front lines of this movement. They represent the diversity of the United States in many ways and also are a first stop for returning veterans reentering the educational system.

Old Critiques and New Responses

Many Americans view the teaching, study, and learning of peace as an unhelpful pursuit, arguing that what we should be concerned about is how to deal with our enemies and preserve American national security. They view the study of peace as the beginning point of a concession to enemies, as well as an incorrect perception of the challenges and puzzles that exist in the real world.[2]

---

2. The premier example may be Bruce Bawer, "The Peace Racket," *City Journal*, 2007 (Summer): 1–7.

It is important to tackle such concerns directly in approaching the systematic study and teaching of peace. One of the first challenges that we hear maintains that the study of peace becomes important only in times of war. The study of peace, some argue, is not an academic discipline of any consequence or substance except when people are politically bothered by government policies, especially concerning national security. This line of argument goes on to claim that students and faculty demonstrate an interest in the teaching and study of peace because they are essentially antiwar activists. If there were not a war, students and professors would not be studying peace. Thus, to study and teach peace is an inherently political, not academic, exercise. The actual focus, this argument concludes, is not honest academic inquiry but, in essence, a dissident social and political commentary.

But such an assertion is actually not borne out by the empirical evidence. Between 1948 and 1980, over 160 peace studies programs were established in the United States. While a significant number were driven by concerns about the tensions between the communist and noncommunist worlds in the Cold War and by research interests in what led to war, most of these peace studies programs were inspired by the nonviolent achievements of Mohandas Gandhi and were reinforced by the experience of the U.S. civil rights movement. And in the late 1960s and 1970s, many of these programs studied how to build a peace system based on world order values, including rejection of war, economic development, affirmation of culture and human rights, and protection of the environment.

When young scholar-teachers completed graduate studies in peace studies at that time, they did so within a traditional disciplinary PhD structure, and not at the master's degree and practitioner level that came into vogue after the 1990s. Their focus was to understand world systems theory, intersocietal communications theory, or contending theories of mediation. They sought to understand how systems that are moving toward greater complexity might do so under conditions of harmony and order rather than of violence. Thus, their actual academic focus was not President Lyndon Johnson and his Vietnam policies. Their main interest was not whether the major powers should be intervening in the affairs of small states. In some respects, peace studies was remarkably apolitical.

The second wave of collegiate peace studies was the growth in programs during the 1980s. According to some critics, this expansion could be explained as a reaction to the arms race policies of Ronald Reagan. However, an examination of the curriculum of programs developed in the 1980s reveals a different focus. New programs that were developed focused heavily on conflict management, mediation, and resolution. This trend reflected the "growth industries" of various sectors in the United States, from environmental mediation to alternative dispute resolution in the legal profession. And most pronounced, of course, was that this new trend reflected the ongoing direct experience of U.S. communities as one outcome of the civil rights era. Conflict resolution programs of the 1980s were the local-global connection as many communities shifted their focus from race to housing, to better schools and economic opportunity. This was done not through riots and demonstrations, and sometimes not even through Martin Luther King Jr.'s approach of civil disobedience. Instead, it came about through the efforts of mediators from the churches, from community relations services, and from other local institutions. The practice of dispute resolution—of conflicting parties learning how to mediate their disagreements—became a desirable skill, for which peace studies programs served as an important base of citizen education.[3]

The final phase of this local-global connection of conflict resolution and the heritage of the civil rights era was bolstered by a nearly twenty-five-year set of events occurring outside the United States. The revolutions of change during 1988 through the early 1990s, with one or two geographic exceptions, were remarkably nonviolent. Bloodbaths had been predicted in some of these situations but did not materialize. Thus, beyond teaching techniques of mediation and negotiation, peace studies investigated how such markedly nonviolent change happened and scrutinized the strategies that proponents of change employed to defeat tyrants. Similarly, there was a need to explore which were the institutions and structures of change in Poland, Hungary, the Philippines, and South Africa.

People in these societies with disparate cultures, religions, and economic backgrounds, many of whom did not have university degrees, had found ways to create nonviolent transitions and institute dramatic changes to their governmental systems. The quarter century of focus on these processes brings us to the people engaged in the Arab Spring of 2011–12. There is little doubt that these actors were studying practitioner texts, like those of Gene Sharp, whose work has been a classic for peace studies courses in the United States for decades. But Sharp and his students consistently conducted workshops in Europe, and their methods were also being taught by the U.S. Agency for International Development (Stolberg 2011).

Another critique about peace studies is that when faculty get in the classroom with students, they essentially profess, "Peace is the answer, so what are the questions? Let there be peace!" Those who make this type of assumption about the teaching in peace studies classrooms fail to appreciate, or even to know about, the open disagreement about peace and the ways to achieve it that parallels and enlivens academic debates about core issues in other

---

3.   For an analysis of these peace studies program trends in varied forms, see Lopez (1989).

disciplines. It is also fair to note that disagreements about the pedagogy and the substance of peace studies have never been confined to academic battles within this transdisciplinary enterprise. Any faculty person who has been to an academic peace conference knows that sometimes the teachers of peace and conflict resolution are poor role models for their field, since our arguments can be deep, divisive, and bitter.

Part of the misunderstanding or misconception may be due to the gulf—if not a directly oppositional disposition—between the concepts of peace and security. We have narrowed the concept and understanding of "security" to mean not only national security in its clearest narrow sense but to mean society untouched by the specter of violence or threats to society. But operating under such an assumption, we fail to recognize that we live in a world where all of us have vulnerabilities to violence. And this shared vulnerability demands a systematic analysis of peace and of the scope of security.

One of the great dangers of the past decade in American society is that we have come to equate peace with security. One of the challenges we thus face, in our communities and in our learning environments, is how to deconstruct security and the dynamic of peace and blend the two more sensibly, beginning by not assuming that the former is preferred over the latter. We then need to find their commonalities and also their disparities. National security elites cannot embrace protesters. National security elites have no interest in exploring the conditions under which suicide bombers see their activities as not only logical but moral, and as a major contribution to the future security of their families and communities. One of the meeting grounds of this tension lies in the concept of human security, and another occurs when we emphasize the "local-global" connection of our guiding concepts and concerns.

To follow the global-local connection through in all our communities invites questions about the activities that we pursue in the name of security globally, and the extent to which these activities enhance security for people locally. Conversely, we must explore whether those factors or forces that provide security for us locally also contribute to security globally. The legitimacy of this approach is that it reflects the realities unfolding currently in the United States, where the post-9/11 situation has led community after community to confront problems of intercultural and interreligious conflict and dialogue. Intercultural councils and various efforts by school systems also try to deal with these dual issues of intercultural peace and security unfolding within their doors.

Since the major problems in the world run across boundaries, to teach that one can protect one's own national security in a world of global *inse*curity is incomplete at best and an outright myth at worst. What we can

protect and foster, and must develop, is *human security*. And so we can anticipate more and more peace studies scholars and more and more students and
faculty studying and researching the concept of human security.

A different point of emphasis in program development—and one in
which peace studies critics can take some solace—has emerged since the
mid-1990s. Like it or not, there are many ways in which the arguments for
peace and its tools of conflict resolution have failed to prevent war or related
violence. The teaching and study of peace is more and more the teaching and
study of how to build sustainable peace *after* violence has destroyed communities and societies.

In these post-conflict situations, there is a need for individuals and institutions focused on rebuilding local peace and security, often within the framework of wider efforts toward global security. These situations demand a coali-
tion of insiders and outsiders who will contribute to institutions that focus on
postviolence peacebuilding in all its micro dimensions. This is why the non-
governmental organization (NGO) community has become so important to
such efforts, and why so many of our students seek internships and jobs in
NGOs: because that's where the action is! In a very real sense, this expands
the pool of disciplines and professions that contribute to peace. Whereas,
in the 1980s and 1990s, the focus was conflict resolution, now it is conflict
resolution *plus* conflict transformation and postviolence peacebuilding.

Postviolence peacebuilding requires our peace studies curricula to include psychologists who understand trauma and healing. We will also need
social psychologists who understand what happens to group identity after
terrible experiences of violence. We will need lawyers who inquire about
who should be held accountable for violence and its aftermath. Anticipat-
ing the devastated economies of a post-conflict society, we will need people
in business and economics who can help lessen the perception of risk that
potential investors have and help them understand how their investment
can indeed bring positive returns. We need students who major in education as well as peace studies to help build new curricula, train teachers, and
create textbooks in war-torn societies, so that the historical explanations and
hate-filled stereotypes that fueled the violence are replaced with more constructive approaches.

Community Colleges and Peace Studies

These conceptual and practical issues of academic peace studies in the
twenty-first century set the context in which community colleges have entered our field. The growing number of community college programs is important for the interdisciplinary field in at least two ways. First, if, as they say,

all politics is local, then surely all concerns about violence, security, and peace are local as well. And those colleges that are created specifically to service the "local" represent an important and growing forum for each of the challenges and points of debate mentioned earlier. Also, community colleges represent a diverse demographic—both in the types of colleges and in those who attend them—that very much intersects with the ideas of the changing nature of security, the dynamic of conflict resolution, the tensions between learning by action and staying in the classroom, and the dilemma of peacebuilding after violence.

Regarding the changing nature of security, this particular phenomenon in all its fragility and fickleness has manifested all too well for many communities the past few years. As some of the most diverse teaching and institutional environments in higher education, community college classrooms allow faculty to make the most of pedagogical opportunities that are right at hand in their students' experience. In rural, smaller community colleges, the debates about the meaning of peace and security discussed above often come up; in larger urban colleges with diverse ethnicities, different discussions reflecting these students' actual experience will unfold.

These pedagogical opportunities permit faculty to explore the early fissures that exist within communities and their experiences with violence and security. Being deeply embedded within these communities, these colleges can explore the ethnic, religious, and class differences that are plainly apparent locally but exist only on a more theoretical level in some university environments. This discussion can also be extended to an analysis of the students' larger global-local connections, such as exploring the dramatic increase in local violence across the Mexican border.

These concerns are amplified by the changing economic climate facing the United States over the past three years. Historically, those who pursue community college often do so while working either full- or part-time because their socioeconomic circumstances do not lend themselves to more expensive options in higher education. Thus, themes of the relationship between a recession-based economic climate, substantial violence, and community conflict abound.

These themes also reinforce the challenges of the changing nature of security issues mentioned earlier. A faculty member in a league liberal arts college or at a midsize private university would be more dependent on *New York Times* headlines to discuss the realities of the economic recession and unemployment with their students than would the average faculty member in a community college classroom. That reality makes a confrontation with the substance and methods of peace studies much more relevant in the community college.

The community college environment is thus ripe for the exploration of different venues in which conflict resolution skills become important. Students can be introduced to the need for tolerance, dialogue skills, and the specification of clear negotiating positions, as well as the utility of mediation and reconciliation. Their experience may show them the importance of community mediation centers that help ethnic groups resolve their disputes. And a peace studies program may provide the experiential learning opportunities for students to build their skills at such a center. In this, students witness the need for more use of alternative dispute resolution mechanisms in the court systems, particularly regarding youthful offenders. Thus, they may have options to study or work in very important reconciliation and mediation options that matter to their local community. Finally, of course, conflict resolution often is an important part of the structure of the local school system, given its first-line status for communal conflict.

Perhaps the most poignant and personal example of the local challenge of peacebuilding after war unfolded at community colleges as we all confronted what it meant to commemorate the tenth anniversary of September 11, 2001. While many of these institutions are geographically and emotively distant from New York or Washington, many focused on how we as Americans assessed our motives, our behavior, and our prospects for success in the multiple wars we have experienced of late. This is an important question of inquiry in its own right that will span courses in political science, philosophy, film, and psychology.

But this question is likely to take on greater meaning at a community college level because these institutions are becoming the first line of entry into higher education for many returning veterans and for family members of veteran households. In the case of returning veterans, there will be both the young persons who decided to skip college and enter the military in order to earn money for college, and those simply seeking to take a course or two in the local environment to "clear their head." Or the class may include students who had joined the National Guard to gain resources to attend college and were "activated" while enrolled. In the most difficult cases, of course, a student may have been stop-lossed and retained for two or three rotations in the wars of the past decade.

I doubt that faculty like me, who have taught in quite different academic situations, will have anything in our yellowed notes or our PowerPoint presentations that would be adequate to this situation. Fortunately, the pedagogy that it calls for reflects the style often discussed by John Paul Lederach as central to conflict transformation itself: it elicits from those in the room their deepest sentiments and preferred worldviews. Then it builds from this reality—not from some predetermined definition—a working description of peace (Lederach 1997).

Moreover, in light of the emerging statistics for family conflict and divorce, community colleges are likely to experience people in the classroom who have dealt firsthand with a veteran who comes back from war quite different from the family member who departed.

The pressures that individuals experience in their life situations often lead them to seek courses such as conflict resolution and peace studies because these classes blend a deeper concern for a wider environment with a close and often painful personal experience. It is the ultimate linkage of the local and the global that peace studies has historically been able to address. Whether this pattern within community colleges will reach the level that I believe it may, thus creating both opportunities and dilemmas for both the classroom and student services, remains to be seen. What is certain, however, is that the community college will be at the forefront of addressing and experiencing the returning U.S. military veteran in ways that other institutions of higher education will not.

A quarter century ago, Chad Alger, one of the patriarchs of modern peace research, wrote an article entitled "Peace Studies at the Crossroads: Where Else?" Alger's intention was to state that peace studies is at its best when it confronts dilemmas and puzzles for which there are no easy solutions. In fact, if we are groping with the tensions between what the theories tell us and our lived experience that brings the theories into question, then that tension and crossroad is exactly where we in peace studies teaching should be. Many of us believed that this tension may have been just a function of the coming end of the Cold War or the shifting dynamic of violence from large nation-state to nonstate actors (Alger 1989).

We could not have been more wrong. In all its cultural, social, and economic dimensions, the intensity of the local-global connection that operates at the end of the first decade of the twenty-first century is beyond what we anticipated decades ago when modern peace studies took form. There are many new opportunities for peace studies in these trends. Tackling them opens the way for more traditional disciplines to bring their core concepts, themes, and findings to bear on peace issues. Moreover, America's recent experience in a large and amorphous global war on terror, along with two specific-theater wars in Iraq and Afghanistan, has presented us with substantial, if not unprecedented, pedagogical and societal challenges.

As a result, our fundamental understanding of what peace comprises or what security comprises has been shaken to its core. As academics who teach in this society, many of us worry that our thinking and our disciplinary tools lag behind the peace challenges of our time. We fear being inadequate to the questions and experiences that our students bring to the classroom. The settings that most directly experience this may be in the college classroom at the community level. This points to peace studies indeed being at a crossroads, because community colleges are the crossroads of America. Alger was correct: where else would we want to be?

References

Alger, Chadwick F. 1989. "Peace Studies at the Crossroads: Where Else?" In Lopez, *Peace Studies,* 117–27.

Lederach, John Paul. 1997. *Building Peace.* Washington, DC: United States Institute of Peace Press.

Lopez, George A., guest ed. 1989. *Peace Studies: Past and Future. Annals of the American Academy of Political and Social Science* 504, no. 1.

McElwee, Timothy A., B. Welling Hall, Joseph Liechty, and Julie Garber, eds. 2009. *Peace, Justice, and Security Studies: A Curriculum Guide.* Boulder, CO: Lynne Rienner.

Smith, David J. 2008. "Global Peace, Conflict, and Security: Approaches Taken by American Community Colleges." *Journal of Peace Education* 5 (1): 63–78.

Stolberg, Sheryl Gay. 2011. "Shy U.S. Intellectual Created Playbook Used in a Revolution." *New York Times,* Feb. 16.

4

Peace, Conflict Resolution, and the Essential Need for International Education

KENT A. FARNSWORTH

If we have no peace, it is because we have forgotten that we belong to each other.   —Mother Teresa

In a world as widely troubled, violent, and unsettled as the one we live in, virtually all of us at one time or another have found ourselves asking, "What will it take to bring peace to the world? Is it even possible? Is there anything I can do personally to contribute to that peace in a significant way? Can I do something to learn to be more successful or skillful as a peacebuilder?"

Among the writers of this book is a general feeling that the answers to these questions lie within ourselves and our institutions and in our obligation as educators to help students, our colleagues, and our colleges understand that the pursuit of peace is a collective responsibility. This chapter suggests that a critical part of the internal process that leads one to be a seeker of peace comes from becoming a globally aware citizen—someone who understands other peoples and cultures well enough to appreciate what motivates them to behave and react as they do. To be seekers of peace, we must first be seekers of understanding. And to understand the rest of the world, we must provide education that is global in scope and emphasis.

Basic Principles of Peacebuilding

Although other chapters discuss the history and development of peace and conflict studies in greater detail, a brief review here of several key principles will help make clear why, if we are to establish a more peaceful world, we must educate a globally competent student. Since the earliest work of peace and conflict resolution theorists such as Johan Galtung and Morton

Deutsch in the mid-1900s, three assertions have been foundational to this area of study. The first and most fundamental is that one cannot pursue peace by attempting to eliminate all conflict, since conflict is an inherent part of human interaction. Writing a quarter century before Galtung and Deutsch, pioneering management theorist Mary Parker Follett maintained that conflict is inevitable wherever people hold differences in beliefs or points of view. She preferred the word "difference" to "conflict" and, in a lecture delivered to the Bureau of Personnel Administration in 1925, asked her audience to see conflict (difference) "as neither good nor bad; to consider it without ethical prejudgment; to think of it not as warfare but as the appearance of difference—difference of opinions, of interests. For that is what conflict means: difference" (Follett 1973, 31). Distinguished peace and conflict scholar Ron Fisher echoes Follett's sentiments that difference is neither intrinsically good nor bad, and notes that "the absence of conflict usually signals the absence of meaningful interaction" (Fisher 2000).

This acknowledgment that conflict is part of normal human interaction leads to a second critical principle of peace and conflict studies: that since conflict or difference will always exist, seeking peace is the process *not* of eliminating conflict but of finding strategies that effectively resolve differences as they arise. Daniel Katz notes that these differences generally arise from one or more of three sources: economic interest, clash in values, or desire for power. Economic conflict involves competition for scarce resources. Values conflict develops when there is recognized incompatibility in beliefs, principles, or commonly held practices. Power conflict is a struggle for influence, with one party wishing to dominate or control another (Fisher 2000).

The third foundational principle important to this discussion is that resolution of conflict, no matter what its origin, can be categorized as a lose-lose solution, wherein none of the parties to the conflict gains satisfaction; a win-lose solution, wherein some parties are satisfied and others are not; or a win-win solution, wherein all parties are satisfied and feel that the particular area of difference has been resolved to the benefit of all. Each of these solutions reflects a balance between how parties weigh their own concerns or interests against the concerns of others involved in the conflict. Peace results when strategies are developed that account for the concerns of all parties and that address them in ways acceptable to each. Matthew Levinger, when describing the process of peacebuilding, notes that "a peaceful society is characterized by the ability to create and sustain *relationships* based on reciprocal respect and a sense of shared interests among diverse elements of the community" (Levinger 2000, 94).

Finding Win-Win Solutions

How, then, do win-win solutions arise? Morton Deutsch observes that "constructive processes of conflict resolution are similar to cooperative processes of problem solving" and that constructive resolution occurs when parties can see their goals as being positively interdependent and their conflicts as mutual problems, and demonstrate this recognition as they interact (Deutsch 2000, 27). The tone and gestures that one brings to the table when seeking resolution help determine whether efforts will be constructive or competitive, and whether the resolution will be one of ongoing contention, compromise, mutual withdrawal, yielding by one party, or a solution that satisfies the concerns of all.

What, then, inclines a party in a conflict to approach the resolution with a desire to seek a win-win solution, rather than one that is only one-sidedly beneficial? Reason tells us that the better we know and understand what motivates another to act in a certain way, the more inclined we will be to consider these motives when faced with a conflict—raising the fundamental question of how we come to know another's motives, beliefs, and attitudes. In essence, how do we learn about those elements of the other parties' lives, cultures, attitudes, and beliefs that would enable us to "think as they do"?

Constructing Understanding

Constructivism, an approach to learning theory championed by Swiss psychologist Jean Piaget and American educator John Dewey, provides a useful model for coming to know others. Stated very simply, constructivism maintains that what we know is "constructed" through a series of progressive and additive experiences, beginning in childhood. Through these experiences, we construct a network, or "scheme," of understanding, into which we fit new information as it comes to our attention through additional experiences. The depth and breadth of our learning and knowledge, and of our ability to understand, appreciate, and infer based on that knowledge, is limited or broadened by the nature and extent of our experiences and by the scheme we create to organize and give meaning to them.

A variation on the constructivist model that has gained significant attention during the past half century, and that was best articulated by Russian psychologist Lev Vygotsky in the 1920s, suggests that the experiences that lead to learning are sociocultural interactions and that learning occurs only within these social contexts. Human action and learning are mediated within a sociocultural context by language, systems of counting and measuring, art forms, maps, and other symbolic conventions that are products of the culture or cultures with which the learner has experience. As learners, our knowledge base is essentially *framed* by our culture, by the culture's symbolic conventions, and by the extent to which we are exposed to other cultures (John-Steiner and Mahn 1996).

If we apply constructivism—and particularly Vygotsky's sociocultural version—to conflict resolution, we recognize that for a party in a conflict to enable a win-win solution, that party must first have some experience with the sociocultural symbols and context of the other parties in order to understand and appreciate what they will view as suitable solutions. As a simple example, consider a neighborhood spat between two families over a dog that continuously digs in the other family's garden. If the families are not acquainted with each other, the offended family (family A) is likely simply to inform the offending family (B) that the dog needs to be restrained or else family A will find a way to get rid of the dog. If the families know each other and have had a long and amicable relationship, family A may be aware that the dog is a generally good-natured and beloved pet of B's two children. Even though the families may have different political views, may attend different churches, and may see the world through somewhat different lenses, family A will still be much more inclined to work with family B to find a way to keep the dog out of the garden without injuring the animal, taking away the children's beloved pet, or damaging the relationship between the two families. The same principles apply to finding win-win solutions to international conflicts. The better we know each other as citizens of differing cultures, the more inclined we become to seek conflict solutions that satisfy all involved.

Building Understanding through Global Education

And yet, as a generalization, Americans know remarkably little about other peoples and cultures and have not made learning about the sociocultural symbols and contexts of our global neighbors a priority in our education systems. Teachers and parents often know as little about the rest of the world as do students, leading children to grow up in a social and cultural environment empty of experiences that teach them about the world beyond their community or national boundaries. As a result, since we have such limited understanding of the values and symbolic contexts that frame others' thinking, Americans faced with international conflicts are ill equipped to seek win-win solutions.

Compare this lack of citizen preparation and understanding with that of two young Dutch teachers the author met in a public market in Cambodia several years ago. Both had just completed their college training to become middle school teachers but had taken six months off to travel in Southeast

Asia before beginning their careers. They were spending a month in each of six countries, beginning in Thailand and traveling through Laos, Cambodia, Vietnam, Malaysia, and Indonesia. When asked why they had chosen to delay their teaching for such a lengthy excursion, they appeared surprised by the question.

"Asia has become increasingly important to the rest of us and to our futures," one said. "If this is the world we are going to be teaching our students about, don't you think it important that we understand it ourselves?"

Unlike these two young Dutch women, students entering community colleges are often particularly impoverished in second-language education; geographic knowledge; world religions, history, and culture; and international travel. Yet for more than half these students, their time spent at the community college will be the totality of their college experience. If community colleges fail to provide some of the global sociocultural context that will broaden students' network of learning experiences, it will not happen. But how can that be done within the framework of the community college's mission, role, and scope?

Seeing the World as Community

Three realities provide ample justification for including global education as an essential component of every community college mission, program, and degree. The first is that our understanding of the new nature of *community* demands it. The second is that if we truly are committed to helping every student succeed, we fail in that commitment if we do not prepare each to function successfully in a world that is increasingly interdependent yet also conflict ridden. The third reality is that peacebuilding and global diplomacy are multifaceted and, at their best, involve high-level officials working in peace talks, treaties, and other agreements; unofficial but influential individuals or groups working to bridge gaps between governments and societies; and people-to-people diplomacy that encourages interaction and understanding to raise awareness at the grassroots level while empowering broader civic action toward peace. The third leg of this multitrack diplomacy can exist only if common citizens have a level of comfort with other cultures that promotes this interaction (USIP 2011).

Our first responsibility as educators is to help students recognize that our community is the world. No matter how rural, isolated, or remote a college community might view itself to be, its businesses, farms, and families are engaged in international commerce. Personal communication devices owned by 80 percent of the adults in the community connect them instantly to global markets, international social networks, and the people who produce and populate those markets and networks. The fruit and flowers they buy are as likely to come from Latin America as from Florida or California, components of their electronic purchases are from Asia, and service support may come from either of these regions. The *community* for virtually every community college has become global, meaning that the successful graduate must be prepared to compete globally as well as locally.

The second reality noted above—that we must prepare each student to function successfully in an increasingly interdependent world—is given greater specificity in a 2006 report by the National Leadership Council for Liberal Education and America's Promise. In this report, a panel of international experts maintains that for twenty-first-century learners, being prepared for the new century's challenges will demand "knowledge of human cultures and the physical and natural world" (AACU 2006). The report maintains that if we fail to provide this basis of knowledge in human cultures and language, we fail to familiarize students with the new *community* in which they will be living and working, and with those who will share this community with them.

The third reality, that diplomacy and peacebuilding are multifaceted endeavors that include person-to-person interactions by common citizens, recognizes that if a segment of the population is unable to participate ably in these interactions, we lose a critical tool in our peacebuilding tool kit. The Institute for Multi-Track Diplomacy, founded by retired ambassador and active peacebuilder John W. McDonald, presents as its first principle that "building strong interpersonal and intergroup relations throughout the fabric of society is essential for promoting a peacebuilding process, engaging people in promoting civil society and assuring the success of a wide range of projects" (IMTD 2012). With almost half of all first-time college students beginning their postsecondary education at community colleges, we greatly compromise our national ability to seek peace if we fail to prepare these students to become engaged in the diplomacy of global conversation. To meet these challenges, institutions must begin the process of reshaping their own internal communities and creating a new culture of their own. Before we can reshape the thinking and experiences of our students, we must change our institutions.

The Role of Leadership

Through a major national community college initiative entitled "Achieving the Dream," aimed at closing performance gaps between students from disparate ethnic and socioeconomic backgrounds, scholars examining the process of institutional change have recognized the need for four essential elements if an institution is to reshape its internal culture. These elements are committed leadership, broad faculty engagement, internal capacity building through professional development in areas related to the desired cultural change, and both willingness and ability to scale up small projects and programs to the level of full institutional involvement. A 2007 study by Gavin O'Connor found that committed leadership was central to internationalization efforts at community colleges. It also found a strong relationship between leadership and faculty engagement in global education, and personal international experience. Without committed leadership, international programming was difficult to implement and even harder to sustain. Even faculty members who had strong interests in developing and supporting international experiences for students had difficulty doing so without strong support from senior administrators and the board (O'Connor 2009).

Resources for Globalizing Learning

When that leadership does exist, colleges committed to creating these experiences for their faculty, students, and leadership team will find that excellent planning resources already exist and are backed by a number of global education support organizations (O'Connor 2009).

Of these, three national associations created to connect college personnel with international ideas, colleagues, and partnerships deserve specific mention: the American Council on International Intercultural Education (ACIIE), Community Colleges for International Development (CCID), and the Midwest Institute for International/Intercultural Education (MIIIE). A fourth noteworthy initiative, conducted in the 1990s but still affecting community college internationalization, was a program of education sponsored by the Iowa-based Stanley Foundation, which defined what "global education" should mean for community colleges and how each might organize to make it a critical mission element. Although there are others, we discuss these four particular organizations and initiatives in detail, as examples of resources that can assist colleges in providing the cross-cultural exposure so critical to peacebuilding attitudes.

In November 1994, the Stanley Foundation, an internationally respected advocacy group for peace initiatives and global education, sponsored the first of two groundbreaking conferences for community college leaders at the Airlie Center in Warrenton, Virginia. Sponsored in collaboration with ACIIE, the conference sought to clarify community college goals in international education and develop a recommended action plan that all community colleges could follow to implement international and intercultural programming (Stanley Foundation 1994). Two years later, a second Airlie conference, entitled "Educating the Global Community: A Framework for

Community Colleges," sought to define what it means to be a globally competent learner and to describe what colleges must do to produce students with these attributes.

Conference participants determined that the globally competent learner

- is empowered by the experience of global education to help make a difference in society;
- is committed to global, lifelong learning;
- is aware of diversity, commonalities, and interdependence;
- recognizes the geopolitical and economic interdependence in our world;
- appreciates the impact of other cultures on American life;
- accepts the importance of all peoples;
- is capable of working in diverse teams;
- understands the nonuniversality of culture, religion, and values; and
- accepts responsibility for global citizenship (Stanley Foundation 1996, 3).

In essence, the globally competent learner possesses the tools needed to seek win-win solutions as differences arise between peoples and cultures.

With the two Airlie conference reports as guides and discussion pieces, Stanley Foundation Senior Program Officer Jack Smith convened a series of state-specific global education seminars in nearly half the states, bringing together senior leadership teams from each college in the state. The seminars acquainted college officials with national organizations and resources that support global education, helped develop campus-specific action plans, and organized statewide college consortia to support continuing activity in international programming and services.

The Missouri Consortium for Global Education continues as a successful example of the fruits of the Stanley Foundation initiative. Serving as a subunit of the Missouri Community College Association, this consortium emerged from the Stanley Foundation's state workshops and has since obtained two federal Title VI-A grants and a Fulbright-Hays project grant that have supported nearly 100 faculty members in gaining international study experience. These faculty members have systematically infused curricula across the state with global content and have expanded foreign-language learning among Missouri community colleges through distance-learning courses in critical language areas such as Arabic and Chinese. College representatives meet quarterly to exchange programming ideas and study-abroad opportunities and to work on collaborative funding opportunities for larger initiatives.

This work by the Stanley Foundation received broad support and encouragement from two of the national associations mentioned earlier: CCID and ACIIE. CCID, organized initially in 1976 as the Community College Cooperative for International Education, continues to provide opportunities for member colleges to develop international partnerships that aid with technical training, economic development work, and faculty and student exchange. In addition to its U.S. membership, CCID includes college representatives from more than a dozen other countries and coordinates international projects around the world (CCID 2012).

Founded within a year of CCID, ACIIE advocated for community colleges in the global arena, with a specific emphasis on faculty and curriculum development. It has since been absorbed into CCID, and its mission of curriculum development now continues as a focus area within the broader consortium. Through membership in CCID, community colleges have sponsored international student and faculty groups' visits to their campuses, placed their own faculty members in international settings throughout the world, and given U.S. students study-abroad opportunities that have fostered the cross-cultural perspectives that are foundational to global appreciation and understanding.

Perhaps the association that now most specifically maintains a focus on curriculum development in international education and on faculty preparation is MIIIE. The institute's stated mission is to support global education through "curriculum and professional development by organizing curriculum workshops, fall and spring conferences, overseas projects for faculty and students, assistance with grant development," and faculty mentoring and professional networking (MIIIE 2012). It annually coordinates a series of faculty study-abroad projects through the Fulbright-Hays program, coordinates international teaching opportunities, and sponsors conferences and workshops that guide teachers through the process of introducing international concepts and themes into their courses.

For institutions interested in enhancing international diversity on campus and sending students abroad, the relatively new Center for Global Advancement of Community Colleges (CGACC) connects colleges with international students interested in studying in the United States and educates these students about the value of beginning their college careers in our community college system (CGACC 2010).

Globalizing Mission

But the availability of national support groups and conference reports that detail the desired attributes of a globally competent learner serve little purpose without commitment to global education at the college level. As with the change agenda sought by the Achieving the Dream initiative, institutional changes in global education will occur only with committed leadership, broad faculty engagement, institutional efforts to build capacity through providing international experiences for both faculty and students, and a willingness to scale up small boutique projects in global education until they become part of the institutional fabric. This chapter began by asking the question "What will it take to bring peace to the world?" As community college educators, we have been bold in proclaiming that we are the education resource for our communities, that the public can turn to us for transfer preparation, for job training, for personal enrichment education, and for community development. But these were mission elements defined by the limited "community" of the twentieth century. As we prepare students for the new, globally integrated community of this century, we need them to know that they can turn to us for a rich and engaging education that prepares them to live successfully in an interdependent world that acquaints them with human cultures and languages and with an understanding of the processes that lead to conflict resolution and enduring peace. If we are to be the true community colleges of the new century, we have an obligation to prepare our students to live peacefully in the community of the information age—a community that includes all nations and peoples. To do less is to fail our students, our nation, and our world. To succeed is to pave the way for a brighter, more promising, and more peaceful future.

References

Association of American Colleges and Universities (AACU). 2006. "College Learning for the New Global Century." National Leadership Council for Liberal Education and America's Promise. www.aacu.org/leap/documents/GlobalCentury_final.pdf.

Center for Global Advancement of Community Colleges (CGACC). 2010. Mission statement. www.cgacc.org/.

Community Colleges for International Development (CCID). 2012. "CCID International News." https://programs.ccid.cc/cci/.

Deutsch, Morton. 2000. "Cooperation and Competition." In *The Handbook of Conflict Resolution: Theory and Practice,* ed. Morton Deutsch and Peter T. Coleman. San Francisco: Jossey-Bass.

Fisher, Ron. 2000. "Sources of Conflict and Methods of Conflict Resolution." International Peace and Conflict Resolution School of International Service, the American University, ca. 1977, rev. 1985, 2000.

Follett, Mary Parker. 1973. *Dynamic Administration: The Collected Papers of Mary Parker Follett,* ed. Elliot M. Fox and Lyndall Urwick. London: Pittman.

Institute for Multi-Track Diplomacy (IMTD). 2012. "Peacebuilding through Collaboration." www.imtd.org/at-a-glance/mission/.

John-Steiner, Vera, and Holbrook Mahn. 1996. "Sociocultural Approaches to Learning and Development: A Vygotskian Framework." *Educational Psychologist* 31 (3): 191–206.

Levinger, Matthew. 2000. "Enhancing Security through Peacebuilding." *Great Decisions, 2010.* New York: Foreign Policy Association, 93–102.

Midwest Institute for International/Intercultural Education (MIIIE). 2012. "Midwest Institute." www.miiie.org/.

O'Connor, Gavin. 2009. Internationalization of General Education Curriculum in Missouri Community Colleges: A Faculty Perspective. PhD diss., Univ. of Missouri St. Louis.

Stanley Foundation. 1994. "Building the Global Community: The Next Step." Conference report, Muscatine, IA, Stanley Foundation. www.stanleyfoundation.org/publications/archive/CC1.pdf.

———. 1996. "Educating the Global Community: A Framework for Community Colleges." Conference report, Muscatine, IA, Stanley Foundation. www.stanley foundation.org/publications/archive/CC1.pdf.

United States Institute of Peace (USIP). 2011. *Peace Terms.* USIP. http://glossary.usip.org/resource/tracks-diplomacy/.

PART TWO

BUILDING
PROGRAMS AND INITIATIVES

5

Global Peace Studies

JEFF DYKHUIZEN AND ABBIE JENKS

*Education is that process through which we glimpse what might be
and what we ourselves can become.* —*Betty Reardon*

Peace Studies in Community Colleges

Many students come to a community college for the education and training they need to find a job. Marie came to Greenfield Community College (GCC) as a human services major. She wanted to get on a career path,
and since she was involved in the social service field after taking custody of
her 10-year-old niece, she chose this major. A nontraditional student, Marie
confessed early on that she was pursuing this course of study because financial support was available for the certificate program, not because it was her
passion. She had come from a home filled with violence, and caring for her
niece had recently cost her her job in marketing. Now she had to reconfigure
her life path. Marie came to GCC with feelings of anger, hurt, and despair,
not only from her personal experience but also because of what she was
seeing in the world. She saw the negative turn that our country took after
9/11: two wars, the economic downturn, and the increasing damage to our
environment. She daily saw the creep of aggression and bullying, and she
was afraid. Someone suggested that Marie take the Introduction to Peace
Studies course, and like many who come to this class, she found that with exposure to new concepts and the possibilities for a new vision, her despair and
anger began to turn into passion and action. This is the transformative nature
of peace studies. She changed her major and never looked back. As she nears
graduation from the Peace, Justice, and Environmental Studies Program,
she plans to enter the field of law and public policy. She is transformed into
an empowered woman in her chosen career and in her personal life. She has
found her voice. Creating a culture of peace has become her calling, and the
field of law will be her vehicle.

Community colleges are uniquely poised to develop curricula and training programs quickly in response to changes in our world. There is growing
recognition that the way we engage in war now causes too much damage to

people and our natural world, and that new and existing methods of destruction and exploitation are neither healthy nor sustainable. In response to these developments, the field of peace studies is beginning to grow, and the role that community colleges play in this movement presents unique challenges and opportunities. Community colleges are wonderful vehicles for offering learning opportunities: they are affordable and accessible in ways that other higher education institutions are not; they draw on the power and the people of the local community, thus serving as an ideal model for democracy in action.

One advantage of peace studies programs at community colleges is that they do not dictate what field a student will go into—they simply, yet powerfully, provide perspective and practical skills. Students in these programs can fulfill requirements for general education, certification, and transfer programs, and in doing so, they also gain knowledge, experience, and skills that will make them at once better citizens and more attractive to transfer institutions and future employers. Whether students are working toward an associate's degree for transfer to a four-year college or to get certification in programs as diverse as nursing, electrical engineering, or elementary education, they can fulfill their general education requirements while also learning about peace. Through engagement in peace studies programs, they will fulfill the general education outcomes of global citizenship, practicing civic engagement, working collaboratively, thinking critically and creatively, and reasoning and acting ethically. Our programs have two primary learning goals: (1) to provide students with an understanding of the complexity of factors that interact to result in either peace or conflict; and (2) to develop the needed skills to become agents of positive change. Hence, whether students are seeking certification in heating and cooling or in respiratory therapy or a liberal arts degree, taking courses in peace studies programs will give them a fuller understanding of how they fit into the complex web of forces in our world and the necessary skills to be actors in shaping it. This knowledge and skill is valuable not only to the students but also to their future employers and our world.

As the field of peace studies evolves it must keep pace with the social issues of the time. One advantage that community colleges have is the flexibility to respond to changing needs in our communities and our world. A specific example: our understanding of human impact on the environment, global climate change, and resource depletion grows. In response, a member of Delta College's Global Peace Studies steering committee recently established a program in wind turbine technology to produce skilled workers to meet a social need in a peaceful, sustainable manner. Thus, the various dimensions of our interconnectedness and the recognition that we must stop violently exploiting our life-sustaining resources are evolving as a focus within peace studies.

Facilitating the Development of an Ecological Perspective

Designing curricula to help students develop a systems, or ecological, perspective is a critical outcome for peace studies programs at community colleges. An ecological perspective recognizes the interconnectedness of all members of a community and recognizes that any network of relationships constitutes a web of interdependence that is the nature of all ecological relationships. When we facilitate such a perspective in our students, they become better able to understand the complexity of factors influencing peace and conflict, and with this knowledge, they are better able to become agents of positive change in our world. A wide variety of activities can be developed and used in peace studies programs to help students develop this cognitive flexibility and perspective. For example, case studies and current events—which require students to examine an issue's technological, environmental, cultural, and geographic influences, as well as its economic, political, and religious dimensions—will help achieve this goal. Systems theory can help students develop a theoretical framework from which to study peace, conflict, and security.

Developing an Ecological Perspective:
An Example Activity

An assignment for the Introduction to Global Peace Studies course at Delta College is an apt example of helping students develop ecological thinking. The assignment requires students to investigate, in-depth, specific dimensions of the 2011 Deepwater Horizon oil spill in the Gulf of Mexico. Working in groups, students research various dimensions of the oil spill: the technology, the environmental impact, geopolitics, energy sources and alternatives (renewable energy), and human complacency and cultural influences. Each group compiles its findings and shares them during in-class discussion. Such detailed research and discussion is crucial to developing many important peacebuilding skills: effective communication, critical thinking, perspective-taking skills, and the ability to recognize the complexity of a conflict condition. Additionally, students see value in listening to, and learning from, others.

Two Models

Greenfield Community College Peace Studies

Community colleges have typically developed their curricula in response to global conditions. Given that our main purpose is to teach, faculty members are especially attuned to creating a curriculum that reflects social changes and world events. This is true at GCC where the idea of creating a culture of peace is a central thread in the program. The Greenfield Community College effort began in 2003 with a single course and has evolved into a full associate of liberal arts option. First conceived in 2006 as the option Peace and Social Justice Studies, it now includes aspects of human ecology and environmental issues and is entitled "Peace, Justice, and Environmental Studies."

After 9/11, it became clear that as first-responding educational institutes, community colleges should play a direct role in addressing issues of peace and sustainability. The work of establishing an interdisciplinary program of peace studies at Greenfield Community College began with a single course: Psychology of Peace, Conflict, and Violence. In this course, students learn how and why humans engage in violent behaviors toward one another. In addition to examining psychological processes—for example dehumanization, groupthink, identity formation, and the effects of trauma, such as posttraumatic stress disorder—the course also explores the important role of healing through reconciliation, compassion, empathy, and forgiveness.

Teaching the course revealed many more critical questions that could be addressed in studying conflict, peace, and peacebuilding. For example, what methods for enacting peace, nonviolence, and conflict resolution already exist? What are the determining factors of war and peace? What are the myths of nonviolence, and how has history shown nonviolent tactics to be successful?

To address these and other questions, we created Introduction to Peace Studies. The course uses an interdisciplinary reader that draws from the fields of psychology, anthropology, religion, economics, history, politics, and the teachings of peace activists and educators. The course investigates the concepts of positive and negative peace and the distinction between direct and structural violence. It explores these and other questions: Is humankind hardwired to commit violence? Is violence ever justified? What is the role of international law and human rights? How can we create more just economic and political systems? What do we mean by "active nonviolence," and what does it look like? Students discuss the ideas of thinkers as diverse as Margaret Mead, Thoreau, Gandhi, Thich Nhat Hanh, William James, Betty Reardon, and Paulo Freire, and they become our teachers. In many respects, this course demonstrates all aspects of what peace studies should do: taking an interdisciplinary approach, developing an ecological perspective, defining a culture of peace, and demonstrating the art and science of social change. Assignments are designed to help students reflect on the material, as well as to give them opportunities to engage in a social action project if they choose.

Two additional courses came about: Conflict Resolution and Mediation, and Peacemaking and Sustainability in Practice: A Seminar in Nonviolence and Social Action. These two courses introduce more theory and also add ways to begin the practice of peace and active nonviolence. Clearly, the study of peace involves understanding conflict in its many forms, ranging from intra- and interpersonal to intra- and interstate. War, the final and most violent of all methods of conflict resolution, confronts us with the big underlying question: will we always engage in war as a way to solve our problems and resolve conflict? To address this question, the second course helps students deepen their understanding of active nonviolence, primarily through the study of those who have developed a belief in the power of nonviolence and have put it into practice. Mahatma Gandhi first introduced the world to the power of nonviolent action by large groups, and he gave the world a template for implementing the power of active nonviolence. The Nonviolence and Social Action seminar also requires students to participate in a service learning project that engages them with the community in learning how active nonviolence works. Projects included sponsoring local speakers, attending grassroots groups working to end the war, working to protect immigrant rights in the community, and other related issues. This course has been renamed Peacemaking and Sustainability in Practice: Strategies for a Sustainable Future, and it borrows from the principles of the Transition Movement, which seeks to build community resilience to weather the challenges of peak oil, climate change, and growing social and economic inequality. It is a grassroots movement whose practices embody nonviolence and is seen as an emerging method for social change.

As the GCC program continued to develop, an emphasis on nonviolence emerged. Few people are offered an opportunity to study the philosophical soundness and practicality of nonviolent action. This theme for creating social change for the greater good came to define the program as a whole and exemplifies the flexibility of a community college in creating a new curriculum that reflects local and global change. Currently, the Arab Spring and the Occupy movement are real-life examples to study, helping students make connections between theory and practice. Learning about individuals and groups who have successfully engaged in nonviolent action to create social change inspires and gives hope. Examples include the Montgomery bus boycott and the suffragists submitting to arrest and jail. Such examples help us envision the possibilities of a culture of peace, show us that humans have untapped capacity for goodness, compassion, and forgiveness, and remind us that methods already exist for resolving our conflicts and differences in ways that meet our needs. Students learn that peace work does not require overpowering others, and that by finding our own power within, we can find our power together. Students learn that another world *is* possible.

The newest version of the liberal arts option in Peace, Justice, and Environmental Studies at GCC draws from the field of human ecology and the need to create a sustainable future. Peace work is deeply connected to the natural world, so clearly our work to create a culture of peace must involve humans' relationship with the earth. Connecting peace, justice, and environmental issues facilitates the development of different ways of conceiving and managing conflicts. In essence, the study becomes a call to create community, to encourage grassroots involvement, and to become part of the solution in ending violence against humans and nature. The new program at GCC includes four peace classes as well as several courses in environmental studies and related sciences.

Regarding transfer and career options, the associate of arts (AA) degree fulfills the requirements for transfer to a four-year institution. The University of Massachusetts Amherst—in the same region as GCC—has two options for either traditional or nontraditional students to create their own independent study that earns them a bachelor of arts (BA) degree. It also has bachelor's degree programs in environmental studies and science, legal and labor studies, justice education, and social work, as well as in education, journalism, criminal justice, and mediation. The University of Massachusetts Lowell, in the Boston area, has just created a BA in peace and conflict studies. Business and entrepreneurial degrees at other local institutions are also possibilities as more programs focus on sustainable business practices. New careers in solar panel installation and other green jobs are also emerging.

The values and skills that accrue from taking even one course in the area of peace studies become a template for new possibilities in any job or profession. They extend into the very real and important work of raising families, being a good neighbor, and building community. As we grapple with the needed changes in our consumptive practices and our economy, more innovative and creative possibilities will open up. What students learn by studying in these programs will translate into real job opportunities, some of them yet to be imagined.

Global Peace Studies at Delta College

The plan at Delta College was to create a full-fledged AA transfer degree and certificate program in global peace studies at the same time, and that goal was realized in the fall of 2010. The idea for the program emerged while two psychology faculty members were attending a weeklong workshop, "Conflict and Cooperation," hosted by the Midwest Institute for International/Intercultural Education. One key presenter at the workshop was a representative of the United States Institute of Peace (USIP). USIP staff then accepted an invitation to visit Delta's campus and met with faculty and administrators, providing advice and guidance for developing a new program. Over the next three years, the two faculty colleagues used modest funds and release time to educate themselves about global peace education. One spent a week studying at the University for Peace in Costa Rica, and the other was accepted into USIP's weeklong seminar for community college faculty and administrators. In addition to other workshops and conferences, supplementary materials were gathered to guide the shaping of Delta's program.

The goal of these two colleagues' three years of effort was to create a high-quality transfer program in global peace studies—one that would provide students with the knowledge and skills needed to become global actors for positive change. After much discussion and thought, the two-year AA degree program was dubbed "Global Peace Studies" (GPS), to reflect the simultaneous emphasis on two educational dimensions: (1) developing a deeper understanding of the complexity of factors that interact to generate peace or conflict; and (2) developing the skills needed to be an agent of positive change in our world.

The program at Delta is very flexible: during the process of creating the program, we were aware that the knowledge and skills developed through the program needed to be applicable to any occupation. Reflecting this practicality, there are four general tracks in Delta's GPS program: international business, human services/social justice, environmental studies, and international relations. Whereas each track fulfills all general education requirements (for transfer to a four-year college or university), a specific three-plus-one transfer agreement was established with a respected business school for the international business track.

Delta's rigorous GPS program requirements enable students to obtain a transfer degree in virtually any field they might choose. It is the only peace studies degree program at the community college level (that we are aware of) that requires a year of foreign-language study. We recognized that many community college students have limited international and cross-cultural experience and that even a single collegiate year of a foreign language provides insight into other ways of thinking and knowing. In addition to establishing cognitive flexibility, tolerance, empathy, and humility, a year of foreign language study will enable students to communicate with, literally, millions of people they otherwise couldn't.

The curriculum for the GPS program at Delta is centered in the corner and capstone courses: Introduction to Global Peace Studies and Leadership for Positive Change, respectively. The introductory course provides the foundation. It uses in-depth case studies extensively (e.g., the Israel-Palestine conflict, the Deepwater Horizon oil spill, corporate control of the food industry, and the campaign for civil rights in the American South). The course also uses films (e.g., *Why We Fight, Encounter Point, A Force More Powerful*) and guest speakers (war veterans, UN consultants, local energy experts, peace activists), who share their stories and guide discussions.[1] The United States Institute of Peace online certificate courses, and simulations such as BARNGA are used to deepen understanding and facilitate negotiation and cross-cultural skills.[2] The primary outcome of the course is not only to understand theory within peace studies but also to identify how it can be used to explain real-life conditions. The assignments and activities are also designed to develop the skills needed to enact positive change.

In the program's capstone course, Leadership for Positive Change, students engage in extensive service learning activities in the community—at women's shelters, safe houses, soup kitchens, and other agencies. Through service at agencies of positive change in our communities, students witness firsthand the impact that poverty, scarcity of resources, policy, and grassroots social action have on human lives. Importantly, the curriculum and activities in this course are structured so that students interact not only with those living in conditions of need but also directly with workers and leaders in the agencies themselves. Hence, students not only witness the impact that inequality has on human lives but also are exposed to functioning community agencies. They experience the realities—the frustrations and limitations as well as the joy of the successes—that are part of working for positive social change. The knowledge and skills gained through these experiences enable them to maneuver effectively within the political structure of any agency, whether at the local, national, or international level.

Although Delta's GPS program is still in its fledgling stage, its structure is based on successful existing programs and the input of knowledgeable educators and peace workers. Through intensive in-class activities and discussions and out-of-class study, service, and reflection, the curriculum in Delta's GPS program provides the knowledge and skills that can empower students to become agents of positive change in any profession, anywhere.

Lessons Learned

Stress the Interdisciplinary Nature of the Program

By stressing the interdisciplinary nature of peace studies programs—that students in *any* field of study can gain the degree or certificate—many faculty members recognize an avenue through which *they* can exercise their passion for educating for positive change. It also helps greatly to invite faculty, staff, and administrators to share ideas and become involved in how the program develops, so that it may meet the needs of our students and communities.

---

1. See Jarecki 2005; Avni and Bacha 2006; York 2000.
2. For the online certificate courses, see USIP 2012. For BARNGA, see Thiagarajan 2006.

It is easy to emphasize the peace studies program's interdisciplinarity by making sure that various campus groups can give input. GCC, for example, has plans to create learning communities combining the Introduction to Peace Studies and English Composition courses, along with other disciplines (for another approach, see box 5.1). Delta's program established a steering committee consisting of faculty from environmental studies, technology, math, political science, English, psychology, and nursing, as well as a librarian, an academic counselor, and the college's dean of instruction and learning. Including individuals from various academic and service areas of the college also ensures "vision" for the program's future by soliciting many perspectives and voices.

Coordinate with Other College Initiatives

Experience has also taught us that collaborating with existing college programs, initiatives, and community organizations results in increased opportunities for students to learn, as well as increased visibility for peace studies programs. Various departments and organizations have much in common with the goals of peace studies programs, and these commonalities can be used for the benefit of all. At Greenfield, for example, the Peace, Justice, and Environmental Studies option worked closely with the Renewable Energy and Environmental Science degree programs to create a collaborative Web site that explains the multiple ways that Greenfield engages in sustainable practices and theory.

On the Web site, each program is described, differences are explained, and next steps for student career paths are outlined. This furthers understanding of the definition and value of peace studies in the context of other disciplines. Also, the student Peace, Justice, and Environmental Action Alliance sponsors the Peace and Pizza film series. The Roots of Peace speaker series is cosponsored with a local community peace organization, and activities for Earth Day, International Day of Peace, and Gandhi's birthday are annual events. A scholarship in the names of two local peace and environmental activists has been established. Similarly, Delta's program works closely with the college's Academic Sustainability Team and collaborates on events with the Office of Student Engagement, such as the annual Global Awareness Program, Earth Day, Women's History Month, and Black History Month. In addition to coordinating with similarly concerned campus programs and initiatives, our programs collaborate with community organizations focused on promoting positive change (such as food banks, homeless shelters, tutoring programs in schools, and neighborhood restoration organizations). These collaborative efforts demonstrate the hands-on, interdisciplinary, and action-oriented nature of peace studies programs. In

Box 5.1: An Honors Approach

Shirin Khosropour teaches at Austin Community College (TX), where she has designated a section of her Introduction to Psychology course "honors" with a concentration on conflict transformation and peace studies. The class, which meets once a week, is directed by students, who are responsible for presenting material. Each student develops a capstone project at the end of the semester. Because of the "peace psychology" focus, the range of topics that students presented (in 2012) included parenting for peace, personality traits and conflict, psychological distress in refugee children, the language of war and peace, child soldiers and reintegration, and conflict resolution and emotional intelligence. This course is planned to be the foundation for a collegewide program.

addition to having a positive impact on our communities, these efforts also empower our students and give them a greater range of opportunities to learn and serve.

Concluding Thoughts

Peace studies programs promote global thinking and enable students to develop the knowledge and skills needed to bring about positive change in our world. Community college peace studies programs foster personal growth and the skills that enable students to respond to conflict in a nonviolent, constructive manner at the personal, local, national, or international level. Such programs are the soil that nurtures the seeds of justice. Community colleges—where nurses and police are trained, where social workers, entrepreneurs, and teachers get the foundation of their education—are the natural place to begin fostering a culture of peace. Through the lens of peace, social justice, and the environment, students can better understand the social and cultural forces that operate alongside science and technology and use them in an integrated and holistic way to manifest a better world. Marie's story is just one of many that demonstrate the transformative power and practical benefits of bringing peace studies to community college.

References

Avni, Ronit, and Julia Bacha. 2006. *Encounter Point*. Just Vision Films.

Jarecki, Eugene. 2005. *Why We Fight*. Sony Pictures Classics. Film.

Thiagarajan, Sivasailam. 2006. BARNGA: A Simulation Game on Cultural Clashes. 25th-anniv. ed. Boston: Intercultural Press.

United States Institute of Peace (USIP). 2012. "USIP Online Courses." www.usip. org/training/online/.

York, Steve. 2000. *A Force More Powerful*. York Zimmerman. Film.

IHU/SSI 120
Introduction to Global Peace Studies
Delta College

Instructor: C. Jeffrey Dykhuizen, PhD
Text: Barash, David. 2010. *Approaches to Peace*, 2nd ed. Oxford Univ. Press.
Other readings will also be assigned.

Course Description: In Introduction to Global Peace Studies (GPS), we will identify sources of peace and conflict, examining the interaction of these influences at the personal, local, national, and international levels. We will explore how economic and political factors, distribution of environmental resources, cultural practices, and human greed and compassion are interrelated. We will examine case studies to distinguish between positive and negative peace and to analyze methods of conflict resolution. We will also engage in cross-cultural training as well as practices designed to enhance emotional self-regulation and perspective-taking skills—skills that are needed to create positive change in the world.

Reading Response Papers: Each week you will be asked to respond, in writing, to several essays from our text and assigned readings. Usually, these readings will not be that long, but they will not be simple. Plan to read each essay at least twice! (I encourage "marking them up" with notes and such!) Questions will be provided (either distributed in class or made available on our D2L site) to guide your written responses and to prepare you for class discussion, which will be based on the readings. Read, think, prep, and write well!

Assignments/Papers: You will also be given a series of assignments throughout the semester, each of which will have its own set of guidelines/instructions. Assignments will typically ask you to do a bit of research, engage in an activity, and reflect on your experiences. We will also typically have in-class discussions based on what you have experienced, learned, and discovered. Guidelines for assignments will be distributed in class or made available on our D2L site.

Final Project: Everyone will have the chance to a give a short presentation on the theme of peace and conflict. There are three options: 1) A Personal Presentation: select something (a painting, tool, song, photo, piece of clothing, sculpture, etc.) that is for you a meaningful symbol or representation of a dimension of peace or conflict in the world; 2) Social Action Project: engaging/acting to enable or promote peace in our world; or 3) Book Report. Each presentation should be 5–7 minutes long, with another 3–4 minutes for questions and discussion. You will submit a two-page summary of your ideas at the time of the presentation. We will sign up for presentation dates around mid semester.

Course Schedule

Week   Example Readings and Activities

1   Introduction to Global Peace Studies: Overview of course
2   *On Aggression* – Konrad Lorenz
        "We May Be Born with an Urge to Help" – *New York Times*
        Discussion: Sustainable Consumption assignment
3   *War and Other Essays* – W. G. Sumner
        "The Causes of War" – Michael Howard
        Movie: *Why We Fight*
4   "A Structural Theory of Imperialism" – Johan Galtung
        Case Study: Israel-Palestine History
        USIP: Online Certificate Course in Conflict Analysis
5   "The Moral Equivalent of War" – William James
        "Defining a Just War" – Richard Falk
        Movie: *Encounter Point*
        "International Law" – David Barash
        "An Insider's Guide to the UN" – Linda Fasulo
        Guest Speaker: UN Development Peace Worker
7   *Getting to Yes* – Fisher, Ury, and Patton
        "A Powerful Peace" – Jonathan Schell
        USIP: Online Certificate Course in Negotiation and Conflict Management
        Guest Speaker: Negotiation and Conflict Resolution
8   "The Land Ethic" – Aldo Leopold
        Case Study Assignment: Deepwater Horizon
        Guest Speaker: Energy Production Specialist
9   "Terrorism Past and Present" – RAND Corporation
        "Dying to Win: The Strategic Logic of Suicide Terrorism" – Robert Pape
        Guest Speaker: Political Terrorism
10   "Human Rights" – David Barash
        "Global Economic Solidarity" – Jeffrey Sachs
        Guest Speaker and Assignment: Regulating Emotional Response
11   "The Clash of Civilizations" – Samuel P. Huntington
        "Refining Security: The New Global Schisms" – Michael Klare
        BARNGA
12   "Civilian Resistance as a National Defense" – Gene Sharp
        "Empire v. Democracy: Why Nemesis Is at Our Door" – Chalmers Johnson
        Movie: *Soldiers of Conscience*
13   "Ahimsa, or the Way of Nonviolence" – Mohandas Gandhi
        "Letter from a Birmingham Jail" – Martin Luther King Jr.
        "Neither Victims nor Executioners" – Albert Camus
        Movie: *A Force More Powerful: The American South:*
                Campaign for Civil Rights
14   Student Presentations
15   Student Presentations

Greenfield Community College
Peace, Justice, and Environmental Studies (PJE)
(Meets Massachusetts Transfer Compact Requirements)

THE DEGREE: Associate of Arts in Liberal Arts

THE PROGRAM OPTION: Offers students an opportunity to understand the relationship between viable economies, equity and justice, peace, and ecological integrity through sustainability practices within the framework of the traditional skills and content of a liberal arts education. It provides an interdisciplinary approach to learning that uses multiple sources and methods for learning and application to everyday life.

YOUR NEXT STEP: Transfer to a baccalaureate degree institution to study any liberal arts discipline, peace and/or social justice studies, environmental studies, or related fields such as public policy, law, education, management, economics, social work, and others.

REQUIRED COURSES   CREDITS
 ENG 101, 103, or 105 English Composition I 3
 ENG 112, 114, or 116 English Composition II 3
 PCS 101, 121, 131, or 141 Personal Communication Skills 3
 PSJ 101 Introduction to Peace Studies 3
 PSJ 120 Mediation and Conflict Resolution 3
 EVS 204 Environmental Justice 3
 PSJ 225 Peacemaking and Sustainability in Practice: Strategies for a
 Sustainable Future 3
 PSY 214 Psychology of Peace, Conflict, and Violence 3
 EVS 101 Environmental Studies: Issues in Sustainability. 3
 SOC 106 The Social Construction of Difference and Inequality 3
Behavioral Science Core 3
 Select one course from the following: ANT 104, ECO 101, PSY 101,
 SOC 101 (recommend ANT 104)
 Humanities Core 9
 History: any HIS course coded HC (recommend HIS 127, HIS 129,
 or HIS 131) 3
 Literature: any 200-level English course except ENG 207 and ENG 208
 (recommend ENG 219, ENG 228, ENG 235, ENG 247, or ENG 248) 3
 A Humanities course with HC advising code and UMass diversity
 requirement code 3
Science/Math Core 11–12
 Choose one course: SCI 120, BIO 103, or BIO 120 4
 Science: one four-credit BIO, CHE, EGR, GEO, PHY, or SCI course
 with NC advising code 4
 Math: one MAT course with NC advising code 3
Peace, Justice, and Environmental Electives 7–10
                         Total 60–64

PEACE, JUSTICE, AND ENVIRONMENTAL ELECTIVES
(if not already used to fulfill required courses)

BIO 103 Ecology 4
BIO 120 Environmental Science 4
ECO 101 Principles of Macroeconomics 3
ECO 113 Environmental Economics 3
ECO 129 Global Trade and Development 3
EVS 121 Gender and the Environment 3
GGY 101 Introduction to Geography 3
HUM 130 Latin American/North American Cultures 3
MAT 114 Introduction to Statistics 3
PHI 206 Environmental Ethics 3
POL 101 American Politics 3
POL 203 American Civil Liberties 3
POL 207 Politics of the Middle East 3
SCI 120 Sustainable Energy: Theory and Practice. 4
PCS 141 Interpersonal Communication 3
THE 108 Interactive Dramatics 3
Any course that meets the University of Massachusetts social and
cultural diversity requirement, marked with an * in the GCC catalog. 3–13
Any language course coded ASL, FRE, SPA 3–13

Green Living Series

EVS 150 The 24-Hour Outdoor Personal Growth Experience. 1
EVS 151 Vision Quest and Rites of Passage 1
EVS 152 Sustainable Agriculture: Organic Gardening 1
EVS 153 Ancient Wilderness Living Skills 1
EVS 154 Earth Education: The Council of All Beings 1
EVS 155 Introduction to Sustainable Energy: Solar Living 1

Sustainable Energy Series

SCI 110 Sustainable Energy Fundamentals. 1
SCI 119 Introduction to Global Warming 1
SCI 118 Greenhouse Gas Assessment 1

Course Descriptions for
Peace, Justice, and Environmental Studies
at Greenfield Community College

PSJ 101: Introduction to Peace Studies (BC) 3 credits
An interdisciplinary study of the concepts of peace and the interplay of cultural, ideological, and environmental factors since the end of the Cold War. This course familiarizes students with the salient concepts of positive and negative peace, peacemaking, and the principles of a culture of peace and sustainability.

PSJ 120: Mediation and Conflict Resolution (BL) 3 credits
A study of the theories of conflict and conflict styles, including how to define issues in mediation, reframing, neutrality and bias, and moving parties to mutually satisfactory resolution. Students explore the role of mediator as a neutral third party who facilitates resolution that is designed by the parties based on their needs. Class includes simulated mediations and has a skill-based component.

PSJ 225: Peacemaking and Sustainability in Practice (BL) 3 credits
An exploration of strategies for social change and creating an ecologically sustainable future. Students study the history of nonviolent and environmental movements and actions, the women and men who promote nonviolence and sustainability, and the cultural conditions under which social change occurs. The course gives special attention to the strategic significance of direct individual actions. Students complete a related service learning component in the form of a placement or action in the wider community.

PSY 214: Psychology of Peace, Conflict, and Violence (BC) 3 credits
A focus on the key concepts of peace psychology: the relationships among violence, social inequalities, peacemaking, and the pursuit of social justice. Topics include ethnic conflict, family violence, hate crimes, militarism, conflict management, social justice, nonviolent approaches to peace, and peace education. Students examine systems of violence and systems of peace. Through lectures, discussions, readings, experiential activities, projects, film, and dialogue, students study the philosophy of nonviolence and develop more complex views of the immediate causes of violence and deeper appreciation for the structural roots of violence, with an emphasis on healing from trauma through reconciliation methods.

Program Adviser: Professor Abbie Jenks, MSW

6

Developing a Conflict Resolution and Peace Studies Program

Implementation Strategies

JENNIFER BATTON AND SUSAN LOHWATER

Establishing lasting peace is the work of education; all politics can do is keep us out of war. —*Maria Montessori*

An ever-increasing number of community colleges in the United States are pursuing the development of a program in conflict resolution or peace studies resulting in a credit-based associate's degree, certificate, or concentration (see appendix B). While the program and course outcomes may overlap, the programs may be called "international education," "global education," "peace studies," "conflict management," or "conflict resolution" or be categorized in another way. The programs encompass a wide range of disciplines, and the conflict resolution and management skill sets—including understanding conflict, understanding how emotions influence conflict, effective communication skills, and problem solving—are integral to every profession and in every area of an individual's life. This chapter provides a general overview of types of peace and conflict programs in community colleges and processes to consider in developing them. It then provides a case study of the development of a certificate in conflict resolution and peace studies at Cuyahoga Community College (Tri-C), in Cleveland, Ohio.

The Process of Creating a Peace and Conflict Resolution Program

The range of academic peace studies offered varies widely, from a single course to a certificate to a degree program. The categories of programs depend on several variables: student demographics, size of the college, interest and focus of the faculty members initiating the program, support from faculty and administration, financial considerations, administrative and curriculum-development processes of the institution, and student interest.

Tri-C committed itself to developing a credit certificate program. The college's planning committee proposed the development of a certificate as the first step in building capacity at the student, faculty, and administrative levels. Its goal was, after establishing the certificate program at two main campuses and proving it sustainable, to develop a degree program. A market survey showed significant interest, both at the college and in the community, to support the development of a certificate. The core courses were initially listed in political science, with the goal of eventually cross-listing certain courses across disciplines. Conceivably, a peace studies and conflict resolution program would be housed in disciplines other than political science, depending on the faculty members creating the classes, certificate, or program.

The electives were chosen from existing courses in various disciplines, provided they already included concepts and theories related to conflict resolution and peace education. While some courses seemed to link naturally with conflict resolution or peace studies, others, to qualify as electives, needed to be altered in their course methodology, theories, and examples. Using existing courses was beneficial since less initial funding for development was required and fewer courses needed to be created and approved. The electives at Tri-C were chosen because several of the conflict resolution outcomes were already explicitly included in the course. Thus, even if a new part-time faculty member was teaching the class, the core values would still be covered. While other colleges have a wider range of electives, such as comparative religion or ecological sustainability, Tri-C did not include them in the list of electives, because as the course outline is currently written, they do not explicitly teach the core outcomes using conflict management methodology, theory, or concepts. The students do have the option to choose other electives and petition the certificate committee to substitute another class for one of the listed electives. In this way, as the certificate program expands, there will be potential for growth into a separate AA degree program or a department for peace and conflict studies.

Challenges

Creating a conflict resolution or peace studies program, like creating any new academic endeavor, is challenging and time consuming. At Tri-C, the process took about two years from conception to offering the first course. A few of the more difficult challenges include the following:

- lack of knowledge and understanding of the field among staff and administrators
- unfamiliarity with the linkages and applications of these concepts to the daily operations in the fields in which the students will be employed

- the need for capacity building to help faculty members integrate these concepts into their current courses
- the amount of time for developing and delivering high-quality marketing surveys and for developing courses

At some colleges, promised support may not materialize, or changes in administrators and faculty may impede progress. When courses are finally offered, recruiting and retaining faculty or attempting to build in-college capacity among current faculty often becomes a challenge. Finally, marketing the new program and attracting and enrolling sufficient students can be challenging.

Naming the Program

Naming the program at Tri-C presented its own unique challenges. Examples of program names at community colleges include "Peace and World Order Studies" (Berkshire Community College), "Global Peace Studies" (Delta College), "Peace, Justice, and Environmental Studies" (Greenfield Community College), and "Peace and Social Justice Studies" (Nashua Community College). A few programs include "conflict" in the title—for example, "Peace and Conflict Studies" (Portland Community College, Northwest Vista College). Classes within these programs indicate the wide range of interests, including the environment, peacemaking and sustainability, mediation, negotiation, ethics, social justice, psychology of peace, leadership, and service learning.

Tri-C named its program "Conflict Resolution and Peace Studies" because some disciplines represented in the community market survey and in the community outcomes process associated the word "peace" with "soft skills" that they did not feel were applicable to their work. When "conflict resolution" was used, the linkages across disciplines were more apparent. On the other hand, some people hear "conflict resolution" and think only of direct physical violence, without considering daily applications. The suggestion of including the word "peace" in the program at Tri-C generated some opposition from those who considered the term irrevocably associated with the social movements in the 1960s and 1970s in the United States. Eventually, the term "peace" was used, though after "conflict resolution."

Incorporating Peace Studies and
Conflict Resolution across the Curriculum

With adequate professional development, infusion of conflict resolution and peace skills into a broad curriculum is relatively straightforward if the faculty members are receptive to the idea and if professional development is provided for those new to the field. The incorporation of the conflict resolution skills set (including understanding conflict, understanding how emotions influence conflict, and learning effective problem-solving skills) may be implemented in two basic ways:

1. The class outcomes—the formal plan for the class, as found in the college catalog and approved by all faculty—may be formally changed to list conflict resolution skills. In Ohio, the state board of education is attempting to adopt new social and emotional learning guidelines to be incorporated in teacher preparation, including skills and concepts for teaching conflict resolution.
2. Alternatively, the faculty may introduce the skill set or the conflict resolution steps into the curriculum in an informal augmentation of the existing topics.

The first method is preferred because all faculty in the discipline would then be required to accomplish the outcomes. The second method is faster and easier, though less consistent. The second approach is also less permanent, and if the supporting faculty members leave, the enrichment of the courses may disappear.

Dr. Kathy Bickmore sets forth a strategy to incorporate conflict resolution skill sets in her 1998 monograph "Curricular Infusion and Integration: Conflict Resolution, Decision Making, and Critical Thinking in 'Academic' Subject Areas" (included after the chapter). Below are other detailed examples of how conflict management skills and peace studies may be incorporated into education and English for speakers of other languages.

Education Courses

Including conflict resolution knowledge, skills, and abilities in education courses is vital because it improves educators' abilities to manage their classrooms more effectively. It also supports numerous state initiatives (including in Ohio), school climate guidelines, social studies standards, and antiharassment and bullying-prevention legislation. To address the large turnover in teachers within their first few years of teaching—in part because of their inability to manage conflict effectively in the classroom—the United States Department of Education's Fund for the Improvement of Postsecondary Education awarded a grant to Temple University. The JAMS Foundation and the George Gund Foundation also provided funding for this initiative. The result was the Conflict Resolution Education in Teacher Education (CRETE) Project, developed by Temple University in collaboration with the Global Issues Resource Center at Cuyahoga Community College, Wayne State University, Cleveland State University, and the Ohio Commission on Dispute Resolution and Conflict Management (Commission). The

Commission was a state government agency that helped the state education agencies build capacity and infrastructure in conflict management through grants, training, and technical assistance to all Ohio public schools, teacher training programs, and universities.[1] CRETE's curriculum for educators includes the primary and secondary school curricula provided by the Commission and the Ohio Department of Education, linking the core concepts across subjects as well as to the state's educational standards and tests. CRETE is a collaboration of colleges and universities, agencies, and conflict resolution education organizations, dedicated to infusing conflict resolution education and social and emotional learning into teacher preservice education.

All fifty states have some form of legislation or state policy recommendations in the areas of conflict resolution education, social and emotional learning, or safe schools initiatives (including bullying prevention). The skills of conflict resolution are frequently already found in the state curriculum standards, particularly in health, social studies, and language arts.

Children's literature is a discipline in which these concepts can be taught and incorporated in education classes or English classes, depending on the institution. At Tri-C, "children's literature" is taught in the English program in a special topics course and in childhood development courses. One high-level education class, Human Diversity in Education, examines relationships between a variety of sociocultural patterns of students and communities. This course considers the causes and possible resolutions for resolving potential conflicts, based on differing expectations, between members of diverse communities. The course description illustrates the connection to conflict resolution outcomes set for the certificate program.

English for Speakers of Other Languages/ English as a Second Language

Incorporating conflict resolution and peacebuilding skills into the English for Speakers of Other Languages (ESOL) curriculum is essential for several reasons. First, the ESOL class typically has students from various ethnic backgrounds, so incorporating and modeling conflict management skill sets is necessary to create an emotionally safe educational environment. Second, students from other cultures often have difficulty adjusting to life in the United States. They experience issues ranging from culture shock to discrimination at school and in the community. ESOL classes have traditionally incorporated readings and discussions on these issues in the classroom to help the students acclimate to a new culture. With the recently increased

---

1. The Commission was eliminated from the state budget in 2011 due to a tight fiscal environment.

focus on the bullying of students—bullying that has, at times, resulted in suicides—and on violence against those deemed different, conflict resolution knowledge, skills, and abilities should be infused into the curriculum so that ESOL students can better cope with the escalating tensions in their lives.

Another salient reason to incorporate conflict resolution skills into the ESOL curriculum is that many international students return to their home countries, where they often fill positions of power in government, non-governmental organizations, academia, or business. If these returning students have gained knowledge of, and respect for, peacebuilding and conflict resolution skills, they will likely transfer these skills to their home countries and use them there, thereby promoting peace in countries around the globe. This transmission is greatly enhanced if implemented by a citizen of that culture.

It is relatively straightforward to infuse ESOL classes and extracurricular activities with conflict resolution skills and peace studies while adhering to the core outcomes that require increased reading, writing, speaking, and listening skills. Most textbook writers and publishers have incorporated activities that address intercultural differences and misunderstandings. Instructors only need to take these activities a step further by introducing the basic conflict resolution steps and then, throughout the academic term, repeatedly asking students in discussions and written responses to consider the various scenarios in terms of the conflict resolution steps. The discussions and writings could be based on activities in the textbook, literature readings, newspaper articles, or the students' own experiences. Even those students who are reticent about openly discussing their emotional responses to their experiences could be encouraged to write about them in journals. Writing can be cathartic. As a means of self-analysis, it is unparalleled.

Often, ESOL students have not been encouraged to develop critical thinking skills, because typical exams in many countries merely require them to recite by rote from their instructors' lectures. Using the conflict resolution steps as a means of discussing the writings or topics promotes critical thinking. The students could discuss possible outcomes and the results of those outcomes. As they become adept at analyzing other situations, they will develop the skills with which they can examine their own personal challenges.

Even courses focusing on grammar could incorporate conflict resolution skills. Different tenses may be used to discuss situations. For example, practice of the past conditional tense could be the basis for discussions that include critical-thinking activities. After describing an unresolved or escalating conflict in the student's life, questions such as these can be useful: Looking back now, what would you have done differently? What else could you have done? What should you have said instead of what you did say? This type of exercise, while strengthening grammar responses, encourages conflict resolution reflection and may encourage more conciliatory responses in similar situations in the future.

Certificate of Conflict Resolution and Peace Studies at Tri-C: The Steps

The first step in developing the certificate in conflict resolution and peace studies was to form an advisory committee and consult with related organizations representing faculty, staff, administrators, student interns from Kent State University's Center for Applied Conflict Management (CACM), faculty at four-year institutions with related programs, and Ohio's Campus Compact (a statewide service learning organization). Kent State's CACM provided Tri-C's faculty with professional development training on conflict management and peace theory, technical assistance on syllabus review, assistance in elective selection, and feedback on the certificate outcomes. After the advisory committee's establishment, a faculty member developed a market survey (internal, of current college students, and external, of potential students in the community), and then the advisory committee developed program outcomes with community focus groups and faculty input across disciplines. Simultaneously, undergraduate peacebuilding and conflict resolution courses from across the United States were surveyed to develop the core courses for the certificate for transferability and to match the program outcomes. Once the program outcomes were designed, the courses were developed to match these, and electives selected that supported those outcomes.

College Process

The advisory committee designing the program should review the institution's curriculum creation and accreditation process. At Tri-C, the certificate in conflict resolution and peace studies was a new type of program not directly linked with any existing program or field but designed to span several disciplines. It thus fell outside the normal developmental pattern, yet many of the same requirements for developing a concentration or a new program applied, such as the development and dissemination of a market survey and a program outcomes mapping and development session.

Market Survey

To demonstrate the need for new programs and certificates, Tri-C requires a market survey. One questionnaire was created for students, and another for distribution to the community's business, health, social services, law, and education organizations, among others. Eliciting responses was more difficult from the public sector than from the students. Still, the community survey was important because it demonstrated the importance of these skills in the business, medical, social services, and other sectors of society, thereby strengthening the argument that the knowledge and skills taught in this certificate program were necessary. E-mail requests to the public often went unanswered until followed by personal requests. Still, the market survey indicated definite interest in, and the need for, the certificate in conflict resolution and peace studies.

Academic Outcomes

While the program's founders were generating, disseminating, and collating the market survey, they also conducted a program outcomes mapping session. Generally, the basic outcomes of peace studies curricula or programs include an interdisciplinary approach to understanding global peace and conflict issues; some form of skills development in proposing and implementing potential solutions; and, ideally, an opportunity to apply the knowledge, skills, and abilities tailored to the student's career choice or major. At Tri-C, the outcomes are defined as follows:

1. *Multilevel understanding of assessing conflict.* Analyze and assess conflict in all its stages and manifestations in order to effectively and ethically intervene to successfully reduce, manage, or resolve conflict.
2. *Results-driven communication.* Listen and use nonverbal, emotional, cultural, and personal perspectives to validate each party's issue or interest and to facilitate de-escalation and engagement moving toward resolution while maintaining a neutral process.
3. *Collaborative community building.* Facilitate community building by engaging stakeholder representatives through collaboration and teamwork while maintaining a safe and objective environment.
4. *Peacebuilding.* Apply problem-solving techniques and knowledge of social and emotional intelligence to analyze and evaluate the roots of conflict (including structural, cultural, emotional, and economic differences) and their effects on individuals to create and sustain a peaceful community.

Nonacademic Comparison

The fourth step confirms the relevance of the program to the nonacademic setting and is important in maintaining the college's relationship with various community entities. This step also enhances the college's ability to monitor and adjust quickly to changes in the community's needs. In developing the Tri-C certificate, community members from law enforcement, business, social agencies, health agencies, government, the nonprofit sector, and education were invited to participate in building the program outcomes and aligning the outcomes with their knowledge of necessary skills for their various career areas. The community members focused on the knowledge and skills that students should possess and the outcomes that students should have as a result of completing the certificate. The core courses were then designed to ensure that students develop this set of skills, abilities, and knowledge through completing the three courses. Then faculty and administrators representing various disciplines and college campuses—keeping in mind the results of the community sessions and the key skill sets identified—began to review existing college courses that might serve as electives. Potential electives were assessed by matching the core objectives listed in the course outlines with the outcomes skill set for the certificate. The program outcomes for the certificate were then compared to potential elective courses. For a course to be considered an elective for the certificate, the course objectives must accomplish the following:

1. introduce concepts, awareness, terminology, principles, or theory
2. review or reinforce those objectives through required practical application
3. demonstrate or provide practice of the objective through skill-building or problem-solving issues

The course and its objectives must include one or more of these designations for the skills taught: "introduce," "review," or "demonstrate." Those evaluating the courses also noted whether the potential elective addressed any of the college's general education outcomes.

The results from the community program outcomes process, the faculty/staff/administrator program outcomes process, and the much larger market survey that was completed first with students across all main campuses and in the broader community revealed the need for a specific core skill set. Those skills included understanding conflict, understanding how emotions influence conflict, communicating effectively, and problem solving in the students' personal and professional lives, across all disciplines and professions. The core courses were developed after first completing a review of undergraduate courses in peace and conflict studies programs across the United States, looking at common outcomes and readings across those courses and consulting with Kent State University's CACM.

The Conflict Resolution and Peace Studies Certificate at Tri-C comprises three required classes whose objectives encompass all the program outcomes developed through the community faculty process listed above. These courses include Introduction to Peace and Conflict Studies, Conflict Resolution Skills, and a service learning class entitled Implementing Peace Studies and Conflict Management Theories and Practices with Service

Learning, with a goal of helping empower students with the knowledge, skills, and abilities to make positive change in their communities. Students must also complete three electives (which they can select from a list of elective courses that reinforce, demonstrate, or introduce the program outcomes) and an academic English class.

Required Conflict Resolution Classes: Introduction to Peace and Conflict Studies

The first core class introduces the theory of conflict analysis and conflict resolution. It examines definitions of conflict, and diverse approaches to resolving it. It explores contemporary studies of individual behavior and social life as they relate to the origins of conflict and to violence as well as to peaceful social change. It approaches specific conflict situations through models of sociocultural dynamics, which will help students see the theories in practical terms. Also, students will be able to recognize theories in the field of conflict resolution and the stages in the life cycle of a conflict.

Conflict Resolution Skills

The second core course is an introduction to the skills of conflict analysis and resolution. This skills-based course is designed so that students will increase their awareness, develop skills, and learn constructive conflict management processes and approaches. Students will explore causes of conflict, conflict styles, and interpersonal conflict communication skills such as assertiveness and active listening. The course will introduce constructive conflict management approaches including negotiation, mediation, nonviolent action, and alternative dispute resolution approaches.

Implementing Peace Studies and Conflict Management Theories and Practices with Service Learning

The third required course is a service learning experience. This course integrates the theories and skills in peace studies and conflict management with service learning. Students gain practical experience, serve their community, and engage with issues surrounding social justice, social service, or conflict management at the local, regional, national, or international level. A minimum of forty hours of service learning is required over the course of the semester. Service learning sites include a mediation program to address student-to-student disputes at the college and the Sustained Dialogue Campus Network (SDCN). The SDCN is a group of eight to twelve students, including two student moderators who have received thirty-two hours of training in facilitating dialogue. They meet weekly to discuss issues of identity on campus—including race, ethnicity, age, ability, and socioeconomic status—and ways to address any challenges that may arise on campus.

Electives

Tri-C has a number of possible electives from which students must choose two or three. These include Cultural Anthropology, Business: Labor-Management Relations, Business: Organizational Behavior, Sociology: Social Problems, Sociology: Honors Social Problems, Speech: Fundamentals of Interpersonal Communication, and Honors Women's Studies: Women and Reform.

These electives were selected from over seventy-five possible courses because the core objectives and course outlines matched the core outcomes skill set identified during the community outcomes session and faculty outcomes session. Students also may petition to substitute another course for one of the listed electives. Electives at other institutions include a wide variety of courses across disciplines as diverse as history, sociology, business, health, education, political science, religion, psychology, philosophy, women's studies, communications, and the environment. At Tri-C, we considered incorporating courses from a wide array of disciplines. The decision to restrict electives to those that clearly indicated the stipulated outcomes was based on the belief that peace and conflict studies has a certain pedagogical and methodological approach, with core theories that need to be taught in order for it to reflect the designated core program outcomes. While many courses have the potential to be taught using peace and conflict theories and methodologies, many times these are not used. Additional professional development is needed for faculty who teach a core elective or a core course, since these theories and methodologies are often not well known or used across disciplines, though they naturally integrate well across the disciplines.

A Comprehensive Approach in Conflict Resolution and Peace Studies

In addition to the certificate in Conflict Resolution and Peace Studies at the undergraduate level, Tri-C is developing supporting conflict management outreach and infrastructure at multiple levels, both within the college for faculty and staff and in the community for various organizations.

An international conference hosted each year brings together educators, students, policymakers, and practitioners from around the globe. A mediation program for student-student disputes is overseen by the Global Issues Resource Center and the Office of Student Affairs. The Sustained Dialogue

Campus Network has also been developed to empower students to address issues of identity, creating more inclusive environments on campus for all students, staff, faculty, community members, and administrators. Moreover, the students have established a peace club, the Student Peace Alliance. Also, Tri-C offers professional development on related topics to the community, faculty, and staff. A collaborative Web site, designed and managed by Wayne State University in partnership with Temple University, houses a wealth of conflict resolution education resources, which are maintained and continually updated. Other resources provided to the community include a special collection of the Cleveland Public Library, housed within Tri-C's Global Issues Resource Center, on topics including international conflict, conflict resolution education, peace education, environmental issues, and diversity and multiculturalism.

Conclusion

Incorporating peace and conflict resolution knowledge and skills into a range of courses and disciplines is not complicated. But it does depend on each faculty member's awareness of the content and methodology. The inspiration for the endeavor may stem from a single person on campus, or it may come from an organization such as the United States Institute of Peace, which has promoted capacity building across community colleges through its seminars for faculty development. Perhaps community college administration will offer additional motivational and methodological training sessions or speakers who can aid faculty and staff in learning and practicing the principles of peacebuilding and conflict resolution. The results of conflict resolution and peace skills training are immeasurable. Each individual reached will incorporate the theories and practice into their professional and personal lives, creating an ever-widening culture of understanding and appreciation for peace in our volatile world.

CURRICULAR INFUSION AND INTEGRATION
Conflict Resolution, Decision Making, and
Critical Thinking in "Academic" Subject Areas
Kathy Bickmore, PhD (1998)

Some **SKILLS, KNOWLEDGE,** *and* **ATTITUDES** *needed for effective*
CONFLICT RESOLUTION

**Communication
(verbal & nonverbal):**
active listening
asking appropriate questions
clear speaking
  (e.g., stating opinions, giving reasons)
critical reading
persuasive speaking & writing
observation, noticing details & clues
identifiying & expressing feelings
dramatizing, role-playing
understanding perspectives,
  viewpoints
communicating w/o same language

Cooperation & community building:
patience
tolerance
persistence
managing anger & frustration
respecting self & others
sense of equity, fairness
strategies for sharing & taking turns
taking initiative
accepting responsibility
comfort with disagreement & multiple
  answers
understanding basic human needs/
  rights
collaboration & teamwork

Recognizing & resisting prejudice:
openness to unfamiliar ideas
comfort with different kinds of people
respect for different viewpoints
familiarity with various cultures
capacity to evaluate fairness
strategies for confronting unfairness

Reasoning & managing problems:
risk taking
clarifying issues & problems
hands-on problem solving
  improvising
  decision making (internal &
  interpersonal)
  consensus building
using voting procedures
recognizing interests, needs & values
analysis (e.g., comparison/contrast,
  themes, breaking complex ideas/
  tasks into parts or steps)
critical thinking, evaluation
recognizing strengths & weaknesses
synthesizing, summarizing main ideas
visually representing ideas & problems
predicting consequences

Peacemaking & negotiation:
identifying long-range & short-term
  goals
inventing win-win (integrative)
  solutions
compromising
asserting, yet knowing when/how
  much to give in
understanding negotiation processes
familiarity with mediation purpose &
  processes
understanding legal/judicial system &
  alternatives
understanding impartiality, neutral
  stance
respecting confidentiality

Concepts for understanding conflicts & problems:
types of conflict, how conflict works
escalation & de-escalation of conflict
social institutions handling various
    types of conflict
perspective, point of view
needs, interests, & positions
identifying common ground, bridging
    difference

A Few Resources:
Bickmore, K. (guest editor, Winter 1997), "Teaching Conflict Resolution."
Special Issue of *Theory Into Practice* (36:1 Arps Hall, Ohio State U., Columbus, Ohio 43210 USA).
Johnson, D. W., & R. T. Johnson (1994), "Constructive Conflict in the Schools."
Journal of Social Issues 50 (1): 117-37.
Macbeth, F., & N. Fine (1995), *Playing with Fire: Creative Conflict Resolution for Young Adults*. Gabriola, BC: New Society Publishers (P.O. Box 189; Gabriola Island, VOR 1XO).
Metropolitan Toronto School Board (1996), *Challenging Ourselves: Towards Equity and Violence-Free Relationships*. Markham, Ont.: Pembroke Publishers (538 Hood Rd. L3R 3K7).
Soley, M. (1996), "If It's Controversial, Why Teach It?" *Social Education* (National Council for the Social Studies) 60 (1): 9-14.

SOME SAMPLE WAYS OF PRACTICING CONFLICT RESOLUTION SKILLS IN ACADEMIC CONTEXTS:

LANGUAGE ARTS & FOREIGN LANGUAGES
- Speaking skills – class discussion acknowledging all personality types; and also group norms, behaviors, and rules; role-play conflict dialogues
- Listening skills – role-play conflict situations in "life" and in "literature"; practice active listening in games, language lessons, and as part of mediation process
- Critical-thinking skills – deduce and establish natural and fair consequences for choices and behaviors; invent/act out different resolutions to conflict role-plays
- Negotiation skills – students make suggestions, encourage feedback, evaluate, and clarify rules and consequences – for classroom and for characters in stories/dialogues
- Perception skills – investigate and write or speak publicly (prose or poetry) about peaceful role models, personal definition, and goals for peace; practice/act out feeling words
- Mock negotiation or mediation between characters in stories/books (primary level) such as fairy tales, *Magic Fish, Cat in the Hat* & *Where the Wild Things Are.*

- Rewrite new resolutions to a story
- Brainstorm/create multiple ways of expressing the same feeling or idea

SOCIAL STUDIES
- Find & evaluate information in news, editorials, and letters to the editor, using/comparing the points of view of different newspapers and newsmagazines
- Study levels and types of prejudice: model and role-play problems and alternative solutions
- Discuss diverse modes of communication, both verbal and nonverbal
- Use/develop various visual materials (such as movies, slides, overhead transparencies) and various verbal modes (such as court simulations, debates): translate words/pictures
- Role-play mediations, United Nations & World Court hearings, roundtable negotiations re: international hostilities – current or world history; identify participants and points of view in each international or intercultural conflict
- Analyze different viewpoints across time or geographic/cultural space, identify common ground, conflicts, and alternative resolutions to human problems in history/geography
- Simulate/practice democratic governance with class policies, elected student leaders, etc.

MATH, SCIENCE & ARTS
- Science – study different points of view, e.g., re: animal preservation (field trips), scientific fact-finding & decision making, e.g., re: oceanography
- Math – graph (& express in ratio/proportion) diversities in community
- Practice estimation & measurement using recipes from various cultures
- Clarify & discuss expectations, e.g., when cooperating is a good idea (using peers as resources, as real scientists and mathematicians do), and when it is "cheating"
- Emphasize practicing/showing problem solving, rather than just getting "correct answers"
- Cultural & historical roots of math and science – how challenges of problem solving have been handled – e.g., biographies of Euclid, who died violently, or Copernicus, who was ridiculed for his discoveries
- Investigate & represent "tough choices" (using graphs, charts, statistics, proportions, etc.) e.g., violence and environmental damage in the community
- Scientific method – inquiry, hypothesizing, careful fact-finding, evaluation of evidence – apply to school & community problems students want to solve
- Geometry – e.g., perspective, optical illusions; logical proofs re: counterintuitive shapes or geometric rules/relationships
- Art/visual – independent creative projects, e.g., educational posters re: animal preservation, advocating human rights, community problems
- Communicating different viewpoints & feelings, notion of "perspective"
- Become familiar with arts from various cultures, arts for various purposes
- Music – experiment with composition, harmony, counterpoint, music to express feelings or communicate themes

Cuyahoga Community College
Conflict Resolution And Peace Studies Certificate

Short-Term Certificate

This certificate will provide the student with the theory and skills of conflict resolution and with an opportunity to implement this knowledge in the community.

This program is designed to prepare students to demonstrate the following program outcomes:

1. Analyze and assess conflict in all its stages and manifestations in order to intervene effectively and ethically and to reduce, manage, or resolve conflict successfully.
2. Listen and use nonverbal, emotional, and cultural/personal perspectives to validate each party's issues/interest, to facilitate de-escalation and engagement, and to move toward resolution while maintaining a neutral process.
3. Facilitate community building by engaging stakeholder representatives through collaboration and teamwork while maintaining a safe and objective environment.
4. Apply problem-solving techniques and knowledge of social/emotional intelligence to analyze and evaluate the roots of conflict (including structural, cultural, emotional, and economical differences) and their effects on individuals to create and sustain a peaceful community.

Suggested Semester Sequence

First Semester		Credits
ENG-1010	College Composition IOR	3
ENG-101H	Honors College Composition I	
POL-1040	Introduction to Peace & Conflict Studies	3
XXXX	Select 1 or 2 electives from list below	3–6
		9–12

Second Semester		Credits
POL-2040	Conflict Resolution Skills	3
XXXX	Select 1 or 2 electives from list below	3–6
		6–9

Summer Semester		Credits
POL-2140	Implementing Peace Studies & Conflict Management Theories & Practices with Service Learning	3
XXXX	Select 1 or 2 electives from list below	3–6
		6–9
	PROGRAM TOTAL	21–30

Select from the list of courses below to fulfill elective requirements:

Electives		Credits
ANTH 1010	Cultural Anthropology	3
BADM 1210	Labor-Management Relations	3
BADM 2220	Organizational Behavior	3
SPCH 1000	Fundamentals of Interpersonal Comm.	3
SOC 2010	Social Problems	3
SOC 201H	Honors Social Problems	3
WST 200H	Honors Women and Reform	3

POLITICAL SCIENCE—POL

POL 1040 Introduction to Peace and Conflict Studies

3 Semester Credits

Introduction to conflict analysis and conflict resolution. Provide solid foundation for further inquiry and application. Examine definitions of conflict and diverse views of its resolution. Explore contemporary studies of individual behavior and social life as they relate to the origins of conflict and violent and peaceful social change. Specific conflict situations approached through models of sociocultural dynamics.

Prerequisite(s): ENG 1010 College Composition I, or concurrent enrollment; or eligibility for ENG 101H Honors College Composition I, or departmental approval: permission for instructor.

POL 2040 Conflict Resolution Skills

3 Semester Credits

Skills-based course in conflict management and resolution. Increase awareness, develop skills, and gain knowledge of constructive conflict management processes and approaches. Explore causes of conflict, conflict styles, and interpersonal conflict communication skills such as assertiveness and active listening. Introduce constructive conflict management approaches including negotiation, mediation, nonviolent action, and alternative dispute resolution approaches.

Lecture 03 hours. Laboratory 00 hours.

Prerequisite(s): POL 1040 Intro to Peace and Conflict Studies or concurrent enrollment.

POL 2140 Implementing Peace Studies and Conflict Management Theories and Practices with Service Learning

3 Semester Credits

This course will integrate theories and skills in Peace Studies and Conflict Management with service learning. Students will gain practical experience, serve their community, and engage with issues surrounding the promotion of social justice, social service, or conflict management at local, regional, national, or international levels. A minimum of 40 hours of service learning required over the course of the semester.

Lecture 03 hours. Laboratory 00 hours.

Prerequisite(s): POL 1040 Intro to Peace and Conflict Studies, and POL 2040 Conflict Resolution Skills

7

Peacebuilding and Conflict Resolution In Two Community Colleges

TU VAN TRIEU AND KARA PAIGE

Peace cannot be kept by force; it can only be achieved by understanding. —*Albert Einstein*

C ommunity colleges are at the forefront of serving the needs of people, businesses, communities, and the nation. Creating peaceful communities is one of those needs, and academic leaders believe that teaching about peace is an essential mission of these institutions. John J. "Ski" Sygielski, president of Harrisburg Area Community College and former board chair of the American Association of Community Colleges, believes:

> Peace and conflict resolution programs are essential to the effectiveness and viability of community colleges. The most significant aspect and core value of many community colleges is diversity. We attract, nurture, and change the lives of people from all walks of life. These individuals are diverse in terms of age, gender, race, ethnicity, sexuality, socioeconomic background, geography, philosophy, beliefs, and core values.... Because community colleges are such diverse institutions, it is natural that we will not agree at all times and that some of our beliefs, philosophies, and core values will clash. When those clashes occur, the community colleges with effective peace and conflict resolution programs will address, overcome, and even learn from the conflicts.[1]

There has not been a standard approach to developing peace and conflict studies programs in community colleges. Therefore, we will share the experiences of two community colleges that focus on teaching and incorporating practical skills in peacebuilding and conflict resolution.

Northwest Vista College

Northwest Vista College (NVC) in San Antonio, Texas, is a part of the Alamo Colleges, which comprise five community colleges. The Alamo Colleges, with enrollment surpassing sixty thousand students each semester, is

---

1. John Sygielski, e-mail message to Tu Van Trieu, Sept. 21, 2010.

the largest institution of higher education in South Texas. More importantly, NVC is in a city that is home to five military bases and a large veterans' hospital. Every semester, faculty teach members of the military, including those returning from, or about to be deployed to, Iraq and Afghanistan. And many students are related to someone in the military. This military presence was a critical factor in developing a program of peace and conflict studies.

NVC's program development began in the spring of 2007, when the college president called a meeting with faculty to solicit their ideas on developing a program in peace studies. The response was overwhelmingly positive, and the continuing interest from faculty and staff made it clear that such a program was both needed and desired. Due to the growing interest and the need for leadership, a faculty member was asked to coordinate development of the initiative beginning in the fall of 2007. With full administrative support, a stipend for the coordinator, and a team of highly dedicated faculty and staff, the program was off to a strong beginning.

In the fall of 2007, a representative of the United States Institute of Peace (USIP) visited the college. He showcased many programs designed for peace studies, spoke personally with the president of the college, and met with students about conflict and peacebuilding. He also led a discussion with community leaders to obtain their vision for a program in San Antonio and to assess local interest. Based on this discussion, the top priorities were to work with veterans and schools, teach skills in conflict resolution, incorporate service learning, and partner with local organizations.

The USIP visit was instrumental in helping the NVC peace and conflict studies committee shape its program. As a result of the visit and the follow-up assessment report issued by USIP, a clear vision began to take hold. But this vision would soon be clouded as the committee tried to create its mission, areas of focus, and course offerings and, most importantly, to decide on the type of program desired (emphasis, certificate, or degree). The committee would reach a consensus, but as with any committee—especially a large one with up to eighteen members including staff, administration, and faculty from ten disciplines—time for debate was needed. Eventually, the following mission was agreed on: "The Peace and Conflict Studies program at Northwest Vista College is to examine issues of social justice and develop skills in conflict resolution through interdisciplinary study. The vision is a program that inspires and educates students to become more fully engaged and knowledgeable citizens of our local and global community." The committee also agreed that the program should have two areas of focus: *social justice*, including equality, justice, human rights, global perspective, sustainability, and economic and environmental issues; and *conflict resolution*, including studying the causes of conflicts, mediation, prevention, and peacebuilding.

The program at NVC is referred to as an "emphasis," which requires nine hours (three courses) for completion. The term "emphasis" was adopted over "concentration" because the curriculum review board argued that "concentration" had a connotation of a state licensing curriculum, making it similar to certificate programs already in place. The review board thought it was also misleading to potential employers, who might interpret the certificate to be a validation of a certain skill set, which our program did not yet provide. The concern was thought-provoking and sparked the following questions: "Is our program *truly* equipping students with skills in conflict resolution?" and "Is that even our goal?" While it was agreed that students would be gaining awareness of issues of justice and conflict, the committee raised a concern about whether students would come away with a skill set that would actually improve their performance in their future careers. Some members agreed that the new program, as designed, was not yet providing such a skill set. The committee felt that addressing these questions was paramount when building a program. It was decided that a long-term goal would be to build a program that trained students in skills that they could use in their career fields.

To receive an emphasis in peace and conflict studies, three hours of the course Humanities: International Studies is required. Six hours from two of the following designated courses are also needed: Social Problems, U.S. History II, Women's Peace Literature, World Regional Geography, Fundamentals of Criminal Law, and World Dance. Fortunately, the courses offered in the program are part of the core; therefore, students can earn the emphasis without needing additional courses, and transferability is not problematic.

The first course offerings came in the fall of 2009, two years after program development started. Much work went into its development, and the many challenges included agreeing on what constitutes a peace and conflict studies course, designation of courses, the approval to designate the emphasis on student transcripts, issues concerning political bias, approval from the curriculum review board, buy-in from additional faculty, and advising students on how useful the emphasis would be for their careers.

Along with the challenges, there have also been many opportunities. Numerous trainings have taken place with a local organization called the Peace Center. The first training, "The Class of Nonviolence," developed by Colman McCarthy, was highly successful, with thirty participants consisting of both staff and faculty. The training provided faculty and staff with a common language to talk about teaching nonviolence. The Peace Center conducted five additional training sessions for employee development day and leadership development training. These trainings focused on conflict resolution skills and had high attendance, averaging twenty-five participants.

Currently, a train-the-trainer model is considered a top priority. A grant team is searching for funding to bring a specialist in conflict resolution to the college. The goal is to have core peace and conflict studies faculty and staff trained to become trainers for the Northwest Vista community. Once the core group has completed the skills training it will offer workshops.

Although faculty members have brought speakers to campus, they have done so for their individual classes. To reach larger audiences and build awareness of the peace and conflict studies program, NVC is designing a speakers' series. For each speaker, students, faculty, and staff will hear a "common reading," based on the speaker's life, work, or service. Some faculty members will embed common readings in their courses, thus enhancing the learning experience for students when they attend guest speakers' presentations on campus.

Finally, to address the importance of veterans in our community, faculty from the peace and conflict studies committee are organizing panel discussions with soldiers who have returned from Iraq or Afghanistan. Faculty members are seeking out community leaders and students enrolled at NVC who have experienced post-traumatic stress disorder or other challenges from their time served in combat. The hope is that when students hear the soldiers' accounts, they will become more aware of the current conflicts and draw attention to the importance of issues that manifest as a result of war. This first panel will lead to future discussions, with the goal of having units of study built around topics such as peacebuilding, effects and consequences of war, and personal experiences.

The program has come a long way, accomplishing much in its first three years. In May 2010, the program had its first student graduate with an emphasis in peace and conflict studies. With continued marketing and after securing a funding source and launching a speakers' series, the number of students enrolled is expected to increase. And yet, a central question remains: is the program providing students with the necessary skills to perform better in their future careers and become responsible global citizens? It is this question that will shape the future of the program at Northwest Vista College.

Howard Community College

Howard Community College (HCC), located in Columbia, Maryland, has about twelve thousand students enrolled in its credit program and over seventeen thousand enrolled in the noncredit continuing education courses. The Mediation and Conflict Resolution Center (MCRC) was originally a nonprofit organization staffed by volunteers during the 1990s. Volunteers were recruited and trained to become skilled mediators in providing community mediation services. In 2001, after years of struggle, HCC agreed to bring

MCRC under its umbrella and established it as a division under Academic Affairs, modeled after Maryland's Salisbury University Conflict Analysis and Dispute Resolution Program.

MCRC is unique in that its initial mandate and focus as a college entity was to provide a community service to Howard County and to help strengthen community partnerships. The services that the Center provides include community mediation, restorative dialogue, and conflict resolution education and training. In its early years, MCRC was also engaged in developing an in-service mediator certification, leading a statewide restorative justice initiative, and facilitating education and discussion on peaceful alternatives to international conflicts.

The long-term vision of both the college and MCRC was to develop an academic program to complement the community service and practical skills-building component. But the academic program was initiated outside MCRC, at a time when MCRC was in its critical first year and a half of developing its community service program. When the AA degree in conflict resolution was developed at HCC, it was the first of its kind among community colleges in the United States. The first conflict resolution course was initiated by the Health Sciences Division (with consultation from MCRC), which saw a need for building conflict resolution skills for students in the health care field. When the AA program was created, the course was cross listed with the conflict resolution and criminal justice programs.

A major challenge with developing the academic program in conflict resolution was that interest had grown faster than MCRC could manage. During the 2004–05 academic year, in order to receive a promotion, a faculty member, who was also an MCRC volunteer mediator, proposed to develop an AA degree in conflict resolution. The faculty member consulted and collaborated with MCRC staff. The developmental process was determined by the promotion project process and its deadlines for curricular review and approval. At the time, MCRC's limited staff and resources were concentrated on increasing case referrals and developing a solid community service program.

After MCRC obtained approval and implemented the associate's degree program, it became apparent that several important modifications were needed to strengthen the program. In hindsight, early investment of dialogue and time among principal stakeholders was needed before MCRC submitted the program to the curricular review and approval process.[2] It became apparent that

---

2. At the time, MCRC's goal was to create a certificate program in mediation and conflict resolution, including a mediation course (for credit) and a mediation practicum course (for credit). But in 2006, the curricular review committee postponed the revision with the new course offerings until a need could be determined. The matter has not been revisited since then.

it is vitally important not to rush the academic development process; however, one important benefit resulted from the degree developmental process: the administration gave MCRC oversight of the conflict resolution degree program.

Since MCRC was originally modeled after the Conflict Analysis and Dispute Resolution Program at Salisbury University on Maryland's Eastern Shore, it was a natural fit to articulate HCC's degree program, also, with Salisbury University. The associate's degree was articulated and established in fall 2006 (see program page at the end of the chapter).

Since the program was implemented, Introduction to Conflict Resolution is offered three times a year, with an average of twelve students enrolled each time. In fall 2007, MCRC added a new elective course, Introduction to Restorative Justice, which is offered once a year and is growing in popularity. Meanwhile, Conflict and Process, a required course, is offered twice a year but continues to have difficulty attracting students. All three courses combine both theoretical and practical skills-building elements.

Since 2009, only a few students have formally declared conflict resolution as a major (Rockefeller 2010). The most common challenge to recruiting students into the AA in Conflict Resolution program is that it "does not directly translate into a paying career" (Rockefeller 2010, 19). Often, programs promote conflict resolution skills as a great asset in the workforce and even suggest possible career paths in their recruitment efforts. For instance, many community colleges with peace and conflict-resolution programs promote that students who complete a conflict resolution degree/certificate/emphasis may find employment in a number of fields, including nonprofit, criminal justice, government, health, education, human resources, business, and international development. But have direct career links been realistically connected with a degree in conflict resolution, and have students been equipped with the necessary skills? If so, would it then be a program's responsibility to connect students directly with a career? While it is too early to tell, HCC's challenges in recruiting and graduating students with an AA in conflict resolution need further evaluation.

HCC's conflict resolution program is unique in that it was first developed to provide a service to the community and then became an academic program, which also complements the service component and focuses on skills development and practice. A strength of HCC's program is that it balances theory with practical skills. Through MCRC, students have the opportunity to develop their skills and practice what they learn in the classroom. Another strength is the solid partnerships that the Center developed both within the college and in the community. MCRC works in partnership with continuing education in offering regular noncredit mediation and conflict resolution training courses. Also, within the college, MCRC was given oversight for all conflict resolution related courses. Communication and collaboration are therefore required between academic departments that might be interested in conflict resolution topics. For example, conflict resolution courses have been cross-listed with health sciences and criminal justice departments. In the community, the Center built a comprehensive network of criminal justice agencies, government agencies, public schools, community organizations and associations, and the general public, from which it receives mediation referrals.

In MCRC's experience, patience and support are vital to developing a solid academic program. The key ingredient to the program's success was the solid support it received from the college administration and the community.

Future Considerations

Community colleges have been leaders in encouraging and promoting lifelong and continuous learning (Smith 2010). Launching noncredit or continuing-education credit courses is an easy and expeditious way to satisfy the growing demands for professional development and continuous learning, because it is often quicker to develop a course for continuing education than through the traditional academic route. And with employers requesting basic conflict resolution skills as core competencies in the workforce, the potential to offer conflict resolution courses through noncredit continuing education is limitless. Many community colleges are already doing it.

While community colleges are offering peace and conflict-resolution courses that generally include a skills-building element, too few are offering a separate mediation credit course. But four-year colleges and graduate programs in conflict resolution include mediation skills as a core course in their programs. Community colleges may want to ask why they are offering mediation courses mostly as a noncredit option, and what the advantages or disadvantages might be in not offering a mediation credit course.

Also, community colleges historically have had a strong commitment to vocational career education. However, it seems that few peace and conflict studies programs focus on, or have a relationship with, vocational education students. Portland Community College has an employment skills training certificate that focuses specifically on conflict management, and HCC's nursing program offers a conflict resolution course that is cross-listed with the conflict resolution and criminology divisions. Vocational programs are popular with students because they lead to a specific career, such as a trade, or work in health care or the information industry. Therefore, foundational conflict resolution approaches could be invaluable for students in vocational and technical schools. The potential for conflict resolution programs to develop a presence and impact for vocational students is great. Not only should vocational programs incorporate conflict resolution at the local level, but they ought to focus on international issues as well. Such programs can even result in students' applying their skills to international service, including joining the Peace Corps, which often leads to international careers.

But for peace and conflict studies to succeed, programs will need to address the real challenge of enabling students entering a program to bridge their education with a career (such as nursing, social work, human resources, computer forensics, or law enforcement), and they will need to provide a practical skills-building element. Alarmingly, a recent Special Report on higher education from the United States Institute of Peace showed that graduate programs in international peace and conflict management are not adequately preparing students for careers in the field (Carstarphen, Zelizer, Harris, and Smith 2010). While there has been much focus on peacebuilding approaches and conflict resolution in the academic area, there has been less emphasis on vocational education.

Programs, whether at the community college, undergraduate, or graduate level, can do a better job of building partnerships with employers, connecting students with specific career opportunities, and providing them with the necessary skill sets. Because employers are requiring specialized training and certifications rather than a traditional master's degree, community colleges have an opportunity to respond to this growing need (Smith 2008). Those teaching peacebuilding and conflict studies in community colleges could perhaps learn from their colleagues in the vocational education department, where the expectation of a career path is often clearer and students have a greater awareness of how to apply their conflict resolution skills. Or would peace and conflict studies programs be better suited to offer stand-alone courses for already established professions? Or do peace and conflict studies programs continue their traditional focus on continuing and community education? As the field of peacebuilding and conflict resolution continues to develop and grow, its approaches will also reflect the diversity of needs and interests.

Community colleges are often quick to respond to the needs of students, the community, government, and businesses. Thus, community colleges position themselves to take a leading role in addressing conflicts peacefully, both locally and globally, and to help develop the field, especially in the area of skills development. Before developing a peace and conflict-resolution program, it is important to assess carefully how it can best serve students: whether in attaining a career in the field or in transferring to a four-year college. Equally important in designing a program is the need to develop and include courses that cultivate and inspire students to become critical thinkers, to be civically aware and engaged, and to develop valuable skills for the workforce.

Conclusions

Peacebuilding education and, in particular, conflict resolution skills are increasingly being offered through interdisciplinary courses at community colleges. More growth is not only desirable for the field but also necessary in this era of widespread globalization. With affordable education in a wide arena of disciplines, community colleges are an ideal environment for program development and growth that can include the concepts of peacebuilding and conflict resolution. Community colleges serve a diverse and often underprivileged population that comprises close to half of undergraduates in the United States. These "democracy's colleges" are a vital part of American life, offering programs that build immensely important skills for a significant portion of the college population.

Continuing/community noncredit education is vital to employers who want to see their employees gain skills in specialized professional development sessions. The appeal of such courses is obvious, since students enrolled in continuing education can attend sessions that are tailored to their needs and complete them in a time frame that meshes with the demands of work. Vocational education programs, while in need of expansion, are on a path to success because they link skills to a specific field of study. This intentional connection is vitally important as employers demand increasingly specialized skills.

Developing a conflict resolution and peacebuilding program at a community college provides many opportunities and benefits to students, faculty, and the local and international community. As students study the courses offered in conflict resolution and peace programs, they become aware of their role as engaged citizens who are better able to handle conflict both in the workplace and in their personal lives.

The program development experiences at both Northwest Vista College and Howard Community College offer useful insights. While both colleges have developed different programs, there is commonality in their success.

We have narrowed down the top five essential requirements for building a peace and conflict studies program:

1. Most important is patience. It is essential not to rush either the community service program development or the academic development processes. Often an eager individual, group, or committee wants to see immediate results, but building a strong program will take at least four years. Timelines should be set to match the program's components, strategies, and implementation phases.

2. Get the administration on board and secure resources. Program development is challenging enough under the best circumstances, and

without a supportive administration, the obstacles may be simply too great to overcome.

3. Cultivate relationships not only on campus but in the community as well. It is imperative to engage and include community leaders in the process of program development. Focus groups can play a crucial role by bringing together local leaders in a venue where they can voice their needs and help steer the program in a direction that builds a skilled workforce.

4. Have a clear vision that is shared by those actively participating in the program. This shared vision should reflect the needs of various departments, students, and the community. Most important of all, the vision of the program must clearly match the needs of the students it serves.

5. And finally, continuously evaluate and adapt the program for growth and improvement.

As educators in peace and conflict studies, we have the responsibility to see that students can launch their careers with a solid foundation, fully equipped with the necessary skills to meet the demands of their chosen profession. Johannes Botes asks, "Can an academic endeavor and professional field still proving its utility afford to turn out large numbers of graduates who might struggle to apply their qualifications professionally?" (Botes 2004).

References

Botes, Johannes. 2004. "Graduate Peace and Conflict Studies Programs: Reconsidering Their Problems and Prospects." *Conflict Management in Higher Education Report* 5 (1).

Carstarphen, Nike, Craig Zelizer, Robert Harris, and David J. Smith. 2010. "Graduate Education and Professional Practice in International Peace and Conflict." USIP Special Report 246. www.usip.org/resources/graduate-education-and-professional-practice-in-international-peace-and-conflict.

MCRC. 2012. "MCRC AA Degree Information." Howard Community College. www.howardcc.edu/visitors/mcrc/AADegree.html.

Rockefeller, Kathryn B. 2010. *MCRC FY2010 Annual Report*. Available by request from Kathryn B. Rockefeller, Director, Mediation and Conflict Resolution Center at Howard Community College. kathyrockefeller@howardcc.edu.

Smith, David J. 2008. "Global Peace, Conflict and Security: Approaches Taken by American Community Colleges." *Journal of Peace Education* 5 (1): 63–78.

———. 2010. "Peace Keepers: Colleges as Teachers of Peace and Conflict Resolution." *Community College Journal* 8 (1): 44–46.

Howard Community College

Arts and Sciences
Associate of Arts Degree in Conflict Resolution

Conflict is part of life and exists between and among individuals, groups, and nations. The program in Conflict Resolution teaches students theory and skills that will help them resolve conflicts in many settings. The Conflict Resolution program will work in partnership with Howard Community College's Mediation and Conflict Resolution Center (MCRC), where students will have opportunities to observe and practice skills with the MCRC. Students will be able to transfer to four-year programs in Maryland and other states.

General Education Core
General education core credits in excess of 36 will transfer as general electives or courses related to the major. Each student's total of general education and required courses must equal at least 60 semester hours of credit.

		Credits
Composition	ENGL-121 College Composition I	3
	ENGL-122 College Composition II	3
Arts & Humanities	Literature Core Course	3
	Fine Arts Core Course	3
Speech	SPCH-110 or SPCH-105	3
History	History Core Course	3
	(HIST-122 or HIST-123 recommended)	
Social Sciences	PSYC-101 General Psychology	3
	SOCI-101 Introduction to Sociology	3
Mathematics	MATH-122 or MATH-138	3–4
Science	Science Core Courses	7–8
	(must include one course with lab)	
Interdisciplinary	SOCI-115 Emerging World Views	4

Required Courses Related To Major

CRES-155/HEED155	Introduction to Conflict Resolution	3
SOCI-102	Social Problems	3
PHIL-103	Intro to Ethics	3
CRES-201	Conflict and Process	3
CRES-202	Dynamics of Social Conflict	3
CRES-225/SOCI-225	Sociology of Conflict and Nonviolence	3
PSYC-202	Social Psychology	3
ECON-102	Principles of Economics (Micro)	3
		61–63

Conflict Resolution 2011–2012
Course Descriptions

CRES-155 Introduction to Conflict Resolution: Science and Art
3 Credits (Interdisciplinary and Emerging Issues Core)

The purpose of "Introduction to Conflict Resolution: Science and Art" is to introduce students both to different perspectives on conflict and to different strategies for resolving it. Conflict will be explored in different contexts, including intergroup, cross-cultural, and international conflict, with an emphasis on interpersonal conflict. Most importantly, students will be asked to reflect on their own style of conflict resolution and the pertinence of the material covered to conflict resolution in their own lives. Course content will include experiential learning and role-play.

(3 hours weekly) NOTE: Also listed as HEED-155.

CRES-201 Conflict and Process
3 Credits

This course provides students with knowledge about different conflict resolution processes—e.g., mediation, negotiation, arbitration, and facilitation. Role-plays will be used to demonstrate the use of these processes and to provide students with an opportunity to practice conflict resolution skills.

Prerequisites: CRES-155/HEED-155. (3 hours weekly)

CRES-202 Dynamics of Social Conflict
3 Credits

This course will explore the social conflict that results from problems such as structural racism, disproportionate minority confinement in our prisons, economic inequality, and gender discrimination, which continue to be social problems that define U.S. culture. These problems have resulted not only in the attention of observers, as noted by Case, but also in major social movements that have had varying degrees of success in making sustainable improvements in human interaction in our society. These four problems in particular, because of their intractable nature, often underlie conflict at the interpersonal, neighbor-to-neighbor, community, political jurisdiction, and ethnic/identity group levels. Particular attention will be paid to case studies that illuminate racism, gender discrimination, and class inequality. Students will generate potential resolutions to cases through the application of dispute resolution theories and techniques.

Prerequisites: CRES-201. (3 hours weekly)

CRES-225 Sociology of Conflict and Nonviolence
3 Credits
This course examines why humans engage in conflict, why violence is employed to resolve conflict, and the nature and practice of nonviolent conflict resolution. Students will explore the social forces that produce conflict–including cultural, economic, and psychological–and the arenas in which conflict occurs–including family, community, nation, and world. Within an interdisciplinary framework (using social sciences and humanities), students will learn the theoretical, historical, practical, and political aspects of violent and nonviolent conflict. Special attention will be given to emerging social and global conflicts, including examination of how or whether these conflicts might be resolved in a nonviolent manner.
Prerequisite: SOCI-101 or SOCI-102. (3 hours weekly) NOTE: Also listed as SOCI-225.

Humanities – 1302
International Studies-Peace and Conflict Resolution
Northwest Vista College

Instructor: Carlos Lopez

Required Books and Materials:
- *Building Peace: Sustainable Reconciliation in Divided Societies,* by John Paul Lederach
- *The Class of Nonviolence,* designed by Colman McCarthy (Web links to readings provided)
- Other handouts or links to reading assignments will be provided in class.

Class Objectives:
- Demonstrate an understanding of the causes of conflict
- Explore relationship between international conflicts, conflict resolution, and the basics for mediation
- Explore how culture, poverty, health, and other social issues could become sources of conflict
- Evaluate conflict resolution and mediation as an agent of social change and social justice
- Learn to contextualize class materials through study cases and role-play scenarios
- Develop leadership and communication skills

Peace and Conflict Studies: By taking this course, you have the opportunity to earn 3 credit hours toward both Peace and Conflict Studies and International Studies. Please ask me more about these programs if you are interested, or visit the following Web site: www.alamo.edu/nvc

Class Requirements:

PowerPoint Team Presentations – Each team will present on its particular political actor in the negotiations process (Israel, Palestinians [Palestinian National Authority – PNA], HAMAS, USA or UN). I will give you detailed instructions and guidelines on the specific information to be covered. There is a 15- to 20-minute PowerPoint presentation required per team. The work should be equally divided among the team members for each to present on the assigned date. Also, a minimum of a 5- to 10-page report of the team's political actor/country is required as part of this assignment.

Negotiations and Team Proposals: On each day of negotiations, each team will come prepared with a 2- to 3-page proposal for negotiations with the opposing team. Each team needs to be prepared to defend its proposals and ready to issue a counterproposal to be debated in class. I, your instructor, will act as the moderator. I will also provide you with further instructions and information for each round of negotiations.

Teams' Final Agreements: During finals week, all teams, whenever possible and based on their semester negotiations, will draft a final document of at least 5 pages with specific agreements reached by all parties specifying the reasons and conditions for each agreed-upon point or issue. Also, and because there may be points of contention for which no agreement could be achieved, each team will draft a 2-page (minimum) document stating what those points of disagreement are and why they could not be resolved.

Team's Dossier Journal: Each team will put together in a binder all the documentation, information, draft proposals, notes, maps, etc., and make up a dossier for the team's work throughout the semester. You can divide these documents as follows: Full Negotiation Rounds, Exercise Negotiations and Practice, Maps, Team's Notes, Draft Proposals, Final Proposals, and anything else you think can be a part of your team's dossier. Your dossier journal should have a cover page with your country's or political actor's name, flag, and the names of the team members. **To be presented and graded each time during negotiations, including on the final day.**

Course Topics/Readings:
Topic: Understanding the Root Causes of Conflict: "Stuck" on Positions
Reading: *Getting to Yes*, Chapter 1, "Don't Bargain over Positions"

Reading: *If We Listen Well*, by Edward Guinan (from "The Class of Nonviolence")
Video clip: "I Shall Prove My Point"

Reading: *Getting to Yes*, Chapter 2, "Separate the People from the Problem"

Reading: "Human Nature Isn't Inherently Violent," by Alfie Kohn
(from "The Class of Nonviolence")

Reading: "Motivations for Conflict: Groups and Individuals," by Frances Stewart and Graham Brown (from *Leashing the Dogs of War*) In-class exercise on Israeli-Palestinian Conflict

Reading: *Building Peace*: Chapters 1 and 2, Overview and Divided Societies The Chapters stay: BUT CHANGE THE LESSON AND VIDEO (Video: *Arab and Jew*)

Conflict, Divided Societies and Genocide: Rwanda
Reading: "Rwanda," (from *Slaughter among Neighbors: The Political Origins of Communal Violence*)
Reading: *Building Peace*: 170–77 (Case: Rwanda)

Topic: Power as a Source of Conflict/ Video: *Why We Fight*
Reading: Machiavelli, *The Prince*, excerpts

Reading: Carl von Clausewitz, *On War*
Short clips on Chile and General Pinochet: *The Judge and the General* and *War on Democracy: Chile*
Topic: Religion and Conflict: Our Understanding of Islam

Reading: The Quran, excerpts
Video: *Muslims*/The Quran and *Muslims*, cont./Exercise: Settlements/ Jerusalem

Topic: The State and Human Rights
Reading: UN Declaration of Human Rights
Video: What Are Human Rights?

Topic: Breaking the Law on Principle: Disobeying Unjust Laws
Reading: Henry David Thoreau: *On the Duty of Civil Disobedience*, excerpts (from "The Class of Nonviolence)

Reading: *Pilgrimage to Nonviolence*, by Martin Luther King Jr.
(from "The Class of Nonviolence")

In-class Exercise: Based on MLK's 6 points on his philosophy of nonviolence, prepare an outline/nonviolent strategy that could be applied to the Israeli-Palestinian Conflict.

Video: *Peace, Propaganda and the Promised Land*
Reading: *My Faith in Nonviolence*, by Mohandas Gandhi
(from "The Class of Nonviolence")

Reading: *Building Peace*: Chapter 5, Process: The Dynamics and Progression of Conflict
In-class Exercise: Israeli forces in Gaza and its violent repercussions to both sides

8

Community Building through a Peace and Social Justice Institute

KAREN DAVIS

We don't have to engage in grand, heroic actions to participate in the process of change. Small acts, when multiplied by millions of people, can transform the world. —Howard Zinn

The steadfast mission of the community college since its inception has been twofold: to give all members of society access to a postsecondary education whose immediate goals are technical or vocational credentials, with which they can, in turn, serve the community; and to provide, through a two-year liberal education, a portal to serve a more global environment. This twofold mission inspires community colleges to integrate academic and nonacademic services that lay the groundwork for the broader purpose of improving or revitalizing the community. Since most community college students' employment and family ties are rooted directly in their communities, the community college can take a more active role in motivating citizenship through work, volunteer service, and civic engagement. The potential is also there to help students recognize their roles in their communities as significant components of the broader global community. Therefore, developing programs or initiatives in which the student population and community interact opens doors of social, political, and environmental engagement whose focus is peace and social justice. This chapter shares my colleagues' and my experiences in establishing and maintaining an institute dedicated to the concepts of peace, social justice, and conflict management, with the shared goal of passing this passion on to our students. While our Peace and Social Justice Institute continues to evolve, our major endeavors include providing courses within a peace and social justice and conflict management framework, sponsoring on-campus activities related to peace and social justice, and hosting a recurring peace week event every fall.

Inspiration

Pasco-Hernando Community College in Central Florida comprises four campuses with about 8,600 undergraduate students and a total enrollment of 10,770, situated in two counties: Pasco and Hernando. Like many other urban developed areas in Central Florida, Pasco and Hernando counties have shifted demographically from retired Midwestern and Northeastern seniors toward younger permanent-resident families with children attending local public primary and secondary schools. Our college is typical of the norm in providing postsecondary education to traditional and non-traditional students who, for various reasons, choose to remain close to home to pursue degrees and certificates that often place them in the local medical, education, and law enforcement workforces, or to pursue higher degrees at four-year institutions. While our college soon will offer four-year degrees in two disciplines, we have so far remained committed to the two-year community college paradigm.

Through a more personal narrative, I hope to provide inspiration along with practical knowledge for any community college faculty or administration interested in establishing an institutional, community-based initiative dedicated to peace and social justice. My narrative begins with my own initial interest in introducing studies in peace, social justice, and conflict managment onto my college campus through a documentary film festival I hosted in the fall of 2002. I solicited submissions on the Internet through a Web site created for this purpose and was overwhelmed by the response from filmmakers all around the United States and as far away as Israel. While viewing these films to make selections for the festival, I was struck by the intense nature of the works from students in significant film studies programs, professional documentarians, and even a well-known fiction writer. Each filmmaker sought to challenge the audience through provocative images of injustice, war, and poverty and to think beyond the all-too-comfortable dictum that war and conflict are part of human nature. I chose films based on those themes that presented opportunities for dialogue among students, college personnel, and the community that went beyond the classroom experience. Our campus, like most other college campuses throughout the country at this time, was affected by a post-9/11 climate of international terrorism and war. Many students, for the first time in their lives, began questioning national and international dilemmas and their own roles on a broader world stage. Hence, I found myself introducing into my film course more films that examined social injustice, war, and conflict management.

While my initial interest in peace studies was sparked by the film festival, my colleagues played an integral role in preparing the climate for the institute. Our most significant inspiration was our students. Since the English and social sciences faculty had neighboring offices, we often engaged in theoretical and pedagogical discussions related to the United States' current wartime status, our students' military involvement (many were leaving for tours of duty in Iraq and Afghanistan) and interest in war and possible conflict resolution, and our roles as educators and even role models and mentors. We all were confronted daily with our students' questions on causes and effects of war, individual responsibility, social and religious involvement, the national response, and the history of war. Motivated by our students' questions, uncertainty over the duration of U.S. involvement in Iraq and Afghanistan, and the immediacy of working with students who were going to war and those who would be returning to our classrooms, we found the need to form a more cohesive group that could address these challenges together. So we decided to organize a group of instructors and, possibly, administrators who shared our goal of establishing a forum for our students, faculty, and community at large. Participants could not only engage in formal academic peace studies but also explore the just/unjust war questions, along with possible actions toward peacebuilding and conflict resolution on a global scale. Through the initiative of our department's associate dean and faculty members from various disciplines, including English, sociology, history, and psychology, we met to plan a more formal structure. Our first task was to brainstorm ideas for developing a peace and social justice curriculum open to all our students. By the end of the meeting, we had faculty commitments to develop peace-related courses, and most significantly, we agreed to include an interdisciplinary Introduction to Peace Studies course. Even though we had no plan for institutional funding, we managed to develop the courses and include them in our schedules.

Courses in the Institute

The first courses in the newly organized Peace and Social Justice Institute were the interdisciplinary Introduction to Peace Studies (taught by psychology, English, history, and sociology faculty), Nonviolent Conflict Resolution and Film, World Religions, Poetry and Peace, and War and Society. The courses were first offered as electives, and all met the required minimum student enrollment. While the film, religion, poetry, and history courses were theme based within the faculty members' disciplines, Introduction to Peace Studies was a cotaught course, presented on a more experimental

Box 8.1: Peacebuilding through Music

In 2008, El Camino College (Torrance, CA) hosted a concert titled "Ambassadors of Harmony: A Festival of Peace" to showcase the college's peacebuilding activities. Joanna Medawar Nachef, the college's choral director, organized the program. The anthem produced for the event, "Ambassadors of Harmony," was later published by National/Emerson Fred Bock Music and is now regularly performed by many choral groups, including for the United Nations Interim Force in Lebanon in 2009.

basis as a new discipline and a team teaching endeavor. Since peace studies is by its very nature a multidisciplinary field, and since team teaching seems a logical approach to a multidisciplinary course, none of us at the time had a comfortable grasp of the foundational themes the field is based on. At best, however, the students benefited from our expertise in our fields of study, and at worst (as their evaluations reflected), they were confused by the instructor rotations. None of us had taken any formal peace studies courses, but our varied fields of studies qualified us to teach an interdisciplinary course. Looking back, I now see this course as the force that anchored us to a collegewide commitment to studies in peace, social justice, and conflict resolution and moved us forward in our strategy. This was the transition from the efforts of an under-the-radar group of professors trying to introduce a serious approach to peace and conflict studies to an obvious and ostensible presence on campus. As a result of our joint efforts and our enthusiasm for the subject matter, the Institute currently includes six courses:

- *War and Society.* This course focuses not only on the rationale for fighting wars but also on the roles of those involved in conflict prevention. It examines the roles of diplomats, generals, journalists, and protestors toward conflict prevention; the roles of women in warfare; and the Vietnam War from the perspective of the My Lai massacre.
- *Art in Peace and War.* This course focuses on the history and use of art in peace and war. It also emphasizes the political use of art as well as how television, film, books, and other media relate to art in peace and war (for an alternate approach in the performing arts, see box 8.1).
- *Poetry, Peace, and Social Justice.* This course examines poetry thematically and technically as it relates to issues of war and social injustice and their alternatives. Also included are culturally diverse perspectives.
- *World Religions.* Inherent in this course is the ideology of peace in most religious practices. The focus is on traditional religions, such as Hinduism, Buddhism, Christianity, Islam, and Judaism, as well as new religious movements.

- *Introduction to Peace Studies.* This course explores the interdisciplinary field of peace studies from various perspectives, including history, political science, literature, philosophy, psychology, sociology, and other fields. There is a strong emphasis on critical-analysis skills relevant to such ambivalent concepts as empathy/apathy, chaos/order, hostility/compassion, and acceptance/intolerance.
- *Nonviolent Conflict Resolution and Film.* This course examines conflict and conflict resolution through documentary and fiction films with political, sociological, and ethical emphasis.

With the successful implementation of these courses, the Institute had a solid academic presence on campus, and the committee was beginning to develop ideas for more nonacademic projects and events to attract the wider student body. It was at this time that I was introduced to the United States Institute of Peace (USIP). I applied for and was accepted into USIP's 2007 intensive weeklong seminar for community college faculty and administrators held in Washington, D.C. My interactions with my fellow community college instructors from across the United States and with the staff and guest speakers at USIP reinforced my knowledge, pursuit, and, most of all, enthusiasm for peace studies and the further development of programs in the Peace and Social Justice Institute. My colleagues in the Peace and Social Justice Institute shared my enthusiasm for creating a student-focused event.

Formation of Peace Week

While some of our students were learning about war through firsthand experience, for most, war was happening far away in countries with very different cultures from their own. Their exposure was through sporadic information from electronic media and network television. Their knowledge of diplomacy and conflict resolution, other conflicts on the world stage, and human rights violations was very limited. Through electronic media and television and, to a lesser extent, print media, students were being exposed more to the controversies surrounding war than to the controversies surrounding more peaceful means to resolving conflicts. Our students were sporting the now trendy peace sign and beginning to ask relevant questions but, at the same time, still seeing war as an inevitable product of the human condition, and conflict resolution as more elusive than ever. Clearly, we had a compelling argument for a student-focused nonacademic event. Although most faculty members can work within their classrooms to promote an on-campus peace-related event (all you need are enthusiastic students and a motivated instructor), working with a budget would expand options and attract a wider audience. But with a troubled state and federal economy, any funding for

Box 8.2: Peacebuilding Fairs

A number of community colleges throughout the country host on-campus peace fairs and community-based conferences.

Arizona Western College sponsored a Peace Expo Educational Conference on the International Day of Peace (September 21) in 2009. The event brought together a range of community groups in Yuma, Arizona, working to promote sustainability and peace.

Bluegrass Community and Technical College holds an annual Peace and Global Citizenship Fair. The 2012 fair brought together local Lexington, Kentucky, organizations that focus on peacebuilding, as well as representatives from the Peace Corps, non-governmental organizations and Iraqi, Burundian, and Guatemalan cultural groups.

Cayuga Community College holds an annual Peace Festival, designed as a community fair, for the Fulton, New York, community it serves. The event has been held since 2011.

Golden West College hosts an annual Peace Conference in Huntington Beach, California. The 2011 daylong event was titled "A Better Tomorrow: Making Peace a Global Reality in the 21st Century." A host of groups, including the International Center on Nonviolent Conflict and USIP, made presentations.

Grand Rapids Community College in Michigan held a Peace and Reconciliation Conference in 2009, sponsored by the college's Irish Studies Program. The event included a keynote address by Nobel Peace Prize Laureate John Hume.

Henry Ford Community College in Dearborn, Michigan, sponsors an annual conference on religion, conflict, and peace. In 2012, the theme of the event was "Walking the Talk to Compassion and Harmony." The Common Bond Institute, Parashakthi Temple, the People's Peace Fund, and the International Humanistic Psychology Association cosponsored the conference.

Since 2009, Lane Community College in Eugene, Oregon, has sponsored an annual Peace Symposium. The themes have varied from local to global issues. The 2011 conference focused on natural resources.

In 2008, San Diego City College sponsored a conference on international relief organizations. The event provided a platform for international relief and peacemaking organizations, based in Southern California and elsewhere, to raise awareness about their mission, work, and accomplishments and to connect students with groups where they might seek internships and future employment.

the Institute was even bleaker. However, a student-focused nonacademic activity fell under the jurisdiction of Student Activities, so through the collaboration between full-time and part-time faculty, Student Activities, and Student Government, we managed to procure speaker funding for an event titled "Peace Week" (see box 8.2 for more examples).

As with most innovations, moving forward with optimism and enthusiasm first and damage control last is the solid, progressive approach. Since most committee members were connected with our students through the classroom, clubs, and extracurricular activities, we were confident through experience that they would be receptive to our agenda. Moreover, we assured the administration that we were not staging any kind of media-drawing politically partisan peace demonstration, but rather a bipartisan forum that would encourage awareness and promote dialogue within our campuswide community and the community at large. We expressed our further commitment to establishing our college as a paragon of peace and social justice by installing a peace pole—a pole inscribed with the message "May Peace Prevail on Earth" in different languages—as part of the international Peace Pole Project campaign on our main campus. Our college president affirmed her support by suggesting that we order not one but three peace poles, one for each campus.

Moving Forward

From the start, the committee's goals were compatible, as reflected in our peacebuilding philosophy: that peace is not simply the absence of war, but a constantly changing and fragile ideology. Peace is threatened when people are not given the opportunity to express, connect, cooperate, and learn to understand one another in an ever more culturally diverse, technologically advancing society and an increasingly volatile global, political, and social climate.

The first Peace Week would reflect this philosophy through guest speakers, faculty and staff lectures and discussion, workshops, a film series, discussion panels, art, music, cultural displays, and entertainment. Through Peace Week, we could challenge students to embrace the notion that war is not an inevitable part of the human condition and that they, as community college students, could contribute to a different dialogue: a dialogue of peace and conflict resolution. We recognized the need to engage students of all disciplines. This, of course, was where faculty involvement became crucial. As most educators know, attracting students to free outdoor events and free food requires little effort—but luring them indoors to attend more time-consuming lectures or film panels is more of a challenge. Most instructors in arts and social sciences can easily include an interdisciplinary lecture, discussion, or film presented outside the classroom as relevant to their discipline. But science and technology instructors, who have more rigid and sequential curricula, are more reluctant to sacrifice class time in favor of an extracurricular activity unless it pertains directly to their lectures. Therefore, we tried to schedule the more science- and technology-focused events during those class times. In this way, many students benefited by participating in events along with their instructors and classmates, while others were enticed through extra credit or entertainment. This is not to imply that students will avoid an academic or informative event unless bribed to do so, but the very nature of the community college as a commuter-based environment where students are often obliged to hold one or more jobs, perhaps while raising a family, makes scheduling extra time into their days a challenge. So we had to work within our students' daily time constraints and focus particular events during specific class times. Students also tend to leave events punctually at the end of the required class meeting to attend other classes; therefore, being attentive to the collegewide course schedule helps us avoid a mass exodus during the middle of an event. Since Florida's autumn weather is quite temperate and we have adequate outdoor space in a relatively contained area on our campuses, Peace Week events are visible to most of the student body. Getting Student Activities' assistance also involved engaging students with refreshments, tile painting, drum circles, and musical performances. Still, all these events related to our mission of peace and attracted students, faculty, and staff throughout the campus.

Reflection

Since we proposed our objectives at a time when our college was seeking ways to expand its course offerings—and before the economic crisis—we didn't encounter any insurmountable obstacles, but we remain committed to continuing the balance between serious dialogue on peace and conflict management in the classroom, outside on the campus, and, ultimately, in the community. Today's financial constraints might hinder the versatility of course offerings, but an argument can be made for the long-term benefits of preparing students for the more globalized job market. Also, expanding our Institute through Peace Week has presented more creative funding opportunities through Student Activities. Student Activities has been instrumental in getting speakers and hosting events, which most faculty members would find quite time consuming when added to their teaching duties. Through more strategic scheduling, we hope to increase student and faculty attendance numbers, but the problem of bringing in the community remains. For our most recent Peace Week, we had the nonfinancial sponsorship of a major Florida newspaper; however, we had little control over how they used our press releases. While they did announce many of the events, they limited their articles in the local section to two of our more controversial speakers—and after the fact. We would have liked to see an article, along with an image, addressing Peace Week's overall peacebuilding goal at the *beginning* of the event, highlighting students' enthusiasm for peace and possibly attracting more community attention and attendance. By engaging the newspaper's staff in the planning stages, we hope to inspire more relevant articles. A collegewide endeavor of this scope needs to secure as much faculty cooperation as possible, along with the marketing department's assistance in promoting the program to the larger community. With this in mind, I recently organized an executive committee of faculty and staff representing diverse disciplines to oversee the Institute's activities and participate in planning Peace Week. Through this committee, we hope to give all departments a voice in the Institute's mission and decision making.

Although we had no immediate plan for the future at its inception, Peace Week has become the college's biggest annual event with the largest Student Activities budget, reaching an estimated eight thousand students on all four campuses. The Peace and Social Justice Institute and, eventually, Peace Week originated from our commitment to peace and conflict management studies. Our mission can be summed up as a collegewide collaboration to prepare students for a technologically advanced global society whose future depends on peacebuilding. But most importantly, we have learned (and corroborated through students' testimonials) the influence that the Institute's efforts have had on the students' awareness of, and active participation in, peace, social justice, and conflict resolution. Student feedback has been inspirational, with comments such as these: "Thank you for what you do to bring Peace Week to our campus," and "I drew a lot out of everything I took part in, and am changed in different positive and intellectual ways because of it." While we hope to connect more with the community at large, our student body remains our immediate priority. Probably the most influential tool in achieving this goal has been language. Through the peace courses and the annual Peace Week event, not only do faculty, staff, and students associate our college with peace, but the terms of peace are assimilated into their vocabulary and, hopefully, their lives. The many speakers, events, and films during Peace Week, along with the peace courses and curricula, show our students how to speak the language of peace, social justice, and conflict resolution in a peace-friendly environment, and empower them to carry this language into their communities. We all see how the climate of an entire country can be all too easily influenced by bumper sticker slogans and faulty logic. Therefore, as educators, we should recognize the influence we have in steering our students away from the language of conflict, hatred, and ignorance and toward language more conducive to positive peace. Through our leadership roles, professional expertise, and dialogue at our institutions, we can generate opportunities in our classrooms, centers, and campus activities to enlist our students in a new peace activism of twenty-first-century conflict management and peacebuilding.

2010 PHCC Peace Week Theme: "Peace Begins with Me"
All events are free and open to the community.

Peace Week, Wednesday, November 3–Wednesday, November 10, is presented by Pasco-Hernando Community College's Peace and Social Justice Institute and Student Activities Department. Events incl ude keynote speakers, presentations, panel discussions, artistic performances, and interactive participation.

This program recognizes that peace is not simply the absence of war but a constantly changing, fragile ideology that can be threatened if people are not given the opportunity to express, connect, cooperate, and learn to understand one another in an ever more culturally diverse, technologically advancing society and a volatile global political and social climate.

Wednesday, November 3
Building a Culture of Peace Panel Display
Jim Schienle, PHCC adjunct instructor

Peace Week Opening Ceremony and Keynote Address
Keynote Speaker
Sheldon Himelfarb, Associate Vice President, Center of Innovation for Science, Technology & Peacebuilding/Media, Conflict & Peacebuilding, United States Institute of Peace

Thursday, November 4
Peace Week Festival
Event features: Peace tile creations, friendship bracelet making, wish bottles, tie-dye shirts, the Giving Tree Music Circle, Chris Jackson (professional flutist).

Peace Begins with Me
Discover ways to focus your energy on calming yourself; learn how others affect you. An introduction to meditation.
Jessica White, Student Activities Director, West Campus

Panel Discussion: Cultural Diversity and Peace
Moderated by Imani Asukile, District Coordinator of Multicultural Student Affairs and Equity Services

Should We All Become Environmental Activists?
Karen Davis, Associate Professor, Language Arts
Discover how environmental changes threaten national and international security and have influenced past conflicts.

Keynote Speaker: T. J. Leyden
As a leading recruiter, organizer, and propagandist for the white supremacist and neo-Nazi movement, Leyden spent fifteen years promoting hate, bigotry, and racism. In 1996, he renounced racism and began working as a consultant to the human rights organization Simon Wiesenthal Center in Los Angeles. He

now devotes his time to speaking at high schools, colleges, FBI headquarters, and police agencies.

Friday, November 5
Faces of Soldiers: Service through Remembrance, and the Place of War in Peace
Andrew Grimmer, student
Art, poetry, and prose project honoring soldiers who have served in Iraq and Afghanistan.

Saturday, November 6
Peace Week Community Festival
Event features: Native Pride Dancers, the Giving Tree Music Circle, food and refreshments, area school Sheet Project displays, peace tile creations, friendship bracelets, wish bottle making

Performance: *Twelve Angry Jurors*, a play by Reginald Rose
A Showcase Repertory Company Production
Twelve Angry Jurors is the approved adaptation of the classic play *Twelve Angry Men* that features a mixed cast of men and women.

Monday, November 8
Religious Fair
We know very little about the role of religion in conflict situations and peace-building efforts. Religion intersects with economic, social, political, and other factors in very complex ways. Faith communities are often arrayed on different sides of the same issue. In order to learn more about realities on the ground, PHCC Peace Week provides an opportunity to visit with local religious leaders and engage in dialogue.

Film and Discussion: *The Moses Code*
Facilitated by PHCC Coordinator of Student Activities Jessica White

Original Play Workshop
Daniel Caron

Keynote: Laughter in Peace Tour
A Muslim, a Jew, and a Christian Enter the PHCC Performing Arts Center . . .
This unique event has received critical acclaim across the continent and promises to be a lot of fun, and an experience guaranteed to break down stereotypes and warm our hearts. According to the *New York Times*, "They had the audience convulsing."

Tuesday, November 9
Thoughts on Peace, Social Justice, and the Western Tradition
Mike Sadusky, Professor, Social Sciences
This lecture will focus on the practice of peace and social justice, primarily in Judaism and Christianity. Some comparisons will be made with Native American spirituality and insights on peace and social justice. If time allows, we will also

include some thoughts on religions of the East. The approach will be biblical, historical, and critical.

Film and Discussion: *Forgiving Dr. Mengele*
Facilitated by Professor Mike Sadusky

Peace Week Festival: Think Globally, Act Locally!
Event features: Peace-Related Organizations—visit the information tables and discover how you can be involved in dynamic initiatives.

Scott Camil
Former member of Vietnam Veterans Against the War, current member of Veterans for Peace, and the subject of numerous documentaries

Film and Discussion: *Scott Camil Will Not Die*
Also showing the documentary *Seasoned Veteran, Journey of a Winter Soldier*

Lecture: Loss of Relevance
Artist and Teacher: David Kastner
A study of the history of history, its context in social relations, social sculpture, bureaucracy, and individual responsibility found in the action of living.

Keynote Speaker
Eva Mozes Kor, Auschwitz survivor and victim, along with her twin sister **Miriam**, of Dr. Josef Mengele's experiments
Eva firmly believes that in our own way, we each can make a difference. She is making a difference by helping people understand what hatred and prejudice can do.

Wednesday, November 10
Civil Liberties and the Patriot Act
Larry Poller, Adjunct Instructor
Peace Week Luncheon: Reflections on Peace Week Activities

9

Teaching Peace through Short-Term Study Abroad

Long-Term Benefits for Students *and* Faculty

VASILIKI ANASTASAKOS

Travel is fatal to prejudice, bigotry, and narrow-mindedness. —*Mark Twain*

In higher education, the need to promote global awareness among students has become increasingly urgent (Nair et al. 2012, 1). Some community colleges are particularly keen on addressing this need since, with their deep local roots, they feel acutely the consequences of global developments such as wars, job outsourcing, and other shifts in the global economy for the communities they serve. Central to the community college mission is preparing students to live and work successfully in today's world with its inexorable link between the global and the local. Increasingly, community colleges are adopting study-abroad programs as part of their larger efforts to enhance students' global literacy. When community colleges successfully combine a curriculum infused with a global perspective, study-abroad programs, and other types of experiential learning, they can become powerful agents of world peace.

Until recently, students who studied abroad were relatively affluent compared to the overall college population and generally went abroad for a semester or a year. As more and more community colleges realized that students from all socioeconomic strata would benefit from studying abroad, they began offering a wide range of short-term programs. Defining "short-term" is not easy, because "they can range from week-long programs conducted during spring break in conjunction with a single course, to three- or four-week programs conducted during January term or in the summer, to longer programs of up to eight weeks that can involve home stays, travel to multiple sites, and service or research experiences" (Donnelly-Smith 2009, 2).

Rather than follow one single formula, community colleges have developed distinctive ways of structuring study-abroad programs, depending on their various strengths, resources, and institutional cultures. Despite the diversity of approaches, community colleges are already playing a major role in transforming the world as they become an integral part of global education. In doing so, they also enrich the lives of all participants—students, faculty, and the entire college community in both the host and home countries—thus contributing to a more peaceful global community. What follows is an account of my professional and personal journey teaching short-term study-abroad courses in Turkey and Costa Rica.

The Need for Teaching Global Literacy

From the very first moment I set foot inside a community college classroom in the late 1980s, I knew that being an effective political science teacher was not going to be easy. I quickly noticed that many of my students approached local, national, and global issues with a strong dose of apathy and cynicism and a sense of disempowerment. Their lack of engagement was very disturbing to me. My personal life experiences had not only influenced my choice of political science as a field of study but had also transformed me into a proponent of nonviolent protest and pacifism. I was born in Greece and had spent my adolescent years living through a repressive and brutal military junta during 1967–74. People from all walks of life were often imprisoned, tortured, exiled, even killed for seeking a return to democracy. When my family moved to the United States in 1972, the country was just going through the painful end of the Vietnam War, dealing with unanswered questions and thousands of physically and mentally broken returning veterans. Moreover, Watergate shook the foundations of our democracy, and people's trust in democratic institutions waned. How was I going to convince my students that democracy was not a spectator sport and that simply voting once every four years to choose the next president was not enough? And if they were not engaged in local and national issues, how could they be convinced that being responsible and peaceful world citizens was equally important? How was I going to make world hunger, poverty, and war real and relevant for them?

In the late 1980s and early 1990s, very few community colleges offered any courses in international relations or global studies, and even basic introductory courses in the field were rare to nonexistent. This would change after two disastrous events, both of which manifested the inexorable link between global problems and local consequences. The first such event was the tragedy of September 11, 2001. Two-year colleges started recruiting faculty with expertise in international relations, and I landed my first full-time, tenure-track job, at Northampton Community College (NCC). The second event—more relevant to my own environment—was the 2001 bankruptcy of Bethlehem Steel, the gigantic company that had been the economic life-blood of Bethlehem, Pennsylvania, where NCC is located. Bethlehem Steel had been the largest employer in the area since the 1850s and one of the most powerful symbols of American industrial manufacturing leadership. It was ironic that these two catastrophic events had made international relations, my field of study and my personal passion, finally relevant.

My students' questions, filled with fear, anxiety, and confusion, became the window of opportunity to infuse my teaching with global awareness. I chose textbooks that addressed the connection between the global and the local, and I linked classroom discussions and assignments to this new reality. I used the Internet to show students the latest global developments, often with horrifying images from faraway places whose names sounded new and unfamiliar to them. Without realizing it, I gradually became a practitioner of experiential learning through service learning projects. I invited guest speakers into my classes: union activists, retired Bethlehem Steel workers, war veterans, antiwar activists, and conflict resolution experts. Whenever possible, I required students to attend campus events with guest speakers who recounted personal stories of life and death. In 2007, Benjamin Ajak, a refugee from Darfur, spoke to our students about losing his family and spending many years in a refugee camp until the age of thirteen, when he and his cousins were able to flee to the United States. The following year, Jacqueline Murekatete, a young college student who was ten when her entire family was killed during the Rwandan genocide of 1994, visited our campus to share her story.

These events affected my students deeply. Although our college's population was fast becoming more diverse, most of my students had not traveled outside the United States. The large majority of them were from middle- and working-class families living in Bethlehem, Allentown, and Easton, Pennsylvania, although increasingly more of them had recently moved to the area from northern New Jersey or New York City. With the relatively recent influx of significant numbers of international students from countries such as Brazil, Egypt, Turkey, Taiwan, and South Africa, the student demographics in our campuses were quickly changing.

Soon, my own teaching would take a global turn. NCC was already a member of Community Colleges for International Development (CCID), a consortium of 160 U.S. two-year colleges that initiates and manages study-abroad programs, international faculty development programs, and conferences focused on global issues. NCC's Office of International Education, which had been extremely active offering cultural enrichment trips to France, Russia, Denmark, and other countries during spring breaks, was exploring the possibility of offering for-credit study-abroad courses through CCID's Troika program. "Troika" is a creative way for community colleges to collaborate, combine their resources, and make study abroad affordable to their students. It is based on the simple concept of having three community colleges carry out a joint course for three consecutive years, with teachers from each college taking turns leading/teaching the course each year. Each participating college agrees to recruit a minimum of four students and to award a minimum of four $750 scholarships ($3,000) for each program annually.

This financial commitment is of tremendous importance, since the average cost of most trips is about $2,500. Although some participating colleges offer scholarships that exceed the required minimum of $750 per student, it is not unusual for faculty and students to organize fund-raisers to further defray the costs. Also, many students use financial aid to cover the tuition part of the course. Participating faculty members are compensated for teaching a three-credit course the year they lead the class; when they are not leading, their travel expenses are covered. Leading is equivalent to teaching the course, from developing the syllabus to grading assignments and submitting final grades. Also, leading faculty are in charge of the logistics of in-country activities, although most decisions are reached by consensus among the faculty team. They collectively design the common course and agree on common readings, assignments, and activities, while allowing some flexibility into the course to meet curriculum- or program-related requirements specific to each participating college. Although CCID membership is not necessary to teach a study-abroad course successfully, the signing of memorandums of understanding by the presidents of the participating colleges does provide the guarantee of strong institutional support and funding for the project.

Turkey: Teaching Peace through Intercultural Understanding

In the spring of 2004, I was invited to participate in a faculty exchange program in Turkey, as a member of a faculty team from NCC, Delaware Technical and Community College, and Howard Community College in Maryland. Later, we were divided into two groups with three members each. One group went to Iskenderun, in southern Turkey near the Syrian border, while our group went to Cankiri University in the town of Cankiri, about fifty miles northeast of Ankara.

Cankiri University has a reputation as one of Turkey's best vocational/technical colleges. Upon our arrival, it became quite clear that our hosts were gracious and amazingly well organized. In addition to giving presentations on Turkish history and education, they had planned a series of visits to local schools and vocational training centers. We met with school principals, teachers, and students; we toured their facilities, including computer, automotive, and electronics labs; and we saw student exhibits in electronics, textiles, art, and engineering. The most fascinating part of the trip was becoming acquainted with Turkish history and culture through visits to local museums, mosques, open markets, and restaurants. At Cankiri University, we attended several end-of-the-year activities involving folk dancing and music as well as a local food competition. After visiting two other colleges in the towns of Nevsehir and Kastamonu, we traveled to Ankara and concluded our trip with four days in magnificent Istanbul.

For me, the trip was particularly moving and transformative. I had received my primary and secondary education in Greece during the 1950s and 1960s and was all too familiar with the "official" historical narrative of Greece: Turkey was the aggressive neighbor, the enemy, the one to fear. Images flashed in my mind: the 1453 fall of Constantinople, 400 years of Ottoman rule, the 1821 War of Independence, and the conflict on Cyprus. This was going to be a challenge. How would my Turkish colleagues react to my being Greek? How would my Greek friends and family react to my trip? These concerns evaporated quickly. In a very short time, I was feeling completely at home. The sights, sounds, food, music, and people all seemed familiar to me. The color of the sky, the smiles on people's faces, the smell of coffee, and the scrumptious Mediterranean cuisine triggered familiar childhood memories. I quickly saw myself as an ambassador of goodwill engaging in citizen diplomacy. I felt empowered realizing that my actions and teaching could promote, even in a limited sense, better understanding and collaboration among our peoples in Turkey, Greece, and the United States.

Upon my return to the States, I began designing the first three-credit study-abroad course, Politics of Modern Turkey. It was my hope that by taking this course, students would not only learn about Turkey's rich history, society, and culture but would also develop a capacity to appreciate ethnic and religious diversity. There was one catch: Turkey is a predominantly Muslim, albeit secular, society. What challenges was I going to face in trying to recruit my first group of students? Despite the fact that nearly four years had passed since September 11, 2001, I expected students to be apprehensive about traveling there.

In hindsight, things were not as difficult as I had imagined. There were occasions when I had to respond to a few anxious parents' e-mails and phone calls regarding trip safety. I invited one student's parents to sit in during the first student orientation to help them feel at ease. After all, this was the first time their daughter or son would spend three weeks far from home without them. I also recall how understanding I had to be when a disappointed student told me that her parents would not help pay for the trip, since they did not approve of it.

The complexity and logistics of coordinating the trip among our three colleges were daunting. The work seemed endless and the hurdles insurmountable. After several months of preparations—and periods of serious doubt whether the project was going to get off the ground—we finally made it: eighteen students and three staff members from three different colleges. From the start, I knew that this was going to be a different type of course: we had no campus, no classroom, no blackboard, and not a single teacher who was an authority on Turkish politics and society. I felt less like a teacher and more like a student—someone who would guide my students to learn but who would also be learning right along with them.

Soon after we arrived, my nervousness subsided—our hosts were friendlier, more welcoming, and better organized than I had any reason to hope. They helped us feel at home in a country whose culture we did not know and communicate with people whose language we did not understand. Through lectures and museum visits, we were introduced to the fascinating civilizations from both East and West that have shaped the social, political, cultural, and religious character of Turkey. Our students became aware of the significant role that Turkey plays in the Middle East and Eastern Mediterranean, and its efforts toward joining the European Union. They were exposed to tradition and modernity, religion and secularism, rural life and urbanization, and the family structure in Turkish society.

Most importantly, they forged strong friendships that would last for many, many years and that would bring several of them back to Turkey—this time on their own, for they had acquired the curiosity of world travelers—to revisit, continue to learn, and spend time with their new friends. Others would welcome their Turkish friends in the United States in the following years, as our student exchange program flourished and some received scholarships for two-year studies in our college. The next summer, I was ready to be the lead teacher. It was another equally stressful year of preparations, culminating in a highly successful and rewarding trip. Little did I know that I would continue preparing and participating in these trips for several years to come, or that I would become a staunch advocate for study-abroad education in my college.

After reading my students' reflective journals and research papers, I was convinced that the course had enhanced their global literacy and awareness. Although the course did not directly address the theory associated with peace studies courses, the three-week trip was a hands-on exercise in multicultural understanding and peaceful coexistence. It allowed my students to grow as individuals and open up to the world around them. Their attitudes and perspectives about themselves and their place in the global community had changed dramatically. They had acquired a deeper understanding and respect for diverse religions, cultures, and traditions, and they had become lifelong friends with people in another corner of the world. Aren't these, after all, among the basic requirements for world peace? Here are some of the thoughts they included in their reflective journals:

> The program has been very beneficial to me as a student and as a person. The experience was like no other that I've ever had in my life, and I wish to see this program continue for many years so more students can have the opportunity that I have had. The places I've been, the things I've touched, and the people I've met are some of the things I hold close to my heart after having traveled over 1,000 miles inside Turkey. For me, this trip has aided me and solidified my aspirations to pursue a degree in International Relations and one day work for a foreign embassy.

> The course not only opened my eyes to a world so similar and yet so different to mine, it also let me touch that world. The experiences of seeing, hearing, touching, and smelling a country that was foreign to me at the time made me realize how fundamentally similar people are, despite cultural or geographical differences. . . I absolutely think study-abroad trips can contribute to world peace. My experience alone has taught me to be more open-minded and to look at things beneath the surface. Traveling to Turkey has made me more compassionate, understanding, and tolerant toward all people. I continue to travel to Turkey since my study-abroad course at NCC. I have traveled there a combined total of six times (two with NCC and four solo trips). After I graduate this May, I plan to move to Turkey. I'm in the process of getting my TEFL certificate, and I hope to teach English at first.

> The trip challenged me on many levels. It challenged me to leave the only place I knew, America. It challenged me to be with other students that I did not know but got to know very well. It challenged me to learn about Islam. As a Jewish American, it was the first time I learned anything about Islam . . . I still travel. I studied in Budapest, Hungary, and in Israel. I am now signed up for the Peace Corps. The Turkey trip opened my eyes to life abroad. I now reach out to others that have a different background than I. My eyes were opened to everything Turkish, and I had to let go of my small-mindedness surrounding American ideals. It was a breath of fresh air to try to understand something besides myself. Once I was able to open myself to others, I found a freedom in me. To this day, I make a friend just by knowing how to say hello in Arabic. Study-abroad trips contribute to world peace by allowing students to develop an understanding of how to relate better to others.

My students' growth was one of the most profound experiences of my teaching career. I remember watching each one of them transform before my eyes with each passing day during our trip and realizing how their lives changed in the long term after we returned to the States. One of them transferred to a four-year college and soon signed up for a semester abroad in Hungary. Another traveled for three months in Costa Rica alone and is now planning to study in China. Someone else contacted me for a recommendation letter for the Peace Corps, and another is completing a master's degree in international education. Yet another left two months ago, with a BA in journalism and a TOEFL (Test of English as a Foreign Language) certification in hand, to spend a year in Turkey teaching English. I became convinced that this short-term study-abroad experience had transformed my students' lives for the long term.

My own transformation was equally powerful and touched every aspect of my teaching. I expanded service learning projects that linked the global to the local, and promoted all types of experiential learning through group work, simulations, and campus events. I felt much more comfortable acknowledging that I did not know everything, and I welcomed spending time outside the classroom with my students. I became a staunch advocate of study-abroad courses and seized every opportunity to speak to colleagues and students about my experiences. For the next three years, I would return to Turkey, guiding more students through this fascinating journey. Eventually, after "passing the torch" to another enthusiastic colleague, I began designing my next study-abroad course: Peace Studies and Conflict Resolution. Destination: Costa Rica.

Costa Rica: Teaching Peace and Conflict Resolution

This was yet another course made possible through the CCID Troika project. Although peace studies courses are increasingly being offered in community colleges, NCC did not yet have such a course. Since peace and conflict resolution had become one of my primary areas of interest, and since I welcomed the opportunity to work with other academics and professionals in the field, I seized the opportunity. In the summer of 2010, after a year of preparation and countless hours of teleconferencing, five educators from Cuyahoga Community College in Cleveland, Richland College (of the Dallas County Community College District), Southeastern Iowa Community College, and NCC traveled to Costa Rica for a site visit. Unlike my first course, Politics of Modern Turkey, this course had objectives directly related to peace and conflict resolution. The course outline clearly stated that the main goals were to teach students the fundamental concepts and theories of the peace studies field and to focus on Costa Rica as a case study of countries attempting to create and sustain a culture of peace.

In June 2011, the first group of students from the three colleges completed the first successful two-week trip to Costa Rica. Their pretrip assignments were heavily focused on peace theory, multitrack diplomacy, and approaches to conflict transformation. During their in-country visit, they attended lectures by Costa Rican academics and presentations by government officials, teachers, and community activists working in the fields of peace education and conflict resolution in schools, prisons, government, and community organizations. They visited the UN-mandated University for Peace, the Costa Rican Ministry of Justice and Peace, Earth University, and the Quaker community in Monteverde. They participated in a service learning project by building a biodigester that will provide energy for one rural community, and volunteered at the Cedes School, run by the Catholic Church in one of San José's poorest barrios. They visited the U.S. embassy and the Arias Foundation (named after Costa Rica's Nobel Peace Prize-winning former president Oscar Arias). They also talked about community volunteerism and social justice with their Costa Rican counterparts at ULACIT (Universidad Latinoamericana de Ciencia y Tecnología), our outstanding partner college in San José. And they immersed themselves in the local culture through their homestays with Costa Rican families.

Even though this was the first of the three years in the Troika project, it was an extremely well run and successful course. This was primarily due to the diligence of the faculty involved, who had spent countless hours over the past year in weekly teleconferences discussing the minute details of the project. Upon the group's return to the States, we collectively discussed at length what worked well for our students and what didn't and started revising and improving the course for the following year.

Conclusion

Clearly, there is no single or simple formula that guarantees success in a study-abroad course. The current literature is clear, however, on the basic ingredients necessary for a short-term study-abroad program to be effective:

- *Clear academic content and faculty familiar with experiential learning methods.* An academically rigorous course with faculty who can help students "connect the dots" between what they read and what they experience is a must (Donnelly-Smith 2009).
- *Integration with the local community.* Students should not be tourists. They should forge strong friendships with their host families and student cohorts, which, hopefully, they will maintain for a long time after their return home.
- *Lectures/presentations by academics and professionals from the host country.* These give students a new, genuine perspective on the country.
- *Reflection, reflection, reflection!* Reflective journaling and structured group discussions are essential. The discussions enable faculty to help students integrate daily what they experience and how the experience relates to course content (Donnelly-Smith 2009).

- *Reciprocity for host country collaborators.* On two different occasions, Turkish community college students visited NCC, HCC, and Delaware Technical and Community College during trips to the United States. We hope that our students will soon have the opportunity to host their friends from Costa Rica.

Undoubtedly, short-term study-abroad courses alone are not enough to meet the urgent need for global awareness and literacy. They must be part of a broader approach to global education and should be combined with service learning and other community-based projects that bridge global and local issues and concerns. And they should be part of a broader campus culture that fosters and celebrates respect for diversity and multiculturalism. Also, study-abroad courses should not be limited to the humanities or social sciences but should be incorporated across disciplines, especially in science and technology.

The challenges of creating and sustaining short-term study-abroad courses at the community college level are many, particularly during times of severe budget cuts in higher education. At NCC, we had minimal prior institutional experience but a strong desire to develop a study-abroad program. Our Office of International Education is very active in recruiting and assisting interested faculty in developing additional courses. We have made tremendous strides in becoming more familiar with the intricacies of planning, creating, and teaching such courses. Since short-term study-abroad courses are largely faculty led, it is essential that they receive strong institutional support as they grapple with the complex nature of study-abroad teaching. Although the course duration may be short-term, the benefits of such programs for our students and our local and global communities will undoubtedly be long-term.

References

Donnelly-Smith, Laura. 2009. "Global Learning through Short-Term Study Abroad." *Peer Review* 11 (Autumn). www.aacu.org/peerreview/pr-fa09/donnelly smith.cfm.

Nair, Indira, Marie Norman, G. Richard Tucker, and Amy Burkert. 2012. "The Challenge of Global Literacy: An Ideal Opportunity for Liberal Professional Education." *Liberal Education* 98 (Winter). www.aacu.org/liberaleducation/le-wi12/nair.cfm.

Study Abroad in Costa Rica 2011:
Peace Studies and Conflict Resolution

The activities below were designed to enhance student understanding of the concept of multitrack diplomacy, which is the focus of the course. Students were exposed to government officials, non-governmental organizations, religious and community agencies, educational institutions, and other entities and individuals, all working to sustain the Costa Rican culture of peace.

Sunday, June 5
7:10 & 8:15   Arrivals in San José, capital city of Costa Rica
Host families will pick students up at airport and transport to their homes

Monday, June 6 (All day at La Universidad Latinoamericana de Ciencia y
                Tecnología—ULACIT, our partner college in Costa Rica)
10:00   Orientation, getting acquainted, team building
11:30   Lunch
12:30   Lecture by Mr. José Pablo Barquero on Costa Rican politics and
        economy
2:30   Process, discuss, presentation planning

Tuesday, June 7
8:00   Travel to United Nations University for Peace (UNUP)
9:00   Lecture on peacebuilding by Christer Persson, Head of Department
        International Law and Human Rights, University for Peace. Tour of
        facilities/grounds/ peace sculptures, lunch
1:00   Return to ULACIT, process UNUP experience
2:00   Presentation by Ricardo Calvo, warden of Cartago jail, on Costa Rica's
        criminal justice system
5:00   Meeting with ULACIT student members of Civics House Club to discuss
        how community service contributes to peaceful communities

Wednesday, June 8
8:30   ULACIT
9:00   Presentation by Mr. Randall Arias, Conflict Resolution Specialist at the
        Foundation for Peace and Democracy, on the role of the Organization
        of American States in the Honduran conflict and the Isla Calero dispute
        between Costa Rica and Nicaragua
10:00   Break
10:30   Process Mr. Arias' lecture
Noon   Lunch
1:00   Visit the National Museum and Art Museum

Thursday, June 9
7:00   Travel to Earth University (EU)
        Presentations/Activities on Peace and Environmental Sustainability
9:30   Urban agriculture project

10:30	Visit Escuela Nuevo Amanecer (actividades de la semana de la paz) in Pocora (participate in school activities celebrating Peace Week)
12:30	Almuerzo at EU
1:30	Visit Jardín Botánico y Etnobotánico
2:30	Community service: Build and install biodigester

Friday, June 10

8:00	Students check in at ULACIT
9:00	Conversation with Pablo Chaverri, ULACIT Service Learning Director
10:30	Visit to the Arias Foundation for Peace and Human Progress
2:00	Visit to the U. S. Embassy—Presentation/discussion on U.S.-Costa Rican relations
3:00	Small group presentations

Saturday, June 11

7:00	Visit Volcán Poás
Afternoon	Shopping at Moravia
Evening	Dinner at Tiquicia, traditional folk dance performance

Sunday, June 12

| 7:00 | Leave for Monteverde |
| Afternoon | Options—canopy walk ($25) or zip lines ($40). Sleep in the reserve lodge |

Monday, June 13

All day	a.m. Explore reserve trails
	Early p.m. Visit of the Women's Coop (Casemcoop) - Mrs. Nery Gómez Mendoza
	Evening dinner and swimming at hotel
	Optional guided night walk

Tuesday, June 14

| 8:00 | Meeting with Mr. Alberto Guindon, son of one of the Quaker settlers at Monteverde and founders of the reserve. History of the Quaker community of Monteverde |
| | Visit Puntarenas on the Pacific Coast, meet with members of youth leadership group, lunch, and explore beach |

Wednesday, June 15

9:00	At ULACIT: process 2-day experience
11:00	Small-group presentations
Noon	Lunch
2:00	Presentation by Ms. Dulce Umanzor Alvarado and Ms. Maritza Ortiz Cortés, Ministry of Peace and Justice, on the role of the Ministry in sustaining/promoting peace in Costa Rica
3:30	Process/Discuss

Thursday, June 16
8:00   Meet at ULACIT and travel to CEDES School
        Meeting with teachers and students; participate in service project in
        English classes
3:00   Reflections on the day's activities
        Small-group presentations

Friday, June 17
9:00   ULACIT, meeting with Ms. Yami Chávez of the Ministry of Education, on
        Costa Rica's educational practices promoting a culture of peace
11:00   Reflections/Discussion
Noon   Lunch
1:00   Lecture by Mr. Manuel Araya on the history of Costa Rica
3:00   Reflections and Farewells

Saturday, June 18
7:30   Tri-C and SCC depart from airport
2:05   NCC departs from airport

10

Redefining Community

Cooperative Vocational Education in Mozambique

SCOTT BRANKS DEL LLANO

The most harrowing thing about poverty is the ignorance it has of itself.
Faced by an absence of everything, men abstain from dreams, depriving
themselves of the desire to be others. There exists in nothingness that illusion of
plenitude which causes life to stop and voices to become night.
—Mozambican poet Mia Couto, Voices Made Night

"**B**om dia!" I shout, peering out through the open window of a beat-up Toyota Hilux truck. A wall of dust rises from the tires and clouds the outlines of three armed guards approaching. AK-47s dangle from threadbare woven straps draped loosely over their shoulders—telltale signs of the twenty-year civil war that scarred Mozambique and left it one of the poorest countries in the world. The red fire of the setting sun silhouettes a massive gateway of dilapidated colonial columns, towering like concrete sentinels from nearly a century of Portuguese rule in this coastal region of southern Africa stretching along the Indian Ocean. The lean, weathered faces of these former soldiers stare into the cab of the truck, which is now surrounded by a crowd of curious onlookers. I explain in broken Portuguese that I am here to conduct a language assessment of cement plant workers, and I pull up to an iron gate that is drooping on rusted chains. There has been no word of my coming, and the armed guards refuse to let an unauthorized vehicle into the plant. But when I invite them to climb in to escort me, wide grins transform their expressions, and they hoist their weapons into the back and jump in. We approach a lone abandoned building under a grove of mango trees, where several men lounge in the grass sharing a smoke. They wear faded blue uniforms caked in gray cement powder. I ask them if they are here for the English program, and without words they lead me into a dank, moldy room.

An hour later, I am watching their faces, sweating and serious in concentration under the dull, blinking glow of a few neon tubes hanging from wires above them. Sounds of cicadas and frogs compete in rhythmic cacophony. I feel the weight of the air, a heaviness that wants lifting. The men sit on the floor, on ledges, perched on old wooden benches, determined to learn a language that might open a pathway to a brighter future. Many of them are soldiers rehabilitating from a violent war that claimed their youth. They struggle diligently now with an English exam after a twelve-hour shift laboring in the cement factory, the night before a national holiday. One man approaches quietly, bent over his wooden crutch—a land mine has blown off one of his legs. His massive, callused hands gently place the pencil and test papers, smeared with sweat and cement grime, on the table before me. He smiles nervously, nods politely, and heads out into the night. I know now exactly why I am here [Mozambique, 1998].

***

Mission and Rationale

Over the past few decades, community colleges have been expanding their concept of "community." One vital outcome of this changing mission is students actively educated to be globally competent learners. A more recent strategy is the export of relevant vocational education- and skill-based programs to improve capacity in developing nations. Community colleges can make enduring contributions to the economic development of such countries, directly affecting global efforts toward peacebuilding. Economic stability and equal access to quality education are essential components to building peace within countries whose histories are plagued with violence. This chapter provides a program model of global peacebuilding through international development to show how cooperative educational exchange produced fruitful outcome in the war-torn country of Mozambique. The purpose is to encourage similar community college projects that use practical grassroots education and training as an effective way to create economic growth and perpetuate global peace.

A vital starting point for growing peace education programs lies in connecting them to the institutional missions. Richland College practices a vision for global education that begins with the awareness that "community" is no longer confined to the local county or even the state where the college is but has rapidly come to encompass the world. Within the college's mission for global education is a goal to extend institutional presence and hospitality to every continent. Richland College created its Institute for Peace in re-

> **Box 10.1: Teaching Peace at Richland**
>
> The push to start a program in peacebuilding can come not only from faculty but also from college leadership. Richland College has supported a peace studies effort since the 1990s, making it one of the early community colleges to do so. The leadership for the program came initially from Dr. Stephen K. Mittelstet, Richland's president from 1979 to 2010. Mittelstet's sabbatical in the early 1990s led to revamping the college's international language program, enlivening its study-abroad efforts, and establishing a global studies program, the forerunner to Richland's Institute for Peace. The Institute strongly emphasizes building sustainable local and world community. Mittelstet says, "Leadership is in large part the *art* of the possible. So is establishing a peace studies program, not to mention establishing peace itself, starting with one's own inner peace." As president emeritus of Richland College, Mittelstet still devotes much of his time to peacebuilding efforts.

sponse both to a growing diversity of students and to the expressed desire of students to become globally competent citizens (see box 10.1). The college's mission, combined with the vision of its peace studies program, is to foster an interdependent and sustainable local and global community that actively pursues peaceable living, resolution of conflict, and respect for human dignity, contributing to the goal of global peace, justice, and friendship among peoples. Peacebuilding through international economic development is a key focus of this educational vision.

Background for the Project

In 1996, a group of community college administrators and faculty members was invited through Community Colleges for International Development to engage with educators in the "new South Africa" and explore ways in which the community college model might benefit the citizens of the post-apartheid country. During this exchange, Richland College discovered that neighboring Mozambique was hungry for educational programs in its struggle for development following a newly signed peace agreement. Throughout the country, there was a cumulative call for vocational training programs and accessible, practical approaches to education that would empower communities and provide tangible skills. In the existing higher education system of bulwark universities that educated small elite groups in somewhat detached programs steeped in colonial pedagogy, this type of training was rare. Embarking on a shared vocational education project presented a concrete opportunity for Richland College to act on its commitment to build a sustainable global community and to further realize its expanded definition of "community." The project also continues to offer a unique model of peacebuilding that moves beyond academic rhetoric and into direct action through community capacity building in an impoverished nation recovering from war and economic collapse.

Mozambique proved to be an extreme case of underdevelopment. At the start of the project, two-thirds of the population lived in absolute poverty, and the infant mortality rate was the second highest in the world. The bloody and debilitating civil war had raged for nearly twenty years, bleeding the country of any hope for economic stability following Portuguese colonialism, which had been a predominantly extractive enterprise. At the signing of independence in 1975, there were fewer than eight hundred Mozambican high school graduates in a country of ten million people. The country has more than twenty-three primary languages and fifty indigenous dialects, and the illiteracy rate in Portuguese, the official language, was close to 95 percent at that time. In 1987, and for many years thereafter, the Population Crisis Committee ranked Mozambique first in the world on a complex index of human suffering. By 1992, annual per capita income was estimated at US$90, the second lowest in the world. A complicated struggle for social reform ensued, marked primarily by dependency on imported aid and expertise, economic destabilization, and a devastating series of floods and droughts. When the general peace accord was signed in 1992, more than one million Mozambicans had died, three million had fled their homes and lands, and eight million faced starvation. More than half the schools and health clinics were destroyed, and the national debt was over three times the national income. Even more menacing was the widespread and ever-present violence, resulting in mass migrations of people and dissolving community structure (Finnegan 1992).

It was against this backdrop that Richland College initiated an educational partnership with Centro de Formaçao Industrial (CFI), a national vocational training institution headquartered in the Mozambican capital, Maputo. One of the national strategies identified for economic development in Mozambique in the late 1990s was English-language acquisition at all levels of education. The Portuguese-speaking nation is surrounded by anglophone countries and was seeking to grow its competitive capacity by increasing fluency in this vital international trade language. This goal was not only a peacebuilding venture but also a strategy for vocational rehabilitation and economic recovery at the grassroots level, which would be expanded to other regions of the country. As a community college with excellent academic programs in English for speakers of other languages (ESOL), Richland College was well equipped to provide curricular models, offer dual-credit classes through extension programming, and, most importantly, facilitate teacher training programs directly with CFI faculty.

Project Overview

The project, given the title Inglés Universal para Moçambique (IUMOZ), International English for Mozambique, initiated a collaborative strategy between CFI and Richland College. Richland committed to providing one full-time consultant, who received a base salary over one long semester, and two faculty members to assist with teacher training during subsequent summer sessions. Faculty members and administrators from the School of World Languages, Cultures and Communications at Richland worked closely with the director of operations and instructors at CFI to pursue three initial actions:

Needs Analysis and Marketing

First, the team conducted a thorough needs analysis and marketing process for the English curriculum model within both the business sector and the existing student population. The team identified five major companies, with a total of over two hundred potential participants, for the first phase. These included Cementos do Moçambique, a national cement-producing company; Aeroportos, employer of the air traffic controllers and staff of the just recently operational international airport in Maputo; Crown Agency Import and Export, border control, customs, and import-export shipping personnel; TVM, the leading national television broadcasting agency; and Mozal, a giant multinational aluminum production company. Human resource administrators and CEOs met to discuss the desired curriculum and logistics of the language program. Communication had presented an obstacle between these professionals and outside investors and international development agencies that wanted to contribute to Mozambique's economic growth. In the case of television broadcasting, most international news was entering the country through the BBC, CNN, or other news syndicates, predominantly in English. Each group sought intensive English and intercultural communication instruction in order to interact with colleagues coming from Australia, the European Union, South Africa, and the United States. English had become the common language for each enterprise. In each case, the team tailor-made courses with specific language objectives relevant to the needs of the workplace and the scope of the industry.

In addition to surveying local businesses, IUMOZ polled student populations in secondary schools and universities to assess their interest in intensive English programs. The survey found that most students were dropping existing courses due to the curriculum's lack of challenge and focus. Nearly all the students surveyed voiced enthusiasm for a practical approach to English learning. Students attributed their motivation for studying English to three primary reasons:

1. English was viewed as the international language, and most investment interests privileged English speakers.
2. The emerging job market demanded English proficiency for career opportunities.
3. All communications and technology networks, as well as most popular music and entertainment media, were in English.

The climate and timing were ideal for engaging students in intensive English learning.

Teacher Training Program

The second strategy of the project identified qualified potential instructors and implemented an ongoing teacher training program. None of the staff had received formal education in English, and most had completed secondary education only and were teaching because they had lived for a time in Kenya, Zimbabwe, or other English-speaking countries. The administrators, including the director of pedagogy for CFI, had only a high school diploma, with no formal training in education. The team conducted regular class visits, followed by discussion of the successes and challenges of teaching. The interviews revealed a need for curriculum development, teaching methodology and learning theory, and, most of all, for workshops focused on lesson planning and classroom management. Based on these requests, the team created and facilitated a series of workshops in program development and instruction.

A subsequent phase of the training involved inviting education students and graduates of the English program at Universidade Pedagógica (Pedagogical University of Mozambique) to join the teaching staff of IUMOZ as interns. The university program had established a sound reputation nationally. This partnership welcomed new and skilled instructors for the business training programs and higher-level intensive English courses and broke down a long-standing barrier that had existed between competing institutions in approaches to English education. The team facilitated a gathering of program administrators from several institutions, including Universidade Eduardo Mondlane, and together created common curriculum objectives and strategies toward improved English education for Mozambique. The outcome was positive, and administrators still meet regularly to assess and revitalize programs.

There were two initial challenges in implementing the training into new classes. The first was to access relevant materials for the new courses. No textbooks were available, nor were publications affordable in the numbers necessary, since shipping to Mozambique was prohibitively expensive. Until this point, CFI and other language centers were using poor photocopies of outdated and used publications donated during the civil war. IUMOZ eventually introduced new materials through donations of textbooks from the United States. Second, scheduling classes presented a challenge, since limited facilities were already operating at capacity. Tuition and fees needed to strike a balance between affordability among students and a pay scale that could attract and keep qualified teachers: about US$200 for three months. Involving instructors and students in creative program scheduling and budget strategies provided another way for all participants to feel ownership and accountability in the program.

Partnerships and Sustainable National Support

In order for the project to become nationalized and locally sustainable, a system of enduring regional support needed to be established. One vital partnership was with members of the British Council in Maputo. Directors of its English programs conducted additional teacher training seminars and opened a resource library for IUMOZ. A second collaboration, with the directors of U.S. Information Services (now the Public Affairs Division of the U.S. embassy) sought to establish opportunities for qualified students and teachers to study in the United States. The team also met with the minister of education to establish a strategy for ESOL education in Mozambique, as well as student exchange abroad. This launched a gathering of members of four government ministries—Education, Higher Education, Labor, and Youth—who discussed their support of English education as a human resource for Mozambique. The minister of higher education affirmed commitment to long-range exchange possibilities with Richland College and other community colleges in the United States.

The most energetic partnership sprang from Nova Generaçao (National Youth Council of Mozambique) which had formed a movement to support independent party delegates in national elections who would focus on issues that face the youth of Mozambique. This movement sees education and professional training as national priorities. During several national elections, key ministers, governors, and even former president Joaquim Chissano participated in the youth assemblies and ceremonies. Political candidates are beginning to view educating and supporting the youth of Mozambique, who make up over 60 percent of the population, as a national priority. IUMOZ participated in these televised political rallies to share its educational vision and encourage national participation in vocational education programs. This youth movement and its enthusiastic rallies have become a powerful force for social change in Mozambique.

Future Developments

The IUMOZ curriculum model was developed through student needs analysis and learner-centered planning. As a result of the new model, teachers accustomed to teaching rote programs have begun to develop new teaching and learning strategies. The breakthrough of English for specific purposes and vocational language training has led more and more businesses to contract new classes for their employees through CFI. Young Mozambicans are hungry for English as an international language to develop their work potential and improve business opportunities. The international English model of IUMOZ serves as a welcome addition for Mozambique.

In an impoverished country such as Mozambique, financial obstacles prohibit students and educators from traveling abroad to study. One solution is to provide further training and assistance in-country. In order to establish national scope for such a program, cooperating with existing universities such as the Pedagogical University and University Eduardo Mondlane is essential. Until the time of the project, university English programs focused primarily on actual degrees in English and very little on course offerings of English as a foreign language. Most courses were geared toward Cambridge certification, whether or not students intended to go to the United Kingdom. Mozambique would benefit greatly from a unified, comprehensive K-12 English-language curriculum. A viable solution is to develop a common English curriculum that can be articulated between institutions. The IUMOZ program provides such a tool.

CFI and the ministers of labor and of travel and tourism are now requesting assistance in developing vocational training programs and shared expertise through the curriculum models of relevant community college programs beyond just those in language skills. Programs such as health occupations, business and marketing, and travel and tourism contribute greatly to national development efforts. The internal players contributing to the success of this project, along with non-governmental organizations and international development organizations, are positioned to partner with community colleges in establishing further resource models for technical and vocational training to increase capacity in skilled human resources for the development of Mozambique. Because of limited resources and infrastructure, most institutions in Mozambique will take many years to reach their full potential and become self-sustaining. Programs such as IUMOZ can make a huge impact on the success of education there. The ongoing opportunities are limitless.

Conclusion

Peacebuilding through international education and development projects furthers the vision of the community college movement and broadens our perception of the word "community" as we create sustainable local and global community. This program model is an example of peace education and international educational exchange that can easily be replicated in many areas of vocational training to enhance international development and build peace in other countries around the world. Two primary conditions that give rise to violence in the world are economic instability and the absence of accessible education. Both these realities have plagued many developing countries for decades. Community colleges in the United States are uniquely poised to respond and fill a void by providing vocational training that is readily available to grassroots populations who form the backbone of struggling nations such as Mozambique. Building capacity and building community within developing countries can help reverse the cycle of poverty and suffering that so often contributes to violence and war.

***

As I climbed back into the truck on that warm night in 1998 and drove away from the cement factory out into the darkness, several of the weary men stood in the truck bed, peering into the headlight beams as we made our way to the main road. The hope in their eyes was the beginning of a break in the long cycle of suffering. During the years since that time, I have witnessed a shift as I follow the stories and progress of hundreds of other participants in the training programs of IUMOZ and CFI. Their lives are slowly improving, and the patterns of despair are shifting to pathways of hope and change. For me, in the end, redefining "community" means embracing our common humanity and lowering boundaries that divide us culturally and geographically. I see a new community emerging in the determined faces of the women and men of this cooperative vocational exchange, and I see the harrowing grip of poverty as described by Mia Couto beginning to loosen, and people no longer abstaining from dreams but envisioning a new and brighter day.

References

Couto, Mia. 1990. *Vozes Anoitecidas*, trans. David Brookshaw. Oxford: Heinemann.
Finnegan, William. 1992. *A Complicated War: The Harrowing of Mozambique*. Berkeley, CA: Univ. of California Press.

IUMOZ—Inglés Universal para Moçambique
(International English for Mozambique)
Centro de Formaçao Industrial and Richland College

Program Mission

One of the national strategies identified for economic recovery in Mozambique since the signing of a peace accord in the 1990s is English language acquisition at all levels of education, with the outcome of building competitive capacity by increasing fluency in this vital international trade language. This goal is not only a peacebuilding venture but also a strategy for vocational rehabilitation and economic development at the grassroots level to be expanded to other regions of the country. The mission of IUMOZ is to provide Mozambican students and professionals with academic and vocational English language skills that contribute to their professional goals and develop responsible citizenship in a rapidly changing global community.

Curriculum Philosophy

IUMOZ will implement an integrated and thematic curriculum that combines English language skill areas of writing, grammar, reading, and listening/speaking. The curriculum emphasizes academic preparation as well as developing vocational language skills to help students succeed in their educational, professional, and life goals. Instruction uses a wide variety of language-teaching approaches, including communicative, situation, direct, grammar-translation, audio-lingual, computer-assisted, and literature-based.

Course Descriptions and Objectives

The course descriptions and course objectives outline the instruction of all skill areas of ESOL. The objectives for each level will be implemented based on the following premises:

- Encouraging students to develop their confidence in their ability to communicate in English
- Instilling in students an awareness of their own and other language acquisition processes
- Developing the ability of students to work in groups (team-building skills)
- Helping students become independent and lifelong learners

Curriculum Design

The program curriculum is divided into four levels from beginning to advanced:

Level One (Beginning)

This course focuses on the beginning level of development of English as a second language, through the thematic and integrated skills of writing, grammar, reading, and listening and speaking for academic preparation. It includes an emphasis on parts of speech, simple and compound sentence structure, spelling rules, and basic verb tenses. Students will develop their vocabulary, learn basic reading comprehension (main idea) and study skills, and practice beginning listening/speaking, specifically pronunciation, stress, and intonation.

Level Two (High Beginning)

This course focuses on the high-beginning level of development of English as a second language, through the thematic and integrated skills of writing, grammar, reading, and listening and speaking for academic preparation. Students will learn to create complex sentences and groups of sentences using logic patterns of English and a variety of organizational structures. They will be introduced to the grammar necessary to write topic sentences and controlled paragraphs, including further study of verb tenses, modals, gerunds, and infinitives. They will expand their reading comprehension (main idea/implied main idea) and vocabulary-building strategies, including recognition of paragraph organization. They will learn to listen for meaning, participate in small group communication activities, and further practice pronunciation and intonation.

Level Three (Intermediate)

This course focuses on the intermediate level of development of English as a second language through the thematic and integrated skills of writing, grammar, reading, and listening and speaking for academic preparation. Students will be introduced to writing as a process and different modes of discourse. They will learn to develop effective paragraphs into essays. They will also continue the study of verb tenses and be introduced to adverb, adjective, and noun clauses. The course will include further reading comprehension and reading efficiency strategies, idiom study, vocabulary expansion, using resources, developing oral communications skills and group projects/presentations, and listening through lectures and note taking.

Level Four (Advanced)

This course focuses on the advanced level of development of English as a second language, through the thematic and integrated skills of writing, grammar, reading, and listening/speaking with an emphasis on academic preparation for college-level coursework. Students will practice writing multiparagraph essays in a variety of modes, develop the ability to analyze complex elements of all grammar points covered in previous levels, and be able to self-edit and correct errors. They will practice advanced reading strategies related to academic topics/literature, refine their listening/note-taking skills, and learn formal public speaking skills through presentations.

PART THREE

EDUCATING PEACEBUILDERS

11

Teaching Global Studies and Peace

Rural versus Metropolitan Community Colleges

JENNIFER HAYDEL AND JOHN BRENNER

If you look at the world from only one vantage point, you risk missing much.
Our lives are enriched when we begin to see things from different points
of view. —Kaiser and Wood 2001

In a recent article, Natalie Harder argues that rural and metropolitan community colleges face different challenges in promoting peace and internationalizing their curricula and campuses. She notes that rural community colleges "experienc[ed] significantly less internationalization than their urban and suburban counterparts" (Harder 2010, 16). For all community colleges, institutional support was the key factor determining the degree of internationalization. For rural campuses, the presence of international students was important; for metropolitan campuses, incorporation of international issues into academic requirements was important (Harder 2010, 16).

This chapter highlights the experiences of two very different community colleges: one a diverse metropolitan institution, the other a monocultural rural college. Jennifer Haydel teaches at Montgomery College (MC) in the Maryland suburbs of Washington, D.C. John Brenner teaches in a rural Appalachian setting at Southwest Virginia Community College (SWCC). Table 11.1 reflects their very different demographics.

Contrary to Harder's findings, Brenner has found that rural institutions do not necessarily need to bring international *students* to campus; rather, they need to find innovative ways to create a global environment for students. Haydel has found that internationalization at a diverse metropolitan community college requires faculty members and administrators to draw skillfully on the experiences and knowledge already present on campus.

Shared Understandings and Goals

In our experience as faculty members dedicated to global and peace education, we have identified crucial similarities. First, we understand that inter-

Table 11.1: Demographics at MC and SWCC

	Montgomery College (Student Profile 2009)	SWCC (Student Profile 2007–08)
Full-time Student Enrollment	26,147	2,585
Racial Distribution	White: 35.4% Black: 29.1% Native American: 0.3% Asian: 15.2% Latino: 12.9% Multiracial: 7.1% Unknown: 0.1% Total non-U.S. citizen: 31%	White: 96.04% Black: 2.32% Native American: 0.38% Asian: 0.43% Latino: 0.19% Other: 0.64%

nationalization of the curriculum comes from dedicated faculty members. Green argues, "Faculty members with an international mind-set draw on knowledge from diverse settings, cultures, and languages to internationalize the curriculum; use integrative skills such as translating, synthesizing, and connection; and are adept at identifying the cultural influences that shape these examples" (Green 2007, 21). Both this chapter's authors reflect Green's expectations.

While our desire to internationalize curricula stems from personal experience, my (Haydel's) emphasis on peace education originates directly from the needs of the students I encounter. During spring 2011, a student came to me during office hours, struggling with the loss of a family member who had been killed in a government crackdown on a peaceful protest in her home country. She asked, "What will happen to my country?" Several times, U.S. combat veterans who served in Iraq and Afghanistan have come to me asking how they can use their experiences to work for international conflict resolution in civilian life. The pain caused by conflict, combined with the deep personal *need* for knowledge about peacebuilding possibilities, creates my students' questions.

David Smith characterizes community college educators as "educators of learners who are often at life's crossroads" (Smith 2003, 1). Since our students plan to transfer, start new careers, or take courses to fulfill a goal of lifelong learning, we have a meaningful opportunity to expand global knowledge and infuse peace concepts into a variety of courses. As Green argues, "with over 52 percent of the first-year students enrolled in community colleges, global learning at the postsecondary level must begin there" (Green 2007).

Smith differentiates between international studies and global studies. While international studies bring international perspectives into a disciplinary lens, global studies embrace and study the interconnections characteristic of the social, economic, political, cultural, and physical worlds (Smith 2008, 69). Both this chapter's authors teach international studies courses—disciplinary courses infused with a global lens—but also participate in *global* studies initiatives. We both have found that students in international studies courses need to explore explicitly how perceptions and multiple views shape international society. As Steven Lamy emphasizes, "*Where you stand depends on where you sit and we all sit in our worldview*" [italics in the original] (Lamy 2007, 113).

We were surprised to discover that we both open our semester with similar activities to address the importance of perception. Brenner has a large map of the world in his classroom to get the students to look at things differently and to challenge traditional ways of looking at the world. The map is the What's Up South! world map, on which the south is at the top. Haydel starts the first international relations class by asking students to draw a map of the world from memory in five minutes. Students analyze their own maps and then discuss the politics behind map projections and global "categories."

In work conducted at the University of Minnesota, O'Donovan and Mikelonis found that a significant challenge to internationalizing courses was "intolerance for ambiguity" (O'Donovan and Mikelonis 2005, 92). When students find themselves having to view the world through different lenses, they struggle to find "the answers." Students will ask, "But which view is the right one?" or "Which theory is correct?" O'Donovan and Mikelonis argue, "Considering the possibility that some tacit assumptions might be distorted, wrong, or contextually relative may be 'profoundly threatening' and even painful to people" (2005, 93). The opening map and perception exercises serve as a continual reminder that our answers often depend on our worldview.

The challenges associated with the intolerance of ambiguity have only heightened as the overall economic challenges facing our students have increased. Even at Montgomery College, with the incredible diversity we experience in our classrooms, students can become defensive when faced with these new perspectives. For example, a recent educational event about global hunger raised a powerful and important discussion on campus. Students who participated in a study-travel trip to India organized a "hunger banquet" to raise awareness about the depth and breadth of global poverty and to raise money to send to educational facilities that provide support to children of the untouchables in India. Some members of the campus community, including many students, questioned whether the campaign should be focused "out there" when there is significant poverty in Montgomery County. Instead of becoming disillusioned, both the organizers and critics of the event used the opportunity to raise awareness *simultaneously* about the extent of hunger in Montgomery County as well as in India. These discussions and presentations at and surrounding the event allowed the college community to explore the *connections* between poverty at home and abroad. Thus, the challenges surrounding internationalization of our campuses and curricula can lead to enhanced awareness of local challenges. One major challenge that those teaching in rural monoculture settings may want to keep in mind is that in our small communities, change does not come easy. People have an attitude about how things are, and their worldview may not be expansive. In these teaching communities, it is a major challenge to get the entire faculty or administration to agree that the curriculum should be internationalized or to support some other major international endeavor. The rural community faculty must be given opportunities to attend internationally related conferences along with those dealing with peace, conflict resolution, and the social impact of current lifestyles. Students learn to appreciate a global view of the world if that view is shared by faculty from all the disciplines in the college. This year, I (Brenner) was encouraged by a nursing faculty member who applied to be a faculty exchange person next year with a faculty member from the Netherlands. This is the first time someone from this department has participated. I anticipate that next year another nursing faculty member will apply, and we may see a focus to their teaching that includes some international elements. Institutions seeking to internationalize will benefit from recognizing that change is slow but enduring.

Krain argues that it is important to "[engage] students' senses in multiple ways" (Krain 2010, 291). We both have also found this multisensory engagement crucial to student success. We have specifically found that pictures taken during our own travels have special resonance for students. Brenner uses pictures of a rural Russian McDonald's and of a dung collector from India to stimulate discussions of globalism and concepts of poverty and peace. Haydel discusses the globalization debates using a picture of a Toyota dealership sitting next to a Berlin Wall memorial, and a picture of an Austrian elementary school mural advocating multiculturalism and tolerance, defaced by a swastika. Regardless of the setting, students seem to appreciate the human connection that the professors' pictures bring to the classroom.

Global Studies and Peace Education in a Monocultural Environment

Although we share common goals, our institutional settings shape the means that we have available for achieving those goals. Brenner's college (SWCC) understood years ago that students required knowledge of the world beyond them. Green (2007) states, "An educational system that pretends the world ends at our national borders cannot be excellent; a quality education must equip students to live and work in a globalized and multicultural world." SWCC created the position of global education coordinator to keep the campus aware of international events and opportunities because SWCC, located in the heart of the Appalachian Mountains, lacked racial diversity in the student body.

Early in my career, I (Brenner) was awarded a group Fulbright grant to India, followed by an Office of Education group grant that investigated the drought and desertification of West Africa. This began a career that has included many trips around the world, working on various academic projects.

I teach a global sociology course at SWCC. Readings and course materials introduce concepts through a global lens, incorporating an international/peace theme throughout. This type of base material allows me to translate my international experiences to students.

I have used videoconferencing to bring the world into my classrooms at SWCC. To do the conferencing requires that both parties have an Internet connection. In 2004, I began videoconferencing with the American Brazilian Association (ABA) School, an English-language school in Recife, Brazil. The Web site for the school indicates its commitment to intercultural communication.

The ABA teacher (Marcus Matos) wants to expose his students to hearing American English, while Brenner wants his students to understand a different culture and society in a nonthreatening, relaxed manner. Thus, the videoconference requires both classrooms to be flexible, since there are slight time differences and technology needs.

One student who participated in the semester-long session with the Brazilians stated, "Those Brazilians know all about our politics; they know our movies and our television shows. But we do not know anything about them." We both believe that this statement is the essence of what we both are trying to overcome in our classrooms. Peacebuilding requires a willingness to learn about the viewpoints and experiences of others; Brenner's students gain this experience through videoconferencing.

Most of the SWCC videoconferencing students have no previous interaction with people from other countries, cultures, or societies. Thus the video connections help them understand themselves as well as the people they are communicating with on the screen. As Emert and Pearson state, "One of the desired outcomes of internationalization is cultivation of an intercultural mind-set and skills in students. Intercultural competence is a key goal of internationalization because it indicates awareness and understanding of culturally diverse others and situations, as well as the presence of behaviors that promote productive and effective communication among and across cultures" (Emert and Pearson 2007, 68).

The videoconferencing has now progressed into a spring break trip for Brenner and his students. The Brazilian teacher arranged for a weeklong homestay visit by students from Virginia. Brown, Pegg, and Shively, who cite work by the Strategic Task Force on Education Abroad, note that "... students who study abroad amount to barely more than 1 percent of the 8 million full-time and 5 million part-time graduates" (Brown, Pegg, and Shively 2006, 277).

SWCC has a Quality Enhancement Plan to make students successful in college. The humanities and social science division's faculty has developed a one hour honors humanities course to encourage student participation. In 2011, the course's theme was "All's Fair in Love and War ... Or Is It?" The course discusses the concept of a just war from the perspective of Christianity, Judaism, Hinduism, Islam, and Buddhism. The diverse materials it uses include Daniel Mendelsohn's *The Lost: Finding Six of Six Million*, Peter Schroeder and Dagmar Schroeder-Hildebrand's *Six Million Paper Clips: The Making of a Children's Holocaust Memorial*, and Glen Stassen's *Just Peacemaking: The New Paradigm for the Ethics of Peace and War*; and films such as *Jerusalem: Center of the World*, *Schindler's List*, *Kundun*, and *Exodus*.

At a small rural college, there are benefits to having a global education coordinator. Serving that function for SWCC, I (Brenner) work to keep the faculty, staff, and administration informed about programs, policies, and opportunities in the international arena. I also create international opportunities for SWCC students and assist faculty through guest speakers, visiting scholars, and academic programs at other colleges. The post also involves working with the college administration to see that concepts of globalization and peace are a part of the year's dialogue and coordinating with neighboring four-year institutions, sharing international visitors to the area and bringing issues of international interest to our college campuses. Each year, I host two or three international scholars on campus and always make them available to faculty for classroom visits and presentations.

I also work closely with international and internship programs at the Southwest Virginia Higher Education Center. In 2009, I participated in a regional trip to China, where I administered the Intercultural Development Inventory (IDI) to the student and faculty participants. The IDI is an online instrument used to determine where an individual is on the spectrum running from ethnocentric at one end to ethnorelative at the other. The results of this small study indicated that after a two week trip to China all the participants had moved along the continuum toward a more ethnorelative worldview.

At SWCC, the position of global education coordinator is a three-year faculty position designating one person as the recipient and distributor of information, campuswide, on global issues. The coordinator has such duties as being a member of state and national organizations dealing with global issues, identifying and participating in regional global activities, hosting and organizing campuswide experiences involving international visitors, seeking sources of international speakers in the region, organizing student-faculty-community international trips, and videoconferencing with international organizations. These duties relate directly to increasing student and faculty knowledge of international events, grants, and opportunities.

The global education coordinator represents the college in Community Colleges for International Development. This organization delivers a semiannual international news journal, which the coordinator distributes throughout the campus. It was through this organization that I learned of a New Independent States grant with Russia. I was the grant evaluator, making three trips to Russia and hosting many of the Russian professors on the SWCC campus. SWCC was only the second community college in the United States to receive such a grant. Because of the grant, the State Department later asked me to create videoconferencing. The end result was the multiple meetings that SWCC students have had since 2004 with a class of students in Recife, Brazil.

In summary, without a global education coordinator on campus, SWCC would lose many opportunities to help the students, faculty, and staff make international connections. In Brenner's experience, community college campuses need to have a specified faculty member who can act as a clearinghouse and a dissemination point for information. I (Haydel) had a similar experience when working at a rural community college in Georgia, but in the large metropolitan environment at MC, internationalization has been led by faculty, staff, and administrators working on different campuses and in different programs. Here, global education efforts have flourished within a network rather than through the work of a designated coordinator. The networking possibilities are endless, but the most important thing is to get on e-mail listings and network within your own campus, area four-year institutions, statewide international groups, and national organizations.

Global Studies and Peace Education in a Diverse Environment

Montgomery College understands that the conditions conducive to global learning and peace education have to be institutionally fostered. Considering the diverse human resources at the campus, MC adopts a decentralized approach, allowing for webs of programming throughout the college. There are three main campuses, and while the campuses differ (see table 11.2), no campus has a majority racial group, and the college hosts a noncitizen stu-

Table 11.2: Demographics at the Montgomery College Campuses

	Germantown	Rockville	Takoma Park	Distance Learning
Student Enrollment	6,571	17,028	7,148	3,458
Racial Distribution	Native American: 0.4% Asian: 15.1% Black: 23.5% Latino: 12.7% White: 42% Multiracial: 6.2% Unknown: 0.1%	Native American: 0.3% Asian: 17.7% Black: 22.4% Latino: 13.2% White: 38.7% Multiracial: 7.7% Unknown: 0%	Native American: 0.2% Asian: 9.7% Black: 50.7% Latino: 12.5% White: 21.2% Multiracial: 5.6% Unknown: 0.1%	Native American: 0.3% Asian: 15.2% Black: 27.4% Latino: 10% White: 43.4% Multiracial: 3.8% Unknown: 0%
Non-U.S. Citizen	26.2%	30%	37.9%	24.9%

dent body of 31 percent. As of fall 2009, students came from 179 countries (Montgomery College 2010b, 28). Two campuses (Rockville and Takoma Park) are essentially urban, and one (Germantown) is suburban.

My (Haydel's) work has led me to twenty-three countries, with the most time spent in Germany and Tanzania. I teach several globally focused courses in the MC Political Science Department, including International Relations, Comparative Politics, Introduction to International Conflict Resolution, and an honors seminar on transitional justice.

Working with the concepts of perception and worldview is fundamental to introducing peace education in the classroom. Students often enter the classroom on the first day ready to defend and argue their viewpoint. Other students enter the classroom with open minds but without the necessary skills for encountering opposing views. Students may need their assumptions disrupted through learning to sit with new ideas. These skills can help students identify the causes of conflict, thereby facilitating an airing of differences that can lead to positive change. Simulations and role-playing reinforce the exploration of multiple perspectives. (See Haydel's International Relations course syllabus at the end of this chapter.)

I draw on the diversity found at MC to give context and substance to what can sometimes feel like abstract international relations concepts. Matthew Krain argues that students respond positively to material that "put[s] a human face on the problem" and comes across as authentic (Krain 2010, 30304). When combat veterans open up about split-second decisions they have made, when former microcredit officers share about the transformations they have seen in clients' lives, and when refugee students tell about their flight, students can put a real face on the theoretical concepts employed in the classroom.

An important caveat about incorporating student diversity is in order. Works by Chesler (1997, 17) and Valeriano (2008) highlight the challenges that international students and students of color can face. Both studies tell of faculty members making assumptions about these students' interests and expertise. Personal stories like those mentioned above should be *optional* and *spontaneous,* fostered by the course structure and classroom atmosphere rather than forced from students.

According to Scott Seider, many students become "overwhelmed by the size and scope of the challenges in the world to which they have been exposed" (Seider 2009, 70). As students learn more, they respond by feeling powerless. This is a consistent challenge in peace education. Haydel has found three techniques to mitigate the sense of powerlessness: use of individualized stories, frank discussion of the limits and possibilities of positive action, and the use of active learning techniques like simulations and role-plays. (See Haydel's course syllabus.)

Beyond the classroom, MC has emphasized themes of peace and social justice. All three campuses have developed programming related to the concepts of peace and social justice, emphasizing interdisciplinarity and local-global connections. For example, Earth Day events included a walk to Germantown's large elm tree (discussing the importance of this tree on campus) and a movie night focused on the Three Gorges Dam project in China, thus connecting global and local environmental concerns and bringing together faculty from math, science, humanities, and social sciences. The Takoma Park campus developed a booklet to support the First Year Experience focus on peace and justice (Montgomery College 2010a).

At MC, any interested faculty or staff member can find avenues to promote the study of peace, social justice, and global studies. Initiatives at MC include a developing peace and justice studies effort; student clubs dedicated to global peace and justice, such as the Senegal Water Project and Microcredit Clubs; Peace Day and Human Rights Day celebrations; faculty fellowships focused on internationalization and diversity; and an International Studies AA program.

Conclusion

We both have found that regardless of the institution, the pedagogical goal for global and peace education is the same: students need to encounter diverse experiences and learn to listen and fully empathize with others. A supportive institutional culture gives faculty the space to infuse the campus with innovative opportunities for peace education.

> **Box 11.1: Extracurricular Efforts**
>
> At Allegany College of Maryland (ACM), psychology professor Kurt Hoffman's Peace Club channels students' interests in social justice issues and gets them involved in global issues. Recently, the club has raised awareness of sexual violence in the Democratic Republic of the Congo, the work of NGOs such as Médecins sans Frontières and OxFam, and the humanitarian crisis in Haiti. Hoffman says that for the club, "peace is more than antiwar . . . we advocate a nonviolent approach to nature and sustainable practices." His success is all the more significant considering that ACM is in a rural part of Western Maryland with limited cultural diversity.

At the same time, we have found that the *means* of achieving these goals varies significantly, which agrees with Harder's (2010) suggestion that rural community colleges internationalize differently from their metropolitan counterparts.

- For a rural college with a relatively monocultural population, faculty and administrators must find ways to bring international experience to students or to take students out of their comfort zones (through programs such as videoconferencing, study abroad, or extracurricular activities; see box 11.1).
- For a metropolitan college with diverse populations, faculty and administrators need to develop programming that enables and empowers students to embrace and learn from the knowledge and experiences already present among the college's students, staff, and faculty.
- The means of institutionalizing global studies and peace education must reflect the needs and culture of the institution. For a rural community college such as SWCC, a global education coordinator is key. For a large metropolitan community college like Montgomery, a decentralized and diffused approach can be effective.

Whether students enter the college aware of the global connections they will encounter or with limited understanding of their own connections to the global environment, international studies programs must emphasize developing attitudinal skills that embrace exploring varied worldviews, tolerating ambiguity, and peacebuilding. As true global denizens, we all need to learn how to respect each other in new ways. This respect begins with developing an understanding of our own culture and progresses to understanding other cultures. In a world that will survive based on shared peace, we all owe it to our students to be collectors and distributors of global knowledge. Whether we are teaching in a metropolitan or rural setting, dedicated teachers must seek appropriate methods of reaching out to students, faculty, and the community to educate them on global concepts such as peace, conflict resolution, and respect.

References

Brown, Jonathan N., Scott Pegg, and Jacob W. Shively. 2006. "Consensus and Divergence in International Studies: Survey Evidence from 140 International Studies Curriculum Programs. *International Studies Perspectives.* 7 (3): 267–86.

Chesler, Mark A. 1997. Perceptions of Faculty Behavior by Students of Color. CRLT Occasional Paper 7, Center for Research on Teaching and Learning, Univ. of Michigan.

Emert, H. A., and D. L. Pearson. 2007. "Expanding the Vision of International Education: Collaboration, Assessment, and Intercultural Development." *New Directions for Community Colleges,* no. 138 (Summer): 67–75.

Green, M. F. 2007. "Internationalizing Community Colleges: Barriers and Strategies." *New Directions for Community Colleges,* no. 138 (Summer): 15–24.

Harder, Natalie J. 2010. "Community College Internationalization Activities in the United States: A Snapshot." *Community Colleges for International Development, Inc. International News* (Spring): 16.

Kaiser, Ward L., and Denis Wood. 2001. *Seeing through Maps: The Power of Images to Shape Our World View.* Amherst, MA: ODT.

Krain, Matthew. 2010. "The Effects of Different Types of Case Learning on Student Engagement." *International Studies Perspectives* 11 (3): 291–308.

Lamy, Steven. 2007. "Challenging Hegemonic Paradigms and Practices: Critical Thinking and Active Learning Strategies for International Relations." *PS: Political Science and Politics* 40 (1): 112–16.

Montgomery College. 2010a. "Peace and Justice: Making Connections through Peace and Justice." Montgomery College Takoma Park/Silver Spring First Year Experience 2010–2011. www.montgomerycollege.edu/Departments/gpjs/Peace%20and%20Justice%20FYE%20book%20TPSS%2008272010.pdf.

———. 2010b. "Special Populations, Fall 2009." Montgomery College Office of Institutional Research and Analysis. www.montgomerycollege.edu/Departments/inplrsh/OIRA%20Other%20Files/Student%20Data/W-Special_Population.pdf.

O'Donovan, K. F., and V. M. Mikelonis. 2005. "Internationalizing On-Campus Courses." In *Internationalizing Undergraduate Education: Integrating Study Abroad into the Curriculum,* ed. Lynn C. Anderson, 9195. Minneapolis: Univ. of Minnesota Learning Abroad Center.

Seider, Scott. 2009. "Overwhelmed and Immobilized: Raising the Consciousness of Privileged Young Adults about World Hunger and Poverty." *International Studies Perspectives* 10 (1): 60–76.

Smith, David J. 2003. "The Community College in Peace and War." *Conflict Management in Higher Education Report* 3 (2). www.campus-adr.org/CMHER/ Report Articles/Edition3_2/Smith3_2a.html.

———. 2008. "Global Peace, Conflict and Security: Approaches Taken by American Community Colleges." *Journal of Peace Education* 5 (1): 63–78.

Valeriano, Brandon. 2008. "The Lack of Diverse Perspectives in the International Relations Field: The Politics of Being Alone." *International Studies Perspectives* 9 (4): 450–54.

South Up Maps. 2001. "What's Up? South!" Wall map. www.odt.org/southupmaps. htm.

International Relations (sophomore level)
Jennifer Haydel
Montgomery College, Germantown

Course Outcomes (derived from common Montgomery College outcomes):

Students who successfully complete this course will be able to:

- use and apply the major terms and concepts in international relations;
- explain the relationship between historical events and the development of international relations as a field of study;
- explain, apply, and interpret the major approaches and theories of international relations;
- analyze the power differentials and opportunity structures affecting the relationships among state and nonstate actors in the international system;
- compare and evaluate explanations for war and prescriptions for peace in the international system; and
- analyze the concept of globalization and apply it to contemporary changes to the international system.

Description of Assignments Used in the Course:

In-Class Activities and Writing Assignments. In-class activities include summaries of student small-group discussions, written responses to quotations and poems getting at that day's topic, and responses to video clips used to illustrate course concepts.

Analysis Paper. During the first two weeks of the semester, students write a paper about the usage of the terms "state," "nation," and "sovereignty" by exploring how the concepts apply to a specific case study. Previous case studies have included Palestine, South Sudan, Abkhazia, and Scotland.

Simulation Activities.
- United Nations Security Council: Students receive two separate assignment handouts for these simulations. Recently, the simulations have focused on (a) the debate over Iran's nuclear program, and (b) the international community's response to the regime in Burma. Students are randomly assigned a specific country (all Security Council members). The students write a resolution and lobby for introducing that resolution into the Council meeting. Then students debate and vote on the chosen resolution. These two simulation topics have provided a contrast for discussing the concepts of nonintervention, sovereignty, and the responsibility to protect, among others.
- Arctic ice cap summit simulation: During the final examination period of the course, students simulate a meeting of key players, including countries, NGOs, and IGOs. The goal of the meeting is to develop a plan for addressing the global changes being caused by the increased melting of the Arctic ice cap. This is a "capstone" activity, allowing students to draw together course themes and apply them to the consequences of global climate change.

Examinations. Midterm and final. Exams include identification questions (requiring a definition and statement of significance for a specific term) and essay questions.

Required Textbook and Required Supplementary Readings:

Required textbook:

Lamy, S. L., J. Baylis, S. Smith, and P. Owens. 2011. *Introduction to Global Politics*. New York: Oxford University Press.

Supplementary Readings (in order of use during the semester):

"Rethinking the 'Third World': Seeing the World Differently." 2010. *Economist* (June 12): 65–66.

"In Quite a State." 2010. *Economist* (April 10): 62–63.

"The Melian Dialogue." 1883. Excerpted from *Thucydides*, trans. Benjamin Jowett, ed. A. P. Peabody. Boston: Lothrop, bk. 5. www.shsu.edu/~his_ncp/Melian.html.

Carr, E. H. 1964 [1939]. "Power in International Politics." In *The Twenty Years' Crisis, 19191939*. New York: Harper Torchbooks, 102–108.

Chollet, D., and J. Goldgeier. 2008. *America between the Wars: From 11/9 to 9/11*. New York: Public Affairs, ixxvi.

Jervis, Robert. 2003. "Understanding the Bush Doctrine." *Political Science Quarterly* 33 (3): 21–34.

Atran, Scott. 2006. "The Moral Logic and Growth of Suicide Terrorism." *Washington Quarterly*. 29 (2): 127–47.

Zambernardi, Lorenzo. 2010. "Counterinsurgency's Impossible Trilemma." *Washington Quarterly* 33 (3): 21–34.

Matheson, M. J. 2006. *Council Unbound: The Growth of UN Decision Making on Conflict and Postconflict Issues after the Cold War*. Washington, DC: United States Institute of Peace Press, 62–64.

Zimbardo, Philip. 2008. *The Lucifer Effect*. New York: Random House, 46087.

Students review the Grameen Bank Web site (www.grameen-info.org/).

Schneider, Howard. 2010. "American Power, Waxing On and Off. *Washington Post*, June 27: B3.

Course Schedule

Unit I: Introductory Themes
- The role of categories and perception in Global Politics
- Guiding Frameworks (Realism, Liberalism, and Constructivism)

Unit II: Conflict Themes
- World Wars I and II, Cold War
- The end of the Cold War
- Emerging trends in the post-Cold War world
- 9/11 and the post-9/11 world
- Transnational terrorism
- Nuclear proliferation
- Afghanistan case study

Unit III: Peacebuilding Themes
- Regional organizations
- United Nations
- International law and judicial responses to crimes against humanity
- Humanitarianism and non-governmental organizations

Unit IV: International Political Economy
- The microcredit movement
- The global response to economic crises

Unit V: Course Wrap-Up
- Unipolarity, multipolarity, or nonpolarity: Where are we headed?
- The global environment and international cooperation

12

Teaching Human Rights and International Humanitarian Law

ISABELLE DAOUST AND CINDY EPPERSON

All human beings, whatever their cultural or historical background, suffer when they are intimidated, imprisoned or tortured. . . . We must, therefore, insist on a global consensus, not only on the need to respect human rights worldwide, but also on the definition of these rights . . . for it is the inherent nature of all human beings to yearn for freedom, equality and dignity, and they have an equal right to achieve that.   —Fourteenth Dalai Lama

The social conditions of the twenty-first century, in particular the interaction of societies with differing cultures, and the ubiquitous reality of social media demand that students develop global citizenship based on a set of knowledge, skills, and values. Human societies' interconnection leads to a greater awareness of human rights issues, especially when conflict and violence draw attention through traditional and social media, and informed individuals begin to consider alternatives to violence.

At least 250,000 people die annually in armed conflicts, most of them internal in nature, and at least 1.5 billion people live in conflict zones on almost every continent on the globe (Geneva Declaration 2011, 14; World Bank 2012). Ninety percent of casualties today are civilians taking no part in the hostilities. While the vast majority of conflicts are internal in nature, social media allow the stories to spread rapidly across the globe. The lines between law enforcement situations, including internal disturbances and tensions, and outright civil war may appear to blur. Ultimately, armed conflict erodes social capital and destroys individuals, families, and communities at

The authors gratefully acknowledge the assistance of the following people in writing this chapter: Tajesh Adhihetty, former international humanitarian law fellow with the American Red Cross and the UN International Criminal Tribunal for Rwanda; Lucy Brown, senior adviser, international humanitarian law and policy, American Red Cross; and Laurie Fisher, senior associate, International Humanitarian Law Education Program, American Red Cross. The views reflected in this paper are those of the authors and do not represent the official position of the American Red Cross or its affiliates.

Box 12.1: Human Rights and Homeland Security

As more community colleges prepare students for careers in homeland security, they can incorporate human rights as an important dimension of understanding international law.

Anne Arundel Community College in Maryland offers a homeland security management degree in which International Law and Human Rights is a course option. The course "introduces students to the scope and sources of international law, jurisdiction and dispute mechanisms in the international community. Students will explore fundamental human rights, focusing on genocide, civil rights, and war crimes. Students will also discuss arms control and the laws of war."

both the local and global levels. This reality clearly cries out for greater understanding of universal norms.

In our interconnected world, Americans simply cannot afford to be unaware of the world's human rights and international humanitarian law (IHL) standards. Thus, learning about human rights and IHL should be a core component of peace, social justice, and conflict studies, as well as homeland security programs (see box 12.1). To understand both theory and practice of human rights and IHL, students must have a basic knowledge of the fundamental concepts that underlie these areas of law and the protection of life and human dignity.

Defining and Teaching Human Rights and International Humanitarian Law

A contemporary view defines "human rights" as "a set of ethical principles which seek to ensure the equal worth of each individual life, and which are applicable to all peoples at all times and in all places" (O'Byrne 2003, 27). This represents the "universal" perspective of human rights applicable to every human being regardless of race, ethnicity, gender, age, sexual preference, religious preference, or national origin. In short, every human being is entitled to rights that are innate and absolute and that cannot be usurped by governments or social agencies.

The universalist view is steeped in a Western worldview and is criticized by some as ignoring non-Western cultural norms. The opposite perspective, the relativist view, argues that human rights should be relative to culture. Some, such as Blair Gibb, claim that the 1948 Universal Declaration of Human Rights—a creation of the newly formed United Nations following the destruction and devastation of the Second World Word—does not represent the cultural norms of all humankind (Gibb 2003).

Three key articles to assign before engaging in a classroom discussion of human rights are Donnelly 2003, Gibb 2003, and Lo 2007. These articles provide students with an overview of opposing perspectives in the global dialogue on human rights. Even though the universalist perspective will be the paradigm focused on in the course, it is important to discuss these differing views in a peace studies course that seeks to develop global citizens.

In 1948, the newly formed United Nations systematically defined specific universal normative standards for all human beings regardless of their nationality, ethnicity, or gender, in the Universal Declaration of Human Rights (UDHR). According to Article 1 of the UDHR, "All human beings are born free and equal in dignity and rights. They are endowed with reason and conscience and should act towards one another in a spirit of brotherhood." The International Covenant on Civil and Political Rights with its two Optional Protocols, and the International Covenant on Economic, Social and Cultural Rights, both adopted in 1966 and entered into force in 1976, codified the human rights laid out in the UDHR. Collectively, these instruments are informally known as the International Bill of Human Rights. Since 1948, nine international treaties have emerged to protect human rights. These instruments and the bodies created to monitor them are available online, as are many tools applicable to teaching in the college classroom (OHCHR 2007).

"International humanitarian law" can be defined as the rules and principles that limit the means and methods of warfare and protect those who do not or no longer take part in the hostilities. Unlike human rights, IHL is applicable only during armed conflict, but its purpose, in part, is to protect what is sometimes referred to as the "hard core" of human rights in times of armed conflict. These core protections include the right to life of protected persons, the prohibition of slavery, the prohibition of torture and inhumane treatment, and the prohibition of any retroactive application of the law. IHL has been primarily codified in the four Geneva Conventions of 1949 and their Additional Protocols of 1977 and 2005. While rules and customs concerning the conduct of armed conflict have always existed, the first attempt to codify the existing laws and customs of war came about when Abraham Lincoln commissioned Francis Lieber to compile the customary rules of warfare for use by the Union Army during the American Civil War. Although the groundbreaking "Lieber Code" of 1863 was limited in time and space, it was swiftly followed by the First Geneva Convention for wounded and sick soldiers on the battlefield, which became an international treaty upon its adoption in 1864. In the following years, the other Geneva treaties came into being to address concerns for the wounded, sick, and shipwrecked members of the armed forces at sea, prisoners of war, and civilians.

The Geneva Conventions have been adopted by all countries of the world and their Additional Protocols by many. The terms "law of armed conflict" and "law of war" are often used interchangeably with IHL. These are military terms that include other treaties regulating the conduct of hostilities and the use of specific weapons, in addition to the Geneva Conventions.

These are the basic principles of IHL:

- **Distinction:** A distinction must be made between civilians and combatants and between civilian property and military objectives. Attacks must be directed only at military objectives (Protocol I 1977, Art. 48).
- **Military Necessity:** A measure not forbidden by international law and indispensable for securing the complete submission of the enemy as soon as possible is considered a military necessity (Dept. of the Army 1956, para 3. a., at 4).
- **Proportionality:** An attack on a military objective must not cause incidental loss of civilian life or damage to civilian property that is excessive in relation to the concrete or direct military advantage sought (Protocol I 1977, Art. 51).
- **Unnecessary Suffering:** The right to choose methods and means of weapons is not unlimited. Weapons of a nature to cause superfluous injury or unnecessary suffering are prohibited (Protocol I 1977, Art. 35).

Although human rights and IHL are complementary, they are distinct bodies of public international law with roots in earlier domestic codes. Neither is a purely twentieth-century concept, although both were dramatically shaped in their current form as a result of the devastation of the Second World War. Both share the overarching goal of protecting human dignity. Therefore, a classroom discussion on "What is human dignity?" and "How do you define human dignity?" is appropriate when challenging students to consider global events from a humanitarian perspective.

Human rights and human rights law apply at all times and are designed (1) to protect the liberty of individuals [first generation], (2) to create equality among individuals [second generation (e.g., right to education)], and (3) to develop fraternity among various groups [third generation] (Vasak 1977). Human rights are often divided into these three generations and begin with the development of civil and political rights; followed by social, economic, and cultural rights; and, most recently, collective or group rights (Vasak 1977). While in theory, human rights law applies to all people at all times, in practice, it applies to all persons subject to the jurisdiction of a state. The gap between theory and practice provides a teaching opportunity. The intent of human rights law is to protect individuals from arbitrary behavior by the state (often referred to as *negative rights*) or to oblige the state to provide for its subjects (often referred to as *positive rights*). Human rights exist during all types of conflicts as well as in law enforcement situations and in peacetime. This makes classroom activities designed around human rights very relevant to peace studies programs.

Again, unlike human rights law, IHL applies only during times of armed conflict, whether international (between nations) or internal (within a nation), although core human rights are always protected under IHL. Another difference is that IHL includes provisions that are not included in human rights law. These provisions include rules on the conduct of hostilities (for example, regarding lawful targeting and killing of combatants or special protections for civilians who take no direct part in hostilities). Certain human rights such as the freedom of speech, movement, and association may be suspended in times of national emergencies or conflict, whereas the core protections of IHL can never be suspended.

A plethora of IHL teaching tools is available through the American Red Cross and the International Committee of the Red Cross (ICRC), including the Exploring Humanitarian Law (EHL) program (American Red Cross 2012; ICRC 2010). EHL was originally designed for secondary school teachers but has been successfully adapted to many college courses. Pedagogical tools to address humanitarian issues (e.g., human dignity; the role of the bystander; child soldiers; war crimes; the use of land mines and other weapons; judicial and nonjudicial options in response to IHL violations, including restorative justice, aid to refugees and displaced persons, treatment of prisoners, and so on) are included in the toolkit, which is free of charge to all educators. Divided into five modules, the materials are designed to engage students in interactive learning around humanitarian issues that are relevant to their lives. Students are drawn to the materials out of their concern for the injustices resulting from armed conflict and for the need for international rules to be applied both within the context of conflict and during peacetime.

Some useful resources on IHL include American Red Cross (2011a, 2011b, and 2011c) and ICRC (2004 and 2009).

Bridging the Information Gap: Why Teach about International Humanitarian Law?

The post-9/11 world requires from students a sound understanding of global realities and frameworks, including international humanitarian law. When elected leaders debate the limits of interrogation in times of war or in the face of terrorist threats, it will not serve for the people these leaders represent to be ignorant of the principles and precedents involved in these debates. When members of the U.S. military find themselves in foreign nations where beliefs, social structures, and cultural expectations differ completely from what they are used to, they need guidelines for choosing their actions and interpreting the actions of others. When journalists working overseas are arrested and jailed, it is important for Americans to understand the human rights and IHL issues at stake.

But the debates that have ensued across the United States' social and political landscape during this same post-9/11 time frame suggest that while people may have become more aware of the existence of IHL—and specifically the Geneva Conventions—they have not necessarily become better versed in IHL's content and significance (Gutierrez, DeCristofaro, and Woods 2012). In a February 2011 public opinion survey conducted in the United States by the American Red Cross, 55 percent of adults (age 18 and older) surveyed felt that they were somewhat or very familiar with the Geneva Conventions. But 51 percent of adults also said they believed that it was at least sometimes acceptable to torture enemy soldiers in order to get important military information (American Red Cross 2011a). This belief stands in direct contrast to the provisions of the Third Geneva Convention, outlining the treatment of prisoners of war, which states in Part III, Section 1, Art. 17, "No physical or mental torture, nor any other form of coercion, may be inflicted on prisoners of war to secure from them information of any kind whatever. Prisoners of war who refuse to answer may not be threatened, insulted, or exposed to unpleasant or disadvantageous treatment of any kind (Geneva Conventions 1949)."

The survey also sampled youth (ages 12 to 17) separately from adults, leading to interesting results. Only one in five youths reported being familiar with the Geneva Conventions, and 59 percent of youth felt that it was at least sometimes acceptable to torture captured enemy prisoners. What came as perhaps the biggest surprise, however, was that 41 percent of youth surveyed believed that the torture of captured American soldiers is at least sometimes acceptable. This was in spite of the fact that seven in ten youths reported having a close friend or relative who has served in the armed forces. In general, the youth surveyed were more likely than adults to find activities violating IHL acceptable.

Most Americans are not aware of the role the United States played in the nineteenth-century codification of rules governing the conduct of war, through the development of the "Lieber Code" under Abraham Lincoln in 1863. Public knowledge of this extraordinary document is extremely low (17 percent of adults, and 18 percent of youth ages 12 to 17). Ignorance of the fact that many rules of war actually originated in the United States hinders acceptance of laws that are often perceived by some in the United States as international "impositions" on American sovereignty (Gutierrez, DeCristofaro, and Woods 2012).

On a positive note, youth in particular expressed a strong interest in increased efforts to educate the public on IHL, with almost eight in ten agreeing that the government should educate youth on the rules of war before they are old enough to vote or to enlist in the military (American Red Cross 2011a).

The dissemination of the rules of war (IHL) as established in the four Geneva Conventions is a fundamental responsibility of each signatory to the Conventions. Each Convention contains an article directing that "the High Contracting Parties undertake, in time of peace as in time of war, to disseminate the text of the present Convention as widely as possible in their respective countries, and if possible, civilian instruction, so that the principles thereof may become known to the entire population."[1] The International Federation of Red Cross and Red Crescent Societies (IFRC) has an obligation to "... assist in the promotion and development of international humanitarian law and to disseminate this law ..." (IFRC 2007). In the United States, the American Red Cross, in support of the International Federation, in accordance with Article 3.2 of the Statutes of the International Red Cross and Red Crescent Movement and as a humanitarian auxiliary to the United States government, plays a key role in disseminating the principles of IHL to the civilian population through its International Humanitarian Law Dissemination Programs, including the EHL program for youth and young adults (ICRC 2007, Art. 3, para. 2). The Department of Defense's Law of War Program mandates training and education for all military men and women (U.S. Dept. of Defense 2006).

Educating for Peace: Classroom Approaches for Teaching Human Rights and IHL

At St. Louis Community College in Missouri, a peace, social justice, and conflict program is under development. A global studies program encourages faculty to infuse courses with content that builds students' global competence as they prepare for a competitive twenty-first century knowledge-based economy. One such course, Universal Human Rights, is an interdisciplinary capstone course that fulfills the requirement of the general transfer studies program for the AA degree. The focus of the course is human rights, but IHL is integrated throughout the course because human rights are always violated during times of armed conflict and are often a point of contention during times of peace when various groups compete for valued resources.

---

1. This requirement is found in Articles 47, 48, 127, and 144 of Geneva Conventions I, II, III, and IV respectively.

The course is designed to impart knowledge, enhance global competence and cultural sensitivity, develop conflict resolution skills, encourage action toward social justice, and provide tools for such action in a safe and secure learning environment.

The course has these objectives:

- comprehend the complicated nature of universal human rights in both theory and practice
- recognize the impact of the media, including social media, to influence human rights in both theory and practice
- gain an appreciation of cultural difference while developing or enhancing a greater awareness of global connectedness
- augment students' global competence
- develop an understanding of, and an appreciation for, international humanitarian law

The course was designed around several assumptions: (1) American students are globally and geographically challenged and, in general, embrace the insular American perspective; global problems (e.g., hunger, poverty, inequality, slavery) exist but are not important in the students' daily existence. (2) Human beings, regardless of culture, have the potential for both good and evil, and regardless of modernity's intent to eliminate moral evil through science, history continues to repeat itself, and human destructiveness (e.g., armed conflict, genocide, displaced persons) continues to exist. Sustainable peace and security are possible if human rights are the universal normative standards that shape social structures and social interaction. (3) Conflict, not violence, is the opposite of peace and is inherent in the human condition. Conflict is often necessary for social change; therefore, it is not viewed as pejorative. (4) The quest to implement human rights as universal and ideal standards that guide social arrangements requires education and constant attention. (5) Peacemaking requires global competence and tolerance for cultural diversity. It is not inherent in most people, but it can be learned. Peacemaking is not without contention and requires perseverance.

Starting the Course

The Universal Human Rights course begins with a discussion on being human. This sounds elementary, but when students are asked "What does it mean to be fully human?" they discover that the human condition is a concept not easily defined. To be fully human, one must be afforded human dignity, which is possible only when physiological needs, security needs, belonging needs, and esteem needs are met (Maslow 1943). When the basic needs for becoming fully human are fulfilled, individuals possess the human capital necessary to participate in a healthy society. When human rights are envisioned, implemented, and protected as "high-priority norms," peace and security, the overall mission of the United Nations and its 193 member states, are more likely to become reality. Therefore, understanding what it means to be fully human is essential to the course by connecting the weekly topics (e.g., modern slavery, child soldiers, displaced persons) to human rights and IHL in theory and practice.

The United Nations' 1948 Universal Declaration of Human Rights (UDHR) and the International Bill of Human Rights are foundational documents in the course. It was not until the 1966 adoption and the 1976 entry into force of two treaties—the International Covenant on Civil and Political Rights, with its two Optional Protocols, and the International Covenant on Economic, Social and Cultural Rights—that human rights were codified into law. Helping students understand the difference between legally protected rights, such as civil rights (e.g., freedom of speech) and human rights (referred to as "high-priority norms"), is a semester-long process (Nickel 2007, 9).

Interactive Learning Environment

Teaching human rights and IHL requires the instructor to use an interactive learning environment that lets students safely explore difficult, unfamiliar, and often uncomfortable topics (e.g., child soldiers, displaced persons, genocide, slavery, trafficking in persons). A culture of collaboration is encouraged, in which the focus is on the students' learning rather than the instructor's teaching. Small-group activities are a common experience in each class meeting. One such activity involves the use of whiteboards or flip charts. First the students explore the weekly topic (e.g., genocide) in small groups. They develop a definition and then create a list of words typically associated with the concept. Students write their definition and list of words on the board or flipchart, share their information, and then engage in a classroom discussion. A series of short lectures and activities on the topic follows. The final fifteen minutes of each class session are reserved for the small groups to revise their first definition and list, which is then posted on the board. If laptop computers are available, students make documents and post them on a course management discussion board, where they remain for the semester and can be easily accessed when needed for review or clarification. If laptops are not an option, the instructor can create a handout summarizing the collective work and bring it to the following class session to provide a five-minute review.

During the course design phase, both faculty and students claimed knowledge and understanding of human rights, but when asked to define and apply the concept, the ambiguous and complicated nature of human rights, along with the multiple layers of understanding (e.g., "I have a right . . ." versus "With each right, I have corresponding responsibilities"), they couldn't. Therefore, the first exercise in the course is a conceptual analysis of human rights. Students are asked to write a short paragraph describing their knowledge of human rights. Typical responses include, uppermost, individual legal protections (e.g., freedom of speech, right to keep and bear arms). The right to marriage is a hot topic, and the lists are typically "me" oriented (e.g., "I have the right to . . ."). As students share their paragraphs, a unified list is created and posted. This list returns to class meetings throughout the semester to provide a visual reminder of the class's collective learning.

In the first class meeting (class sessions last 2.5 hours, once a week), the instructor holds a large umbrella over her head and asks students to imagine that she is in the middle of an intense rain storm. She then asks, "What is the purpose of the umbrella?" After discussing their answers, students are reminded that human rights are like an umbrella in the sense that they provide protection. The instructor then turns the umbrella over to show the spokes and spine, explaining that the umbrella keeps people dry but only if the metal rods that give it structure are in working order. If the rods are missing, bent, or broken, the umbrella will not provide protection. The spokes and spine symbolize the international, regional, and domestic instruments that codify the various human rights set forth in the UDHR (a nonlegally binding document) and the International Bill of Human Rights (the legally binding instruments). A volunteer then draws an umbrella on the flip chart or board. Students attempt to name the rods as other types of rights (e.g., political, civil, social, and so on). Then the professor lectures on Vasak's three generations of human rights and Nickel's families of human rights (Vasak 1977; Nickel 2007, 93–95). Students then complete the exercise, labeling all the spokes of the umbrella from the content of the lecture. This exercise provides a visual tool that can be used throughout the semester. If the umbrella analogy is not appealing, try a large box filled with several smaller boxes, individually gift wrapped. The small boxes represent other types of rights, and the large box symbolizes human rights. This analogy has been used at the last class period, where the large box is wrapped as a package to represent something valuable and desired (i.e., human rights). The package is unwrapped and opened to find smaller packages that are marked "political rights," "civil rights," "social rights," and the like. As each smaller package is removed, the students discuss their collective knowledge of each right, including the purpose of each right, the generation or family it belongs to, the legal instruments that protect or provide it, and the impact the right has had on human existence.

Instructor's Professional Development and Teaching Tools

Because the course is interdisciplinary and incorporates the latest violations of human rights (in Syria, for instance), it requires the instructor to constantly increase her knowledge of theory and practice from various disciplinary and cultural paradigms and current world events. Institutions such as the United States Institute of Peace, American Red Cross, International Committee of the Red Cross (ICRC), United Nations, and non-governmental organizations (NGOs) provide many of the crucial tools for teaching the course. Curricular ideas and materials are available, often free of charge, from the Web or Internet.

Teaching this subject matter requires no particular expertise in human rights or IHL. Educators can guide students in defining their thoughts, and they can reach answers together. The educator's role thus becomes that of a mentor by *exploring* the subject with students. It is important to keep in mind that with these topics, there may be no easy answers—many questions that challenge you and your students are also debated by leaders and legal experts around the globe.

Educators in human rights and IHL will likely share similar goals and use similar interactive techniques. They may also share challenges in addressing complex questions raised by students. An excellent starting point for introducing human rights or IHL in the classroom is to encourage students to use stories from local, national, and international media to help them recognize events and issues involving human rights and IHL in their communities, country, and world. The goal is to raise students' awareness of the humanitarian or human rights perspectives and of the need for human rights standards and humanitarian norms. Torture and slavery are topics that prompt a classroom discussion on human dignity and the roles of bystanders as witnesses to behavior that violates it. News stories that can be applicable to one or more of the thirty articles in the Universal Declaration of Human Rights are more common than most realize. Students are encouraged to use common media sources (e.g., television news, newspapers, YouTube, Facebook, Google) and alternative media sources that they often are not familiar with, such as ICRC Media Room, BBC News, National Public Radio, and UN YouTube Channel. By introducing and using unfamiliar media outlets, students discover that their common sources (e.g., Wikipedia) are not always academically sound.

An interactive approach will allow educators and students to explore together difficult questions that may not have easy answers. Educators could find themselves unable to answer students' challenging questions on the spot. It may be useful to designate a place where difficult questions raised by students can be recorded and displayed on a "no easy answer" sheet. Even though some questions may not have an immediate response, possible answers might emerge at a later stage during the course.

While traditional lecture-based techniques are often used to impart knowledge of human rights and IHL, educators may also choose to use interactive classroom techniques. These can include brainstorming, small-group discussions, role-playing, examining dilemmas, reading stories, looking at photos, using multimedia, or attending events. The main advantage of these types of teaching methods is that they encourage students to play an active role in the learning process, thus helping them better understand complex topics at a deeper level of comprehension. Students can stay actively engaged in current events related to IHL by following the American Red Cross IHL twitter feed "@RulesOfWar" (Khurana 2012).

With these teaching methods in mind, the American Red Cross has developed a free curriculum for educators interested in introducing IHL in their classrooms: the EHL toolkit. While EHL was initially designed for students at the secondary school level, it is currently being used in community colleges and four-year institutions around the United States. Because of its flexible and modular nature, community college educators use several of the EHL activities and lessons to enrich their courses. For example, resources from EHL can be integrated into a number of courses such as criminology, human rights, international relations, international law, history, political science, peace studies, sociology, psychology, and homeland security.

Introducing multiple perspectives (e.g., civilian, combatant, government) and exploring dilemmas can also be useful teaching methods. The use of various dilemma scenarios presented in the EHL curriculum introduces students to the complexities of making ethical (and lawful) decisions in times of armed conflict or in fulfilling and respecting human rights. Through stories, videos, and news accounts, students will realize that every decision has consequences, some of which cannot be anticipated, and that people often have very different perspectives and opinions on certain topics. To use the technique of dilemma analysis effectively, educators must analyze two questions with students: (1) "What is the dilemma here?" and (2) "What are its consequences?" The Red Cross EHL curriculum offers a chain-of-consequences exercise that can be useful in analyzing dilemmas. In academia, the term "critical thinking" has come to mean, for many, "I'll be critical of everyone who doesn't agree with my perspective." It is important, therefore, to teach our students that "critical thinking" doesn't mean being critical of anyone different from oneself but rather listening to perspectives that are different from one's own, seeking alternative perspectives, and discovering how multiple perspectives can broaden one's worldview. Critical thinking in its true sense is crucial to developing global citizenship skills.

Modeling classroom behavior that demonstrates respect for human dignity is also necessary. There will be times when students disagree with each other or with you. It is important that students respect others' views. Modeling respectful behavior in the classroom is an important part of teaching about human dignity, the ability to consider multiple perspectives, and, more generally, human rights and IHL education.

Conclusion

Teaching a human rights or IHL course requires a constant focus on the concept of human dignity, which begins in the classroom by creating and accepting nothing less than an environment of tolerance and safe inquiry. The course should follow the spirit of the Universal Declaration of Human Rights, which states, "Recognition of the inherent dignity and of the equal and inalienable rights of all members of the human family is the foundation of freedom, justice and peace in the world" (United Nations 1948, Preamble, para. 1). Many tools are available through organizations such as the Red Cross, the United States Institute of Peace, the United Nations, and numerous NGOs that provide their materials online, free of charge. These tools will enrich the journey your students take with you in discovering the connection between human rights as "high-priority norms," IHL, and peacemaking. By studying the theory of these bodies of law and comparing it to the practice of human rights and IHL, students will enhance their global competence and critical thinking skills while learning how to manage copious sources of information and evaluate competing perspectives.

References

American Red Cross. 2011a. "Development of International Humanitarian Law." Fact sheet. Smith 12 (Daoust and Epperson) clean.docx www.redcross.org/images/MEDIA_CustomProductCatalog/m3640105_IHL_Development.pdf.

————. 2011b. "International Humanitarian Law and Human Rights." Fact sheet. www.redcross.org/images/MEDIA_CustomProductCatalog/m3640107_IHL_HumanRights.pdf.

————.2011c. "Summary of the Geneva Conventions of 1949 and Their Additional Protocols." Fact sheet. www.redcross.org/images/MEDIA_CustomProduct Catalog/m3640104_IHL_SummaryGenevaConv.pdf.

————.2011d. "Survey on International Humanitarian Law." Research conducted by ORC International, March 2011. www.redcross.org/images/MEDIA_Custom ProductCatalog/m12940087_Survey_on_International_Humanitarian_Law. pdf.

————.2012. "Exploring Humanitarian Law: A Guide for Teachers." www.redcross. org/ehl.

Dept. of the Army. 1956. *Field Manual 27-10, the Law of Land Warfare.* Washington, DC: Government Printing Office.

Donnelly, Jack. 2003. "Human Rights Are Universal." In *Opposing Viewpoints: Human Rights,* ed. Laura K. Egendorf. San Diego: Greenhaven Press.

Geneva Conventions of 12 August 1949. 1949. www.icrc.org/eng/war-and-law/ treaties-customary-law/geneva-conventions/index.jsp.

Geneva Declaration. 2011. "Global Burden of Armed Violence 2011." www.geneva declaration.org.

Gibb, Blair. 2003. "Human Rights Are Not Necessarily Universal." In *Opposing Viewpoints: Human Rights,* ed. Laura K. Egendorf. San Diego: Greenhaven Press.

Gutierrez, Brad A., Sarah DeCristofaro, and Michael Woods. 2012. "What Americans Think of International Humanitarian Law." *International Review of the Red Cross,* no. 884. www.icrc.org/eng/resources/documents/article/review-2011/ irrc-884-gutierrez-decristofaro-woods.htm

International Committee of the Red Cross (ICRC). 2004. "International Humanitarian Law: Answers to Your Questions." Brochure. www.icrc.org/eng/resources/ documents/publication/p0703.htm.

————.2007. Statutes of the International Red Cross and Red Crescent Movement. www.icrc.org/eng/resources/documents/misc/statutes-movement-220506.htm.

————. 2009. Film: *International Humanitarian Law: A Universal Code.* Film. www. icrc.org/eng/resources/documents/film/f00981.htm.

————. 2010. "Exploring Humanitarian Law: A Virtual Campus." www.ehl.icrc. org/.

International Federation of Red Cross and Red Crescent Societies (IFRC). 2007. Constitution, Section 1, Art. 5, para. 1 (B) (c), revised and adopted by the Sixth Session of the General Assembly, Rio de Janeiro, Brazil, 2326 Nov. 1987. www. ifrc.org/Global/Governance/Statutory/Constitution_revised-en.pdf.

Sigmund, Eric. 2012. "@RulesOfWar." www.twitter.com/rulesofwar.

Lo, Jieh-Yung. 2007. "Universalism Challenged: Human Rights and Asian Values." *On Line Opinion,* Feb. 1.

Maslow, Abraham. 1943. "A Theory of Human Motivation." *Psychological Review* 50 (4): 37096.

Nickel, J. W. 2007. *Making Sense of Human Rights.* Malden, MA: Blackwell.

O'Byrne, D. J. 2003. *Human Rights: An Introduction.* San Francisco: Pearson Education.

Office of the United Nations High Commissioner for Human Rights (OHCHR). 2007. "The Core International Human Rights Instruments and Their Monitoring Bodies." www2.ohchr.org/english/law/index.htm#core.

Protocol I. 1977. Protocol I Additional to the Geneva Conventions of 12 August 1949. www.icrc.org/ihl.nsf/CONVPRES?OpenView.

United Nations. 1948. Universal Declaration of Human Rights. www.ohchr.org/EN/UDHR/Pages/Language.aspx?LangID=eng.

U.S. Dept. of Defense. 2006. Directive 2311.01E, 9 May 2006, updated Nov. 15, 2010, certified current as of Feb. 22, 2011. www.dtic.mil/whs/directives/corres/pdf/231101e.pdf.

Vasak, Karel. 1977. "Human Rights: A Thirty-Year Struggle: The Sustained Efforts to Give Force of Law to the Universal Declaration of Human Rights." *UNESCO Courier* 30 (11).

World Bank. 2012. "Fragile and Conflict-Affected Countries." http://web.world bank.org/WBSITE/EXTERNAL/PROJECTS/STRATEGIES/EXTLICUS/0,,menu PK:511784~pagePK:64171540~piPK:64171528~theSite PK:511778,00.html.

Capstone IDS 201: Universal Human Rights (4 Credit Hours) Syllabus
St. Louis Community College—Meramec
Cindy Epperson, PhD, Professor of Sociology

Required Textbooks: Nickel, James W. 2007. *Making Sense of Human Rights*, 2nd ed. Blackwell.
Satrapi, Marjane. 2003. *Persepolis: A Story of Childhood*. Pantheon.
Additional readings as assigned

COURSE DESCRIPTION: The course utilizes an interdisciplinary approach to examine human rights as universal, ideal standards guiding social arrangements. Students will explore (1) the difference between human rights in theory and in practice, (2) the philosophical and theoretical paradigms framing human rights as ethical standards, (3) the relationship between human rights and international law, (4) the link between human rights as universal standards and peacebuilding, and (5) the major players in the world community's discourse on human rights. The continuous struggle to implement human rights will be examined as students actively explore world events and relationships in the twentieth and twenty-first centuries. This research-oriented course requires weekly reading, writing, research, and review of various media resources.

COURSE OBJECTIVES: At the conclusion of this course, the student will be able to:
1. Describe and explain the universal nature of human rights.
2. Demonstrate global competencies and the ability to translate cultural views.
3. Apply the process of globalization (capitalism, postindustrialization, technology, availability of media, and modernization) to twenty-first century universal human rights.
4. Explain the impact of the media and the Internet on human rights.
5. Describe the global status of women and children and their crucial role in universalizing human rights as ideal standards.
6. Critically assess the *International Bill of Human Rights* and the nine international instruments designed to legally protect human rights.
7. *Explain* the success and failure of the United Nations to address human rights.
8. Demonstrate an ability to manage massive volumes of information, including copious Internet and news resources, in order to juxtapose the various perspectives on human rights as universal standards.

COURSE ITINERARY

Week 1: Lecture, Discussion & Activities: Being Human, Human Dignity, and Human Rights
Readings: Chapter 1 and Appendix 1; "Chronology and Events in Human Rights," in Ishay, Micheline R. 2004. *The History of Human Rights: From Ancient Times to the Globalization Era*. University of California Press. And "What Are Human Rights?" at www.ohchr.org/EN/Issues/Pages/Whatare HumanRights.aspx.

Week 2: Lecture, Discussion & Activities: Universal Human Rights: The Movement

Readings: Chapters 2 and 3; Opposing Viewpoints "Human Rights Are Universal," "Human Rights Are Not Necessarily Universal," and "Human Rights Must Be Culturally Relative." *Universal Declaration of a Global Ethic* and *Universal Declaration of Human Responsibilities,* available at www.scu.edu/ethics/practicing/focusareas/global_ethics/laughlin-lectures/global-ethic-human-responsibility.html

Maslow's Hierarchy of Needs, at http://psychology.about.com/od/theoriesof personality/a/hierarchyneeds.htm

Week 3: Lecture, Discussion & Activities: Nature of Human Rights in an Era of Global Connectedness—3 Generations of Rights, Families of Rights, and the List Question

Readings: Chapters 9 and 10 and Appendixes 3 and 4; Endorois, at www.witness.org/index.php?option=com_content&task=view&id=511&Itemid=44 "Human Rights by Country," at www.ohchr.org/EN/Countries/Pages/Human RightsintheWorld.aspx

Week 4: Lecture, Discussion & Activities: United Nations and Human Rights Instruments

Readings: Chapter 4; "United Nations and Global Security" in *CQ Global Researcher;* "The United Nations Is Necessary to Stop Human Rights Abuses," and "United Nations Does Not Respond Effectively to Human Rights Abuses" (*Opposing Viewpoints)*

Week 5: Lecture, Discussion & Activities: International Human Rights Law Application

Readings: Chapter 6, "The Difference between Human Rights Law and International Humanitarian Law," at www.icrc.org/eng/assets/files/other/ihl_and_ihrl.pdf

"International Human Rights Law," at www.ohchr.org/EN/ProfessionalInterest/Pages/InternationalLaw.aspx

International Criminal Court (Rome Statute of the International Criminal Court—1998)

Week 6: Lecture, Discussion & Activities: Work: An Equality Right

Readings: Chapter 8, "Labor Rights as Human Rights," "Decent Work as a Human Right," at www.realizingrights.org/index.php?option=com_content&view=article&id=365&itemid=134 www1.umn.edu/humanrts/edumat/IHRIP/circle/modules/module10.htm

Week 7: Lecture, Discussion & Activities: Poverty, Hunger, and Sustainability

Readings: Chapter 9, World Food Programme, at www.wfp.org; "Uses of Global Poverty," at www.gwu.edu/~soc/docs/Eglitis/Global_Poverty.pdf "Food as a Human Right," at www.choike.org/documentos/Food_Human_Right.pdf

Week 8: Lecture, Discussion & Activities: Migration, Refugees, and Displaced Persons

Readings: pp. 131-3, UNHCR at www.unhcr.org/cgi-bin/texis/vtx/home, "Aiding Refugees" (2009) *CQ Global Researcher,* and Internally Displaced Person (IDP) at www.internal-displacement.org/8025708F004D404D/(http-Pages)/CC32D8C34EF93C88802570F800517610

Week 9: Lecture, Discussion & Activities: People as Commodities: Slavery

Readings: *Modern Slavery* in EBSCO electronic database, "Global Crime Case: The Modern Slave Trade," in *The Futurist,* Nov.Dec. 2008, www.wfs.org

Week 10: Lecture, Discussion & Activities: People as Commodities: Human Trafficking

Readings: *Department of State Trafficking in Persons (G/TIP) Report,* www.state.gov/j/tip/rls/tiprpt

Week 11: Lecture, Discussion & Activities: Armed Conflict and Genocide

Video: *Witnessing Darfur* and *Defying Genocide*
Readings: *Eight Stages of Genocide Briefing Paper* by Gregory Stanton, USIP Genocide Prevention Task Force Report, UN Genocide Convention, and NGO Genocide Watch at www.genocidewatch.org/

Week 12: Lecture, Discussion & Activities: Armed Conflict and Peacekeeping

Video: *Peacekeepers*
Readings: *UN's Role in Armed Conflict, UN's Chapter 7 Mandate* at www.un-documents.net/ch-07.htm; *UN Peacekeeping Factsheet,* MILOB Training Institute 2010, at www.peaceopstraining.org/our_courses/cotipso/partner_course/736; *World Peacekeeping* in CQ Global Researcher electronic database

Week 13: Lecture, Discussion & Activities: Armed Conflict and Children as Soldiers

Video: *Child Soldiers in Sierra Leone* and ICRC's *I Don't Want to Go Back*
Readings: *Child Soldiers* by Mike Wessells, *Teaching about Contemporary Conflict in Community Colleges: The Child Soldier Crisis,* by David Smith, *Convention on the Rights of Children,* at www.unicef.org/crc/index_understanding.html, and UN Child Soldiers Factsheet at www.unicef.org/emerg/files/childsoldiers.pdf

Week 14: Lecture, Discussion & Activities: Peacebuilding

Readings: United States Institute of Peace *Peacewatch* and *Special Reports,* available at www.usip.org/resources-tools; and *Enhancing Security Through Peacebuilding,* by Matthew Levinger, available from www.greatdecisions.org

Week 15: Lecture, Discussion & Activities: Human Rights—Is "Universal" possible?

Readings: "The Road Not Taken," by Robert Frost
"You must be the change you wish to see in the world."—Mahatma Gandhi

Exploring International Humanitarian Law

College/Organization: Sample syllabus developed by the American Red Cross, International Humanitarian Law Education Program (International Services Department, National Headquarters, Washington, DC)

Course Description

Where does IHL fit: This material can be taught as a stand-alone course or integrated into a variety of disciplines and subject areas, including human rights, peace-and-conflict studies, history (U.S. and world), international studies, political science, ESL, world languages, sociology, psychology, philosophy, religion, ethics, premilitary and prelaw studies, and teacher education.

Methodology: Multiple teaching methods are used, including discussion; brainstorming; the concept of "no easy answers"; using dilemmas; role-playing; using stories, photos, and videos; writing and reflecting; interviewing; small groups; and gathering stories and news.

Course objectives: To explore and understand (1) central questions underlying international humanitarian law (IHL); (2) the concept of human dignity; (3) the effect a bystander can have on the actions of others, humanitarian acts; (4) why rules are needed in armed conflict; (5) the basic rules of IHL / relationship to human rights law; (6) the historical development of IHL; (7) the plight of child soldiers and evolution of laws to protect them; (8) restrictions on the use of certain weapons in war; (9) identifying violations of IHL; (10) recognizing dilemmas that may arise in combat situations; (11) the difficulties in respecting IHL when the difference between combatants and civilians is unclear; (12) the factors that could lead to serious violations of IHL; (13) the different judicial ways of dealing with war crimes (e.g., national, international, "hybrid" courts); (14) nonjudicial approaches that states have chosen to deal with IHL violations; (15) the scope of humanitarian action needed to meet human needs arising from displacement (refugees and internally displaced persons); how IHL protects the lives and human dignity of prisoners; (17) the dilemmas and ethical issues faced by humanitarian workers; and (18) applying acquired knowledge to design a project that promotes human dignity.

Course Requirements

1. **Class attendance and active participation:** Attendance is expected and requires preparation by completing reading assignments.
2. **Weekly readings:** This course requires **weekly** reading of class assignments, awareness of current events in the news, review of various media resources, class attendance, and group work.
3. **Potential research topics:**
   - How has the United States contributed to the historical development of IHL (including the Geneva Conventions) since the first Geneva Convention in 1864? How did U.S. experiences during the American Civil War contribute to the development of IHL internationally?
   - Compare two countries that addressed IHL violations in two very different ways. What is the situation today in each country?

- Examine a recent situation where there was a violation of IHL. If you were an international leader, what would you suggest to help the country move forward?
- Research a current ethical dilemma faced by an NGO. If you were the executive director, how would you resolve the problem?
- Examine a current war or humanitarian crisis. Pretend that you are the executive director of an NGO of your choice. How would you respond to the needs of the vulnerable?
- Design an NGO that helps either former child soldiers or prisoners of war. How would you address their needs and help them reintegrate into society?
- Research different professions and technical skills needed by international NGOs and humanitarian workers responding to complex emergencies (natural disasters and conflict situations) internationally.

Required/Recommended Texts and Other Materials
- "Exploring Humanitarian Law," at www.redcross.org/ehl
- Dworkin, Anthony, Roy Gutman, and David Rieff. 2007. *Crimes of War*. New York: Norton. Also at www.crimesofwar.org
- Fact sheets, films, and miscellaneous other resources referenced within the weekly course schedule

Course Schedule

Week 1: The Humanitarian Perspective
- Introductory discussion: Images and perceptions activity, what is human dignity, armed conflict and attempts to limit it (EHL, Introductory exploration, i, pp. 4–6)
- What can bystanders do? (EHL, Module 1, 1A, pp. 4–23)
- Looking at humanitarian acts (EHL, Module 1, 1B, pp. 24–28)
- Extension activity (debate/discussion): Why not outlaw war? (EHL, Introductory exploration, i, pp. 7, 10–12)

Resource: http://ehl.redcross.org/curriculum/introduction/resources/EHL-intro.pdf
Resource: http://ehl.redcross.org/curriculum/module1/resources/EHL-Module1.pdf

Week 2: Limits in Armed Conflict
- Limiting the devastation of war (introduces the basic rules of international humanitarian law and the relationship with human rights) (EHL Module, 2A, pp. 4–20)
- Codes and traditions over time (EHL Module 2, 2B, pp. 21–33)

Resource: http://ehl.redcross.org/curriculum/module2/resources/EHL-Module2.pdf

Readings:
Fact sheet: Summary of the Geneva Conventions of 1949 and Their Additional Protocols: www.redcross.org/images/MEDIA_CustomProductCatalog/m3640104_IHL_SummaryGenevaConv.pdf
Fact sheet: The Development of IHL:
www.redcross.org/what-we-do/international-services/educating-future-

humanitarians/ihl-tools-resources

Week 3: Child Soldiers
- Focus on child soldiers (EHL, Module 2, 2C, pp. 34–47)
- Extension activity: Children and gangs (EHL, Module 2, 2C, p. 39)
- Extension activity: Current events/youth action (EHL, Module 2, 2C, p. 40)

Resource: http://ehl.redcross.org/curriculum/module2/resources/EHL-Module2.pdf

Film: *I Don't Want to Go Back*
http://ehl.redcross.org/curriculum/module2/C-resources.php

Readings:
Fact sheet: Child soldiers: www.unicef.org/emerg/files/childsoldiers.pdf
www.redcross.org/what-we-do/international-services/educating-future-humanitarians/ihl-tools-resources
Crimes of War, pp. 95–99

Week 4: Limits on Weapons
- Focus on weapons (EHL, Module 2, 2D, pp. 48–69)
- Widespread availability of weapons (EHL, Module 2, 2E, pp. 70–83)

Resource: http://ehl.redcross.org/curriculum/module2/resources/EHL-Module2.pdf
Film: *Landmines Keep Killing*
http://ehl.redcross.org/curriculum/module2/D-resources.php

Readings:
Crimes of War, pp. 62–63, 93–94, 304–306, 324–327
Unregulated arms availability, small arms and light weapons, and the UN process (26-05-2006 Report, Background paper, ICRC)
www.icrc.org/eng/resources/documents/misc/small-arms-paper-250506.htm#a1
The Skeleton in the Closet – Survivors of Armed Violence (Centre for Humanitarian Dialogue)
www.hdcentre.org/publications/skeleton-closet-survivors-armed-violence
Fact sheet: Landmines: www.redcross.org/what-we-do/international-services/educating-future-humanitarians/ihl-tools-resources

Week 5: The Law in Action
- Identifying violations of IHL (EHL, Module 3, 3A, pp. 4–14)
- Chains of consequences (EHL, Module 3, 3A: p. 7)
- From the perspective of combatants (EHL, Module 3, 3B, pp. 15–27)
- Research/discuss a current event that is an example of an IHL violation

Resource: http://ehl.redcross.org/curriculum/module3/resources/EHL-Module3.pdf

Reading:
Crimes of War, pp. 103, 104–106, 119–120, 218–219, 341, 403, 415–416.

Week 6: Case Study on My Lai
- Who is responsible for respecting IHL? (EHL, Module 3, 3C, pp. 28–32)
- Begin case study: My Lai (EHL, Module 3, 3D, pp. 33–57)

Resource: http://ehl.redcross.org/curriculum/module3/resources/EHL-Module3.pdf

Homework: An Essay (EHL, Module 3, 3C, p. 31)

Week 7: Case Study on My Lai (Continued)
- Continue case study on My Lai (EHL, Module 3, 3D, pp. 33–57)
- Debate: Who is guilty? (EHL, Module 3, 3D, p. 38)

Resource: http://ehl.redcross.org/curriculum/module3/resources/EHL-Module3.pdf

Film: *What We Did at My Lai*
http://ehl.redcross.org/curriculum/module3/D-resources.php

Week 8: Dealing with Violations
- Rationales and options for dealing with IHL violations (EHL, Module 4, 4A, pp. 4–18)
- Judicial options (EHL, Module 4, 4B, pp. 19–41)

Resource: http://ehl.redcross.org/curriculum/module4/resources/EHL-Module4.pdf

Readings:
Fact sheet: Prosecution of Violations of IHL:
www.redcross.org/images/MEDIA_CustomProductCatalog/m3640110_IHL_ProsecutionofViolations.pdf
Fact sheet: International Criminal Court:
www.redcross.org/images/MEDIA_CustomProductCatalog/m3640111_IHL_ICC.pdf

Week 9: Dealing with Violations (Continued)
Resource: http://ehl.redcross.org/curriculum/module4/resources/EHL-Module4.pdf
- Continue judicial options (EHL, Module 4, 4B, pp .19–41)
- Nonjudicial options (EHL, Module 4, 4C, pp. 42–59)
- Extension activity: A torturer confronts his misdeeds (EHL, Module 4, 4C, p. 46)

Reading: www.ictj.org/about/transitional-justice (an overview of transitional justice)

Week 10: Responding to the Consequences of Armed Conflict
- Needs that arise from the devastation of war (EHL, Module 5, 5A, pp. 4–13)
- The experience of fleeing (EHL, Module 5, 5A, p. 8)
- Planning a refugee camp (EHL, Module 5, 5B, pp. 14–25)
- Restoring family links (EHL, Module 5, 5D, pp. 42–51)
- Extension activity: People who have been forced to flee their homes (EHL, Module 5, 5A, p. 9)

Resource: http://ehl.redcross.org/curriculum/module5/resources/EHL-Module5.
pdf

Film: *Forced from Home*
http://ehl.redcross.org/curriculum/module5/A-resources.php

Reading:
www.unrefugees.org/site/c.lflQKSOwFqG/b.4950731/k.A894/What_is_a_
refugee.htm

Week 11: Responding to the Consequences of Armed Conflict (Continued)
- Prisoners of war (EHL, Module 5, 5C, pp. 26–41)
- Suggested class discussion: Detention, torture, and the rights of prisoners of war
- Extension activity: The difficulties faced by a prisoner after being released (EHL, Module 5, 5C, p. 31)

Resource: http://ehl.redcross.org/curriculum/module5/resources/EHL-Module5.
pdf

Film: *Light in the Darkness* http://ehl.redcross.org/curriculum/module5/C-
resources.php

Reading:
Crimes of War, pp. 159–164, 328–332, 400–401

Week 12: Responding to the Consequences of Armed Conflict (Continued)
- Overview of humanitarian organizations: Their work and guiding principles
- Ethics of humanitarian action (EHL, Module 5, 5E, pp. 52–60)
- Resource: http://ehl.redcross.org/curriculum/module5/resources/EHL-Module 5.pdf
- Research a career with a humanitarian organization. What skills are required?

Weeks 13 and 14: Career Week and Wrap-Up
Guest speakers from aid organizations and discussion of careers in humanitarian assistance
Where do we go from here? How can awareness of, and compliance with, IHL be improved?

Teaching Resources for Faculty:
- 2011 Survey on Knowledge of Americans on International Humanitarian Law: www.redcross.org/images/MEDIA_CustomProductCatalog/m12940087_Survey_on_International_Humanitarian_Law.pdf
- Legal guide for educators, glossary, books, videos, Web sites: http://ehl.red cross.org/resources/
- *International Humanitarian Law: A Universal Code* (video) www.youtube.com/user/icrcfilms#p/search/1/jwqRo4Xkix8
- *Photo Gallery:* www.ehl.icrc.org/index.php?option=com_joomgallery&Item id=544
- *Women Facing War*—series of 11 short clips: www.icrc.org/eng/resources/documents/film/f00685.htm

- *From the Field clips* – series of 8-minute films focused on what it's like for civilians living in war-affected areas: www.ehl.icrc.org/index.php?option=com_conten t&task=view&id=576&Itemid=566
- IHL Bibliography – quarterly publication on ICRC Web site that can be useful to develop and strengthen IHL knowledge as well as to provide academic institutions and research centers with relevant up-to-date information on hot issues being dealt with by academic authors. www.icrc.org/eng/resources/documents/misc/icrc-ihl-bibliography.htm
- Solis, Gary D. 2010. *The Law of Armed Conflict: International Humanitarian Law in War.* New York: Cambridge University Press.
- IHL Answers to Your Questions: www.icrc.org/eng/resources/documents/ publication/p0703.htm

13

Listening as the Foundation of Peacebuilding

Teaching Peace in the Humanities

SARAH ZALE AND JANE ROSECRANS

Listening creates a holy silence. When you listen generously to people, they can hear truth in themselves, often for the first time. —*Rachel Naomi Remen*

To create an effective curriculum that optimizes student success, a teacher must begin with a clear pedagogy. The authors of this article share a pedagogy based on empowering students to learn *how* to think rather than *what* to think. Although we teach in the humanities department at community colleges that have no peace programs in place, we consider ourselves peace and social justice teachers. We are both English teachers, and our experience spans a number of disciplines in the humanities: college composition, creative writing, literature, and religion. This report highlights the teaching of two very different humanities disciplines. Sarah Zale will focus on teaching peace and social justice in a college composition course, and Jane Rosecrans will focus on teaching peace through courses in religion.

Teaching Peace and Social Justice in College Composition: Sarah Zale

The Equity and Social Justice Program at Shoreline Community College (SCC) includes a certificate program that focuses on developing awareness about multicultural issues within the United States, including the ways that power, privilege, and institutional biases affect various racial, social, cultural, gender, sexual orientation, and disability groups. Communication strategies are taught for working through conflicts. The Equity and Social Justice Program does not have a peace studies program, although one is under development. Students in my required English composition course have been testing the foundational curriculum for this program.

While a composition class seems an unlikely venue for spearheading a peace studies program, instructors and strategic planners for the college welcome a vehicle to develop their commitment to academic internationalization and to address problems that arise from global connections. SCC's general education outcomes for global awareness reflect a sense of exigency for students to understand the consequences of "global interdependence of diverse societies . . . of events that have led to contemporary global conflict . . . and of the economic forces that have led to the interdependence of national economies and the resulting imbalance of distribution of wealth." Using a strategy that David Smith calls "the experiential approach" for creating a peace studies program, my English composition course "transcend[s] the traditional course and focus[es] on 'doing' peacebuilding, thereby providing hands-on experiences that students can apply in their lives and careers" (David Smith 2010).

Final Projects: Taking What Is Learned to the Community

At the end of the quarter, the students present what they have learned to the campus and local community in a final project presentation. All classwork is preparation for this event. Through community-building exercises, written self-reflection, dialogue, and skits, they have explored issues of power in the world and their personal lives. They have chosen an oppressed group, as defined by one of the thirty articles of the Universal Declaration of Human Rights, and compassionately listened to the story of someone from that group. In an essay, they have analyzed three specific ways of learning about their chosen oppressed group: library research, compassionate listening, and an interview with an authority. They have written a persuasive essay to document the ways, during the quarter, that they have acted as an ally for an oppressed individual—what Allan Johnson calls being "on the hook" (Johnson 2006, 123).

Setting the Foundation

During the first minutes of the first class, I stand with my students in a circle. I turn to the student on my right and clap my hands. He turns toward me and does the same. We then clap each other's hands. Next, he turns, repeating my example with the person on his right, she does the same, and so on around the circle. *What has this got to do with teaching or learning?* It's fun, they think. Other than that, they struggle to come up with an answer.

After a week or so of starting class with similar exercises, the students start to "get it": *In order for me to succeed, I have to connect in spirit and mind and action with the person next to me. For us to succeed, we must make contact and be aware of, be in tune with, one another. We are all connected.* It is a message that echoes what Martin Luther King Jr. stated in a 1963 speech at Western Michigan University: "For some strange reason, I can never be what I ought to be until you are what you ought to be. You can never be what you ought to be until I am what I ought to be. This is the interrelated structure of reality."

One student writes, "Looking back, it is easy to see why the exercises were an important part of being able to change privilege and oppression. By getting to know each other's names, personalities, and experiences, we built the necessary trust to talk about serious topics. This helped me realize that in order to fight oppression, the first step is to build relationships with the people you interact with."

Relevance to Peacebuilding

Peacebuilding must start with self-reflection on our own feelings and values, an awareness of the biases we hold, and insight into what triggers us to respond in any given way. The path to peacebuilding begins *within*. Andrew J. Bacevich says as much when he explores the reasons for U.S. involvement in wars: "The impulses that have landed us in a war of no exits and no deadlines come from within" (Bacevich 2008). He is suggesting that the United States as a whole should employ self-reflection, but the process must begin with each individual. The path to peacebuilding starts with oneself and then with one other. Then with a community. Then a country. The classroom is a place to learn how the process can work.

The theme for my English class is "Privilege, Power, Difference, and Oppression." Through community-building activities, training in compassionate listening, and theater for nonactors, we create a classroom environment in which students feel safe and at ease discussing controversial topics in an atmosphere of open academic inquiry with respect for diverse people and perspectives. We build community and trust so that everyone feels comfortable practicing solutions to difficult and potentially emotional conflicts in order to build our communication skills and understand possible alternative behaviors. The students come to understand that they are more alike than different.

Compassionate Listening: A Practice in Conflict Resolution

My connection with the Compassionate Listening Project began on a peace delegation to Israel and Palestine, where we listened to the stories on both sides of the conflict (Compassionate Listening Project 2012). As Jane Rosecrans discusses later, listening and dialogue with the other is the foundation of peacebuilding: "By knowing the other, we advance peace."

The issue whether compassionate listening has any credibility for addressing serious world conflicts imbues the class discussions throughout the quarter. It is the integration of Theatre of the Oppressed into the curriculum that changes their minds (Pedagogy and Theatre of the Oppressed 2012). Theatre of the Oppressed, a form of interactive theater that turns nonactors and audience members into actors, was created by Brazilian Augusto Boal in the mid-twentieth century and evolved from Paulo Freire's pedagogical theories of oppression (Freire 2009). Its goal is to promote social justice and critical thinking by challenging oppressive systems. Like compassionate listening, it inserts individuals into the heat of experience to discover who they are and what they think and to practice options for conflict resolution. Compassionate listening provides the tools to help students discover healing, win-win solutions to conflicts presented in Theatre of the Oppressed.

Yes! *Magazine: "Take Back Your Education"*

My students submit their essays to the Exemplary Essay Project of *Yes!* magazine for possible publication on the home page and education Web site and in the online education newsletter. The essays of four of my students have been published over the past few years. Cherese Smith's "The Racist in the Room" took first place in the fall 2011 National Student Writing Competition, college/university category and was published in February 2012 (Cherese Smith 2011).

Typically, the students write essays in response to articles in *Yes!* issue 51: *Learn as You Go: Why Life's Best Lessons Are Outside the Classroom.* Daniel Fireside's "Life's Best Lessons Are Outside the Classroom," with its introduction to Paulo Freire, and the RSA Animate "Changing EducationParadigms," by Sir Ken Robinson, get the students on their way to developing skits, photography, music, and interactive games for their final projects, where they assume the role of student educators who take their learning to their communities (Fireside 2009; Robinson 2010).

Benefits of Learning Outside the Classroom

Social activism realized as community involvement is a critical aspect of the course. The "service" of compassionate listening is a particularly personal one, more similar to David Sobel's "place-based education" than to service learning (Sobel 2005). It requires a search process as intimate as finding a friend. Most students don't know who or what they are looking for until they find it. They begin with a walk through their campus or home community to *see*, perhaps for the first time, an injustice in their surroundings. Then they find a place of their own choosing within that environment to make a healing difference. Yielding power to the students to develop their own projects is a demonstration of Paulo Freire's problem-posing education, which diverges from patterns found in a "banking model" of education (Freire 2009, 79). The problem-posing model empowers students with a sense of freedom, coupled with *responsibility* for their own learning, to think in new ways relevant to their relationships with the world. It does not assume that teachers have currency called "knowledge," which they deposit in empty accounts called "students"—a definitive characteristic of the banking model. Freire values learning as the knowledge that students gain from *conscious* and *intentional* inquiry: "[Teachers] must abandon the educational goal of deposit-making and replace it with the posing of the problems of human beings in their relations with the world" (Freire 2009, 79).

Relevance to Teaching Composition

I am often asked, "What does all this have to do with teaching composition?" I reply that language is all important in helping students figure out what they think and how to express it. The practice can be empowering and humanizing. Students learn to craft their words into writing that has the power to touch, understand, and connect with others. Writing that exhibits a strong, passionate voice, mindful of a specific audience, can change the world—a process that begins with changing the self and then the world of at least one other person. Departmentalizing the teaching of writing apart from its connection to educating a whole, humanized being is shortsighted. Sir Ken Robinson, knighted by the queen for his contributions to creativity, the arts, and education, contends that our educational system is outdated and incapable of sustaining the human capacity (at its peak around age 6) for the divergent thinking necessary to address the complex—and volatile— problems facing the modern world. Research, he suggests, indicates that "education" destroys that capacity (Robinson 2012).

I want my students to learn writing skills, but more than that, I want to help them become (1) good citizens in a diverse and complex world, who listen thoughtfully to others, ask the hard questions, and respond reasonably, fairly, and compassionately; (2) achievers who will work hard in the workplace, home, community, and greater world, and social activists who believe in their own power to make the world a better place; (3) specialists in a field of study, and generalists of a broader education so that they understand how everything is related to a bigger picture; (4) visionaries who honor the unseen—the imagination and the spiritual—and who are fanciers and creators of the arts; and (5) critical thinkers who can analyze the lessons of the past and understand the challenges of the future, who are not mere receptacles of information but who can think for themselves in new ways. I want them to be problem solvers, eager to take on the responsibility of creating a world that offers equal opportunities for a good life. My goal for education is to create citizens committed to imagining and fostering a world that continually and creatively renews itself.

In 1977, James Boggs voiced concern about issues of economy, rather than justice and human development, driving the educational system to produce *workers* and not *citizens* (Boggs 2010). The students in my English 101 class are learning the skills to help them succeed in jobs, but they are also taking important steps in becoming *citizens* who understand their responsibility for creating a just and peaceful world.

Teaching Peace through Religion: Jane Rosecrans

Though I have long been involved in teaching peace in a variety of ways, it wasn't until I began teaching courses in religion that I understood the importance of the relationship between religion and peace. Understanding the world's religions helps students better understand violence as it erupts around the world, and understand this violence in its cultural and religious contexts. According to the foundational memo of the *Journal of Religion, Conflict, and Peace,* because of the increasing mobility of economic globalization, "learning to live well with religious and other differences becomes a need for everyone, not just for the residents of a few exceptional places" (Journal of Religion, Conflict, and Peace 2010). The relationship between the understanding of world religions and the development of peace has increased the profile of world religions courses, and such courses are required by many colleges and universities. One textbook actually embeds the relationship between religious understanding and peace in its title: *Understanding World Religions: A Road Map for Justice and Peace* (Smith and Burr 2007).

Understanding the world's religions also enables students to accept members of new faith traditions as the United States continues to grow in religious diversity. As a result of increasing religious diversity, interfaith dialogue becomes integral to establishing and maintaining long-term peace. In 2007, the United States Institute of Peace published an important resource on interfaith dialogue—*Unity in Diversity: Interfaith Dialogue in the Middle East*—which focuses on the relationship between interfaith dialogue and peacebuilding in Israel, Palestine, Lebanon, Egypt, and Jordan. But interfaith dialogue need not be limited to foreign communities of faith that are enmeshed in protracted violence. Interfaith dialogue is important in establishing peaceful practices between religious communities in America as well. Diana Eck, in her groundbreaking book *A New Religious America: How a "Christian" Country Has Become the World's Most Religiously Diverse Nation,* argues for a new understanding of pluralism, one that "goes beyond mere plurality or diversity to active engagement with that plurality" (Eck 2001, 70). In this new pluralism, "spiritual dialogue" grows between members of different faiths (Eck 2001, 377). By *knowing* the "other," we advance peace.

Community colleges are especially poised to teach religion and thereby to teach peace, because we often serve as a gateway to education for many immigrants and their adult children. In addition, community colleges prepare students for a wide variety of careers in their local communities, and many of these jobs require their employees to interact with customers who are both ethnically and religiously diverse. My own college is a diverse community college with international students from over seventy countries and numerous religious traditions. My college offers numerous courses in religion, and the two courses I teach, Religions of the World and Religions in America, have become increasingly popular as more disciplines—mostly recently nursing—require them. I have taught both courses in order to increase students' understanding of religions other than their own, to increase religious tolerance and understanding, and to promote interfaith dialogue. I do this by incorporating into my courses the sixteen "habits of mind" developed by Arthur L. Costa and Bena Kallick. According to Costa and Kallick, "A 'Habit of Mind' means having a disposition toward behaving intelligently when confronted with problems. When humans experience dichotomies, are confused by dilemmas, or come face to face with uncertainties, our most effective actions require drawing forth certain patterns of intellectual behavior" (Costa and Kallick 2000).

I use these habits to help students approach religious controversies and thereby expand their religious understanding and tolerance. In doing this, I am helping students engage in peaceful practices and support the resolution of differences rather than the escalation of violence. In the fall of 2010, I used the "habits" to help students approach the controversy over the building of an Islamic center near Ground Zero in New York City. The controversy began in May of that year, and the debate over the center escalated throughout the summer and into the fall semester. The debate at that point had produced a particularly virulent response from some Americans. Critics referred to the center as a "mosque" and suggested that it would be located on the site where the World Trade Center towers once stood. Others suggested that the center was to open on September 11, 2011, the ten-year anniversary of the 9/11 attacks. Much of the controversy focused on the center's founder, Imam Feisal Rauf, who "justifyi[ed] acts of terrorism by blaming the United States for the oppression of Islamic regimes" (Factcheck.org 2010). Many of my students opposed the building of the center, citing many of the allegations described above.

I introduced them to the list of habits of mind, and we worked through them as a way to think through this religious controversy. For the purposes of this discussion, I will focus on five of the sixteen "habits of mind" as identified by Costa and Kallick (2000):

1. managing impulsivity
2. thinking and communicating with clarity and precision
3. striving for accuracy
4. thinking interdependently
5. remaining open to continuous learning

As a class, we worked through the habits of mind, and students researched specific questions once we had determined how to apply the habits to this particular problem.

Managing Impulsivity

Students confessed that Americans who get their news from ratings-obsessed cable media often draw conclusions too quickly, resulting in misunderstandings and tension that subside only after all the facts have been considered. After researching the controversy online and working through audio links of cable news coverage, the students came to see that many of the "facts" were simply made up in order to fuel the controversy. We could find no support, for example, that the center was a "command center" for "Islamic jihadists." Nor could we find any legitimate source stating that the center would open on the tenth anniversary of 9/11 or that it was a so-called victory mosque— an allegation made by some cable news stations. Students also understood that persistance was key to finally locating salient facts, which are not always obvious or easy to find.

Thinking and Communicating with Clarity and Precision

In discussing the controversy, students could see how the use of hyperbole and overstatement created problems and fanned fires. Accusing the imam of supporting sharia law, for example, or referring to the center as a "command center" tended to stir rather than calm anxiety. Many of those involved in the controversy seemed to be unaware of the language they used or simply did not care; others tended to use inflammatory language for political purposes. Through research, my students discovered that the "mosque" was actually an Islamic center that would house a mosque and that its construction was actually based on the YMCA model. They were able to reexamine the language that had produced the controversy and realized that had that language been more thoughtful and clear and less hyperbolic, much of the controversy would have been avoided.

Striving for Accuracy

This habit of mind enabled students to research the various contested facts, and they learned how to identify credible sources of information. For example, they consulted the Internet site Factcheck.org, a project of the Annenburg Public Policy Center of the University of Pennsylvania. Their most surprising discovery had to do with the imam at the center of the controversy. Feisal Rauf, they learned, was no radical jihadist but a Sufi Muslim—a member of a Muslim sect persecuted in several Muslim countries, including Pakistan, where several attacks on Sufi shrines had recently occurred (Dalrymple 2010). In fact, many of my students not only changed their opinion of Imam Rauf but came to admire him. They also understood the emotional power of falsely accusing—or labeling—a Muslim of being a "radical jihadist," especially in our post-9/11 environment.

Thinking Interdependently

This habit of mind proved to be one of the most transformative for my students. They were accustomed to responding to controversies in isolation or with people who thought as they did. Many of them recalled dinner discussions with family or casual conversations with friends in which false information was reaffirmed by those around them. Few of them had spoken to someone who thought differently, and *none* of them knew a Muslim personally. In class, however, they were forced to confront differences of opinion and to exchange information as they helped one another figure out what was true and what wasn't. It was especially helpful for my Christian, Jewish, and nonreligious students to be in class with Muslims who described their own reactions to the controversy. Not only did they understand that it is dangerous to draw conclusions in an echo chamber, but they learned to consider points of view different from their own.

Remaining Open to Continuous Learning

At the end of this exercise, my students understood that remaining open to continuous learning is important. Circumstances and perceptions change. Sometimes even facts change. It is always important to remain open to new information that changes how we view the world around us. This habits-of-mind exercise took two weeks to complete, and my students came to understand the importance of time in developing a point of view on any subject, but especially on controversial subjects such as this one. They also understood that just because they drew a particular conclusion at a particular moment in time did not mean that that conclusion must remain the last word. They now knew from experience that such conclusions would very likely continue to evolve as new information came to light.

Conclusion

Both of us have learned that teaching peace means teaching content by adopting a pedagogy that teaches peace and social justice. Sarah Zale does this by teaching Paulo Freire's problem-posing pedagogy and compassionate listening, and Jane Rosecrans does this by teaching the sixteen "habits of mind." By framing our courses in pedagogies of peace, whether we teach college composition or creative writing, literature or religion, we teach peace.

References

Bacevich, Andrew J. 2008. *The Limits of Power: The End of American Exceptionalism.* New York: Henry Holt.

Boggs, James. 2010. "Living for Change: The Next Development in Education." *Michigan Citizen,* June 12, 2010. www.boggscenter.org/fi-glb-06-12-2010_j_boggs_education.html.

Compassionate Listening Project. 2012. "The Compassionate Listening Project." www.compassionatelistening.org.

Costa, Arthur L., and Bena Kallick. 2000. "Describing 16 Habits of Mind." Institute for Habits of Mind. www.instituteforhabitsofmind.com/resources/pdf/16HOM.pdf.

Dalrymple, William. 2010. "The Muslims in the Middle." *New York Times*, Aug. 16, 2010. www.nytimes.com/2010/08/17/opinion/17dalrymple.html.

Eck, Diana. 2001. *A New Religious America: How a "Christian Country" Has Become the World's Most Diverse Nation.* New York: HarperOne.

Factcheck.org. 2010. "Questions about the 'Ground Zero Mosque.'" Annenberg Public Policy Center, Aug. 26, 2010. www.factcheck.org/2010/08/questions-about-the-ground-zero-mosque/.

Fireside, Daniel. 2009. "Life's Best Lessons Are Outside the Classroom." *Yes!* Sep. 9, 2009. www.yesmagazine.org/issues/learn-as-you-go/lifes-best-lessons-are-outside-the-classroom.

Freire, Paulo. 2009. *Pedagogy of the Oppressed.* New York: Continuum International.

Johnson, Allan G. 2006. *Privilege, Power, and Difference.* New York: McGraw-Hill.

Journal of Religion, Conflict, and Peace. 2010. "Foundational Memo." *Journal of Religion, Conflict, and Peace.* www.religionconflictpeace.org/about.

Pedagogy and Theatre of the Oppressed. 2012. "18th Annual Pedagogy and Theatre of the Oppressed Conference: *Interpreting the World, Changing the World.*" http://ptoweb.org/.

Robinson, Sir Ken. 2010. "Changing Education Paradigms." RSA Animate. www.youtube.com/watch?v=zDZFcDGpL4U&feature=player_embedded.

———. 2012. "Changing Paradigms." Royal Society for the Encouragement of Arts, Manufactures and Commerce (RSA) Edge lecture. www.thersa.org/events/vision/archive/sir-ken-robinson.

Smith, Cherese. 2011. "The Racist in the Room." *Yes!* magazine. www.yesmagazine.org/for-teachers/essay-bank/fall-2011/the-racist-in-the-room.

Smith, David. 2010. "Peace Keepers: Colleges as Teachers of Peace and Conflict Resolution." *Community College Journal* 81 (1): 44, 46.

Smith, David Whitten, and Elizabeth Geraldine Burr. 2007. *Understanding World Religions: A Road Map for Justice and Peace.* New York: Rowman and Littlefield.

Sobel, David. 2005. *Place-Based Education: Connecting Classrooms and Communities.* Great Barrington, MA: Orion Society.

Shoreline Community College

School of Humanities and Social Sciences

ENG: Analytic Writing
Course Syllabus

Instructor: Sarah Zale

5 Credits
Course Description: Critical analysis of diverse texts. Emphasis on analytic reading, writing, and discussion and on developing argumentative essays based on textual analysis, with attention to style, audience, and documentation.

Required Texts
- Pearson (Publishing) Custom Library: *Readings on Social Justice*
- Pearson MyCompLab (www.mycomplab.com)

Course Outcomes
Students who successfully complete English 101 (earning a grade of 2.0 or above) will be able to demonstrate the following competencies:
- Rhetorical Knowledge
- Critical Reading, Thinking, and Writing: Demonstrate understanding of the interaction among critical reading, critical thinking, and writing for different purposes
- Knowledge of Processes: how to generate topics, revise, proofread, self- and peer assess
- Control of Conventions: Demonstrate control of mechanics, academic conventions

Course Theme: *Social Injustice: The Problem; Compassionate Listening: A Solution*
Social injustice is present in our world. The labels "privileged" and "disadvantaged" are consistently associated with groups of a particular race, class, gender, age, religion, ability, appearance, language, or sexuality. If unearned or undeserved, the privileging and disadvantaging of any person or group becomes *unjust*.

Martin Luther King Jr. said, "*Injustice anywhere* is a threat to *justice everywhere*." If he was right, it seems that each of us stands to gain (or sustain) justice for our own lives if we struggle to (1) understand *and* (2) act against injustice.

The fact that the theme title of this class will give focus to compassionate listening and social justice raises the question "Is it possible to change the injustices of the world merely by listening to the stories of people who experience these injustices?"

In readings and discussions, we will examine the connection of social justice and compassionate listening. In attempting to better (1) understand social injustice, we will explore the issues raised in weekly readings and discussion and in three longer essays. In attempting to better (2) *act* against injustice, you will develop a service-learning final project outside the classroom.

Community Involvement Requirement: *Radical Act of Education*
Students are required to pick a topic of social injustice and become involved with an individual or group who has experienced one of the thirty injustices as defined by the Universal Declaration of Human Rights. Also, they will receive training in compassionate listening (www.compassionatelistening.org) to help them accomplish the community involvement requirement.

Outcomes for Course Focus
Beyond the basic skills listed in the course outcomes, students will
- learn the skills of free listening and compassionate listening
- take their learning outside the classroom (i.e., involve themselves in the community with their oppressed group and authorities working in the field)
- experience how learning and action, particularly issues of responsibility, may be examined in the classroom and applied in the outer world
- learn the value of the arts, historical and cross-cultural, as a tool that complements rhetorical argument
- demonstrate, through a radical act final project, that they are critical thinkers and problem solvers who are responsible, at least in part, for their own learning

Three Essays
Essay 1:
- Read John Taylor Gatto's "Take Back Your Education" (issue 51 of Yes! magazine, fall 2009): "Nobody gives you an education. If you want one, you have to take it." Design a plan for a radical act related to an oppressed group, in which you "take back your education."
- Present various forms of literacy (defined broadly to include the arts) from which you learned about your chosen oppressed group (e.g., video, photos, poetry, music).
Essay 2:
- Assess the five specific ways you learned about your chosen oppressed group: library research, compassionate listening, interviews, observation, and radical act.
Essay 3
- Respond to prompt question: What have you learned this quarter about social injustice, and how can you be part of the solution?
- Use class readings, information from essays 1 and 2, and your presentation of your radical act to the community to support your thesis.

J. Sargeant Reynolds Community College

School of Humanities and Social Sciences

REL 240: Religions in America
Course Syllabus

Instructor: Dr. Jane E. Rosecrans

Course Description: This course introduces students to the history of religion in America and to its ongoing influence in American society. We will focus on the history of Judaism, Christianity, Islam, Hinduism, Buddhism, and Taoism in America. We will also explore new religious movements and current controversies and challenges. The purpose of this course is to foster interfaith dialogue and to explore religious diversity and pluralism, the role of religion in America, and the relationship between religion and both public and foreign policy.

Required Texts:
- Lippy, Charles. *Introducing American Religion*. New York: Routledge, 2009.
- Eck, Diana. *A New Religious America: How a "Christian Country" Has Become the World's Most Diverse Nation*. New York: HarperOne, 2001.

Major Topics Covered:
- Religion among Native Americans
- Judaism in America
- Christianity in America
- African American Religion
- Understanding Islam in America
- Hinduism in America
- The Rise of Buddhism in America
- Religion and Women
- Religion and the Courts
- Religion and Public/Foreign Policy
- Religion and Culture
- Today's Challenges
- Building Bridges

Written Requirements
Students will keep a journal over the course of the semester in response to readings, audiovisual materials, and class discussions. Students should aim for two to three pages per week. Students will produce three essays of approximately five to seven pages, one focusing on religion in American history, a second focusing on new religious developments in the twentieth century, and a third on current controversies. Finally, students will produce a take-home final exam, which will ask them to reflect on what they have learned over the course of the semester.

Place-of-Worship Site Visits

Students will make a site visit to a place of worship in a religious tradition other than their own. The Ekoji Buddhist Sangha in the Fan, the Islamic Center in Bon Air, and the Hindu Center of Virginia in Glen Allen are all possibilities. Students will observe worship services and tour facilities and meet with members of the community. A separate handout with in-depth discussion of assignment requirements will be provided.

The Pluralism Project

In addition to our textbook, I will be using numerous materials produced by the Pluralism Project at Harvard University. The Pluralism Project provides a wealth of information, audiovisual materials, and links on the Web site (www.pluralism. org), and I highly recommend that students use it as a resource.

The 16 Habits of Mind

Habits of mind are dispositions that characteristically intelligent, successful people employ skillfully and mindfully when confronted with problems whose solutions are not immediately apparent. Historically, the habits of mind have been used to help students and others develop successful approaches to learning. I will use these characteristics in a different way, because I believe they also embody an approach to learning about other people, other cultures, and other religions that results in a more civil, thoughtful, and peaceful discussion of how religion affects American society and its place in the world. We will discuss these habits at length in class and use them as a way of developing community and as a lens through which we encounter others, especially those different from ourselves. These are the habits of mind as identified by Costa and Kallick:

1. Persisting
2. Thinking and Communicating with Clarity and Precision
3. Managing Impulsivity
4. Gathering Data through All Senses
5. Listening with Understanding and Empathy
6. Creating, Imagining, and Innovating
7. Thinking Flexibly
8. Responding with Wonderment and Awe
9. Thinking about Thinking (Metacognition)
10. Taking Responsible Risks
11. Striving for Accuracy
12. Finding Humor
13. Questioning and Posing Problems
14. Thinking Interdependently
15. Applying Past Knowledge to New Situations
16. Remaining Open to Continuous Learning

14

Field Training for
Humanitarians and Peacebuilders

PAUL C. FORAGE

Humanitarian action, far from being solely a question of international security,
can support peace and reconciliation.   —Sadako Ogata

atural disasters, technological catastrophes, and armed conflicts remain an unfortunate reality of our modern world, and aid agencies
and disaster relief organizations have long recognized the need for
training skilled humanitarian practitioners. Every generation calls for organizing better and more comprehensive training in the humanitarian sector—training that not only analyzes humanitarian operations but also advo-
cates "getting it right" in the field by teaching, studying, and promoting best
practices. A British survey of humanitarian community training needs noted
that humanitarian non-governmental organizations (NGOs) are often envi-
ous of the elaborate training structures that military and other governmental
organizations have to promote the best tactics, techniques, and procedures
among military field operators. So far, the United States has no parallel educational structure for humanitarians that combines rigorous field training
with solid academics, although many humanitarian organizations, colleges,
and universities are realizing the need for better training and field expertise
(ALNAP 2002, 45).

An ideal educational capability combines conflict analysis with a progressive program of training events and field exercises in partnership with the organizations and agencies likely to be found in the real world of humanitarian
work and disaster relief. These include humanitarian NGOs, international
organizations such as the Red Cross and the United Nations, and national
agencies such as the U.S. Agency for International Development and the
armed services. Some schools and organizations hold tabletop simulations
of the strategic and operational levels of humanitarian operations, and a few
even go outdoors, but little training is done at the practical level for the
field operator, and very few training exercises are geared to preparing aid
workers and peacebuilders and their military counterparts—the very people

Box 14.1: Peace and Stability Operations

Peace operations is a newly emerging field. The most well-known program is the master's program at George Mason University. A peace operations curriculum trains students to work in global environments emerging from violence. But coursework in the field need not be limited to graduate programs. Northern Virginia Community College (NVCC) offers Introduction to Peace and Stability Operations. The course, regularly taught at two of NVCC's campuses, introduces the concept of co-ordinated public, private, international, and nonprofit sector responses to conflict, post-conflict, and natural disaster international humanitarian emergencies with the objective of returning states and regions to peace and stability.

entrusted to "get it right" and build peace from the ground up when sent overseas.

Community colleges in the United States are especially well positioned to provide this combination of academics and practical training. Many have unique resources and capabilities that can be harnessed to develop peace-building and humanitarian education for real-world practitioners (see box 14.1). Unlike universities, which lean toward the study of policy and the intricacies of administering and managing emergency services, community colleges place the practitioner first. They already train more than 80 percent of America's first responder community, including law enforcement, fire service, emergency management, nursing, and medical services personnel. Also, many community colleges across the United States have state-of-the-art facilities for training first responders. These facilities include emergency operations centers; mock police stations, courtrooms, and fire stations; burn buildings; collapse structure simulators; motor vehicle ranges; firing ranges; and tactical villages.

The Challenge for Educators

The challenge for community college educators and administrators is to imagine how their existing resources can be engaged to provide the training needed for new generations of humanitarian aid workers operating in future disasters and international crises. Table 14.1 reveals that many of the skills required of humanitarian practitioners can easily be matched up with faculty interests and competencies at a community college. For example, many law enforcement educators understand security training needs, especially in areas such as community policing, situational awareness, information gathering, and threat analysis. And they often have the technical expertise to teach subjects such as hostage survival, explosive-device awareness, incident management, and radiotelephone procedure.

Table 14.1: Comparison of Core Competencies

Comparison of Eight Civilian Peace Operations Training Courses

	Competency	PPC	SAIT	SSAFE	eCentre	ZIF	OSCE	IPT	Svetlina
1	Incident Command	–	–	–	–	–	–	–	X
2	Project Management	X	–	–	–	–	–	X	–
3	Conflict Analysis	X	X	–	–	X	X	X	X
4	Humanitarian Negotiation	X	–	X	–	X	X	–	X
5	Human Rights	X	–	–	–	X	–	X	X
6	Cross-Cultural Awareness	–	X	X	–	X	–	X	X
7	Case Studies	X	–	–	–	–	–	X	–
8	Checkpoint Procedures	–	–	–	X	X	–	–	X
9	Land Navigation	X	X	–	X	X	X	–	X
10	First Aid	X	–	–	X	X	X	–	X
11	Mass Casualty Response	–	–	X	–	–	–	–	–
12	Landmine/UXO Awareness	X	X	X	X	X	X	X	X
13	Hijacking/Hostage Survival	X	–	–	X	X	X	–	X
14	IED/Ambush Survival	–	X	X	X	X	–	–	X
15	Emergency Evacuation	X	X	X	–	–	–	–	X
16	Convoy Operations	–	X	X	–	–	–	–	X
17	Radio and Voice Procedure	X	X	X	X	X	X	X	X
18	Safety and Security	X	X	X	X	X	X	X	X
19	Security Risk Management	X	–	X	X	X	X	X	X
20	Critical Incident Management	–	X	X	X	–	–	–	–
21	Off-road Driving	X	–	–	–	X	X	X	–
22	Camp Management	–	–	–	–	–	–	–	–
23	Mass Care	–	–	–	X	–	–	–	–
24	Media/Public Relations	X	–	–	X	–	–	–	X
	Course Length (in days)	14	4	2	12	12	5	14	14

Abbreviations

PPC	Canada—Pearson Peacekeeping Centre—Civilian Core Competencies in Peace Operations
SAIT	International Organization for Migration—Security Awareness Induction Training (Iraq)
SSAFE	United Nations—Secure and Safe Approaches to Field Environments (Afghanistan)
eCentre	United Nations eCentre (Asia-Pacific)
ZIF	Germany—Center for International Peace Operations
OSCE	United Kingdom—Pre-Deployment and Assessment Training Course
IPT	Austria—International Civilian Peacekeeping and Peacebuilding Training Program
Svetlina	US/Macedonia—Summer Institute on International Disaster Relief and Humanitarian Assistance

Note: An "X" indicates inclusion of a competency or skill taught in the training program.

Our approach was to present the practical subject matter of our program to as wide a faculty audience as possible and bring together the different campus constituencies—in health sciences, social sciences, law enforcement, and fire science—to address the multidisciplinary and cross-professional challenges posed by complex emergency and large-scale humanitarian disasters. We found that one clear advantage of focusing on field training for humanitarian operators is that this made it easier for faculty to imagine the practical application of the subject matter. At the same time, given the multidisciplinary nature of humanitarian response, we also realized that it is important that all faculty, regardless of their subject expertise, share a common understanding of basic humanitarian principles and activities. To facilitate this, we put in place a certification protocol that includes a short list of key reference materials and a shared humanitarian field operations pocket guide for study, and a short but comprehensive written test that all instructors must take before participating. We also encourage new faculty members to participate in the exercise planning process and observe experienced instructors in the field.

Building a Humanitarian Field Training Curriculum

At Indian River State College (IRSC), members of our planning team developed a sequence of courses that lead up to an annual capstone field-training exercise, which merges ongoing classroom work with field experience by simulating a complex humanitarian crisis. In 2005, we designed a four-day mock deployment to a fictional country, dubbed "Atlantica," that had suffered a large-scale natural disaster such as a hurricane or an earthquake, in additional to ongoing intercommunal strife. Our concept was to turn about fifty acres of our public safety campus in Florida into a large-scale simulation of a complex emergency that requires students to spend much of their time understanding the situation—conflict analysis—and conducting negotiations with a variety of stakeholders before they can even begin the actual disaster relief work. Little of the real work is classroom based—everything is conducted in the field for four days straight. The exercise was called ATLANTIC HOPE (see box 14.2).

Similarly to many Model UN simulations, we designed a detailed political, social, economic, and geographic guide to Atlantica for our student humanitarians and peacebuilders. The guide provides reference information for students and faculty on the positions of several different Atlantican factions, U.S. government agencies present in Atlantica, international organizations, local intermediaries, and other fictional NGOs and includes abbreviated how-to instructions and checklists to remind students of key concepts and essential skills in disaster relief and humanitarian operations.

Early on, we decided to concentrate on both peacebuilding and practical humanitarian work, based on our belief that in the process of stabilizing a crisis, the two cannot be separated. (Arguably, aid work focuses more on immediate humanitarian needs while peacebuilding addresses long-term underlying issues.) We also faced practical time constraints. There is simply not enough time to train students from the ground up to be expert techni-

Box 14.2: Lexi Almy: Peacebuilding in Africa

Lexi Almy is a testament to the powerful impact that community colleges can have in laying a peacebuilding career path. Lexi participated in the ATLANTIC HOPE simulation at Indian River State College while a student at Northern Oklahoma College (NOC). As a result of her experience and the inspiration of faculty at NOC, she went on to Oklahoma State University, where she is studying subjects that will prepare her to work in the humanitarian field. She spent the summer of 2011 in Sierra Leone conducting field research in community and sustainable development for Njala University, and in the fall she interned for the UN High Commissioner for Refugees, working in displacement camps in Kenya. She comments: "The professors I encountered at Northern Oklahoma College are the ones to thank for enabling my studying and working internationally. They didn't just teach me the necessary curriculum; more importantly, they taught me how to live."

cal responders, such as technician-level qualified urban search-and-rescue or water/sanitation experts, even though we run the exercise around the clock. We decided to provide a training environment unlike any other in the United States: one that concentrates on the political complexities of complex humanitarian crises. This choice has the advantage of including more campus constituencies than would a simple technical exercise focused on a narrow range of skills. Students must think about the *reasons* for acting and not just *what to do*.

International Experience

Realizing the physical and cultural limitations of training in the United States, we also decided to build on our experience and work with government agencies and academic institutions in the Balkans. We did this for several reasons. We had developed a relationship with the Macedonian government as a result of a peace studies conference in 2001, and the Macedonian Ministry of Defense offered the use of its training facilities, personnel, and equipment. And the peace agreement achieved between the two major ethnic communities in Macednia following the crisis in 2001 gives our students an excellent opportrnity to examine firsthand how peace building works in the real world. Despite the expenses of international travel, we felt that the advantage of working with our colleagues in Macedonia outweighed any disadvantages: rather than having Americans on an American campus pretend they are foreigners, we could fly overseas and work alongside Macedonian students and faculty in a truly cross-cultural context.

In May 2007, we conducted the first Summer Institute on International Disaster Relief and Humanitarian Assistance in Macedonia with students and staff from IRSC and Northwest Missouri State University, together with the Institute for Defense and Peace Studies at the University of St. Cyril and Methodius in Skopje and the Macedonian Ministry of Defense. IRSC worked with the Ministry of Defense to identify and secure the needed physical assets and facilities at the ministry's Krivolak Training Center in central Macedonia. We also established an annual planning conference between all the academic participants and an advisory board of seasoned humanitarian practitioners to examine our exercise evaluations, review plans for the scenarios in Florida and Macedonia, and suggest additional content.

Five years later, the Summer Institute and its field training exercise, called SVETLINA (or Light), has evolved into a highly textured simulation of a complex emergency. The Institute begins with American students from across the United States flying to Fort Pierce, Florida, for two days of pre-deployment training as members of a fictional humanitarian organization called International Humanitarian Action, or IHA. This prep work includes completion of all paperwork, communication of all exercise guidelines, and a series of team-building and practical training drills conducted at the IRSC public safety training facilities. The U.S. students and faculty then depart for Macedonia as a team. As soon as they clear Border Control in Skopje, Macedonia, the exercise begins. At the airport, they are paired up with Macedonian students, and together the integrated team departs for the mock disaster area in "Atlantica." Along the way, they are escorted by the Atlantican Army—simulated by a platoon of heavily armed Macedonian military police—as they proceed through a series of checkpoints to their austere temporary accommodations in military barracks. Once they arrive they get a series of briefings from local IHA representatives on the current situation in Atlantica, including a disaster status update, safety briefings, and meetings with mock relief agencies and U.S. embassy officials.

Over the next five days, the team is trained or refreshed on a number of critical skills on which they will be evaluated over the next two weeks. These include not only operational security, first aid, and specific disaster response skills but also peacebuilding skills including conflict analysis and negotiation. The U.S. and Macedonian student participants are expected to begin building or expanding their "humanitarian space," or operating environment, for themselves as soon as they arrive. The government of Atlantica will attempt to divert their aid to communities of its choice, and the armed opposition will attempt to co-opt the humanitarians to promote its political agenda. Student IHA teams could be harassed or threatened. They will also need to sort through the intricacies of the U.S. and international interagency process as they encounter a variety of different agency representatives and conflicting advice and information, often role-played by senior instructors. Meetings and negotiations with all these parties are held throughout the day and late at night. While much of this could be simulated in a comfortable classroom in the United States, putting together all the pieces necessary for success, in as authentic an operating environment as possible, with all the attendant personalities, challenges, and frictions, is the real advantage of this training.

Service Learning

As the IHA teams work throughout the first week to expand their operating environment, improve their relationship with all Atlantican stakeholders, and gain access to an earthquake-stricken village, they are also given time to conduct a humanitarian needs assessment of three real agricultural villages near the Krivolak Training Center—an area notionally controlled by the Atlantican government. The students are divided into three IHA teams and are asked to develop a detailed profile of each community and identify its needs. The fictional IHA headquarters in New York then issues a request for proposals for a microscale community development project suited to the village, as well as an assessment of the mission's time and budget constraints. Each student team then prepares a grant proposal, which it forwards to "New York" for approval.

While the IHA teams wait to see which project will be approved they prepare to respond to disaster at the earthquake village—in reality, the stone ruins of a Turkish village near Krivolak. The process is complicated and delayed because the teams must first secure approval from the Atlantican civilian authorities and the Atlantican army as well as the armed opposition—who, in this case, control the village and its surrounding territory. Eventually, all parties agree, and IHA is given conditional humanitarian access to the village. Once the student IHA teams rescue or recover the victims of the disaster—role-played by local villagers—they must then care for the injured in an adjacent internally displaced persons, or IDP, camp, which includes basic medical facilities and which they must set up and operate according to international standards. The role-playing villagers are coached and supervised by on-site observer-controllers to present the students with a variety of personal, political, legal, and medical problems to solve while they reside in the camp. Security problems are also simulated as combatants infiltrate the camp at various times. All these issues are construed to provide learning opportunities for the participants to think about longer-term relationship building and not just quick-fix tactical solutions.

International Humanitarian Law

An additional layer of complexity introduced into the exercise during the second week is the practical application of international humanitarian law. As the student IHA teams interact with the stakeholders in the course of their negotiations the armed factions reveal that some of their soldiers are being held captive by the opposing side. They ask if IHA can look into the prisoners' condition and help secure their safe return. This initiates a series of discussions among the students on how to go about this and whether they even should. This dimension of their mission is important for the students, because it changes their relationship with the Atlantican armed factions and offers them an additional way to bring together the interests of the negotiating parties. The students quickly learn during their first week on the ground that the desperate plight of the earthquake-stricken villagers may not be enough to override the stakeholders' political concerns. But once they reach an agreement with both factions the IHA teams then conduct a series of visits to the prisoners held by each side and report on their conditions as they try to apply International Red Cross guidelines. Because the armed opposition in Atlantica has no fixed facilities, these visits are often conducted under difficult conditions late at night. The IHA students begin to realize that a prisoner exchange might be a way for them to increase their humanitarian space and might enable a confidence-building measure that could initiate peace talks between the armed factions.

As the SVETLINA exercise nears its conclusion the students, having rescued the survivors of the earthquake village and successfully operated an IDP camp, set about their last two tasks: an IHA-approved reconstruction project for one of the three real villages, and an exchange of prisoners between the Atlantican army and the armed opposition. If the students have done well, they may even get the belligerents to agree to a cease-fire. If not, the prisoner exchange may still be possible. The prisoner exchange and small-scale reconstruction project allow the exercise to end on a positive but realistic note—there is no expectation that a mere two weeks in Atlantica can bring about lasting peace between the combatants. But the process does provide a hands-on illustration of how peacebuilding works step-by-step, bringing together interests, encouraging a positive peace, and transforming conflict.

Lessons Learned

The past five years of humanitarian training exercises have taught us several important lessons. First, our students come from all age groups and academic backgrounds in emergency services, social sciences, and humanities but share a common interest in humanitarian service. Their ages have ranged from eighteen to fifty-four, with many in their early twenties and female. The austere conditions living in tents in Krivolak, the sleep deprivation, and the simulated violence and hostility have not discouraged them. Not only are they highly adaptive, most want to experience the exercise again. Repeating students do pose a dilemma for the instructors, since these students are more familiar than newcomers with the events we stage for them, but by changing the major scenario events and adding more complexity every year, it is relatively easy to accommodate them. We have also discovered that the best students can later serve as assistant observer-controllers to the faculty. To facilitate this, with the United States Institute of Peace's support, we are developing a train-the-trainer program to recruit and train the best of these returning students.

The recruitment of supervising faculty, however, is a more difficult problem. With the growing interest in humanitarian studies, many academics are studying and researching different aspects of this emerging field. At the same time, as noted earlier, humanitarian agencies demand recruits with practical field experience as well as academic qualifications. But it is difficult to find humanitarian academics willing to endure the austerity of Krivolak. Those most willing tend to have extensive field experience of their own, either in humanitarian service or in military operations. A few days on a farm somewhere in the United States is nowhere near an adequate test of either student competency or faculty capabilities—despite its rigors, everyone knows that a brief U.S.-based event will be over soon no matter what happens. As a result, we position our Florida exercise as preparation for participants to the SVETLINA weeks in Macedonia—the ultimate crucible, short of a real deployment, of their capacity to handle humanitarian field operations.

Two weeks is not enough time to produce trained specialists. Still, the Summer Institute, structured as a capstone event, can serve those who have already obtained expert training elsewhere. For example, practicing doctors and nurses interested in international humanitarian service have joined our training exercises. Moreover, a recent report by Peter Walker of the Feinstein International Center at Tufts University and Catherine Russ of RedR UK polled more than 1,500 practitioners around the world to explore the possibility of creating a humanitarian profession, and the role that higher education might play (Walker and Russ 2010). The top four knowledge categories identified by these practitioners were needs assessment, safety and security, international humanitarian law, and program monitoring and evaluation. These four categories ranked two to three times higher in importance than specific technical knowledge areas such as public health, water/sanitation, logistics, and food/nutrition. The top three humanitarian skills this group identified were the ability to multitask, team building, and negotiation and mediation.

Because of the Summer Institute's professional validity, its graduates report that their experience has benefited them in the field and in their careers. Several have graduated and joined state or municipal emergency management agencies, and others have gone on to serve in humanitarian agencies overseas. Some report relying on the safety-and-security training to get them through difficult circumstances overseas. Three Summer Institute graduates from IRSC accompanied an aid organization to Haiti immediately after the tragic earthquake of January 2010. There they worked with Jordanian and Brazilian peacekeepers and U.S. troops to organize food convoys and points of distribution in Port-au-Prince, using their practical training in mission planning, civilian-military relations, safety and security, and negotiation.

The Summer Institute on International Disaster Relief and Humanitarian Assistance, with its training exercises in Florida and Macedonia, is one way educators can meet the challenge of using existing resources in new and innovative ways to promote active learning in humanitarian operations and peacebuilding. Key to its success was finding common interests between faculty members on campus who typically might not otherwise interact. With a little imagination, finding these common interests opens up new opportunities for collaboration. Based on the positive response of their students to these capstone training experiences, our colleagues at other colleges have felt encouraged to develop or add to their programs in emergency management. It is a field that embraces all aspects of the public safety and public service professions and also has much in common with the humanitarian and peace communities, including the value it places on training exercises. Humanitarian aid response, peacebuilding, and long-term development are mirrored in the domestic sphere by emergency management's emphasis on mitigation, preparation, response, and recovery. We look forward to finding new ways to bring these communities together using the unique resources offered by democracy's colleges.

References

Active Learning Network for Accountability and Performance in Humanitarian Action (ALNAP). 2002. *Humanitarian Action: Improving Performance through Improved Learning.* London: Overseas Development Institute.

Walker, Peter, and Catherine Russ. 2010. *Professionalizing the Humanitarian Sector: A Scoping Study.* London: Enhancing Learning and Research for Humanitarian Assistance.

15

International Negotiations Modules Project

GREGORY P. RABB AND JOYCE KAUFMAN

When you negotiate an agreement, you must remember that
you are also negotiating a relationship. —Harold Nicolson

Faculty members, especially in the community colleges, often face the challenge of teaching their materials to nontraditional and diverse groups of learners, who want to apply the information from their classes to further their education and careers. For the faculty member, this also often means finding ways to engage students that not only challenges and excites them but also makes them active participants in their own learning. Simulation is one technique that has been employed successfully to meet these challenges (for another resource, see box 15.1).

This chapter presents a case study of the International Negotiations Modules Project (INMP), a computer-assisted simulation of international negotiation developed specifically for community colleges.[1] When it was created in 1996, the program had the following stated educational goals:

- to use Internet technology as a tool for teaching
- to use the simulation to internationalize across the curriculum
- to help improve students' reading, writing, and critical thinking skills through an emphasis on written communication
- to encourage students to work in teams and learn from one another
- to help students understand complex international issues
- to enable students to better understand different countries and cultures

Although it was not stated at the time, the application of the simulation also changed the pedagogy, not only of the classes where it was introduced but of

---

1. The INMP was created and piloted from 1996 through 1998 with funding provided by a grant from the U.S. Department of Education Fund for the Improvement of Postsecondary Education (FIPSE), grant award P116B50043. It grew from a collaboration of a number of institutions, including the University Maryland ICONS Project and California Colleges for International Education.

Box 15.1: A Virtual Consortium for Peace

The Global Consortium for Sustainable Peace (GC) (http://theglobalconsortium-forsustainablepeace.org) established by John Haas at Cerritos College in 2001, works to bridge cultural and political divides by raising college students' aware-ness of global issues. GC is currently linked to 112 community colleges in Cali-fornia and has collaborated with institutions in 12 countries around the world to produce programs on the Arab Spring, the Holocaust, civil war in Zimbabwe, and Burmese political prisoners, among others. GC has worked with USIP, the Carnegie Endowment for International Peace, the United Nations, the U.S. De-partment of State, Al-Quds University in Jerusalem, and the Simon Wiesenthal Center. Using Webcasting and local cable, GC programs can be broadcast to 2.5 million students in California and around the world.

other classes as well, as faculty became more comfortable with this nontradi-tional and student-centered approach to learning.

The INMP has been running simulations every year since its creation and has spawned a number of other adaptions of the program. This chapter explores the INMP as one approach to teaching about current international issues and shows how it has been applied successfully at Jamestown Com-munity College (JCC) in rural upstate New York.

Background of the INMP

The INMP was an adaptation of the International Negotiations Project (INP), a variant of the University of Maryland's International Communi-cation and Negotiation Simulations (ICONS) Project, which was created in the late 1970s to adapt the new Internet technology for political science classes at the postsecondary level. At that time, the ICONS project was one of the first to use Internet technology as a tool to enhance the teaching of political science (Wilkenfeld and Kaufman 1993; Kaufman 1998). To quote the ICONS Web site, "The ICONS project ... is an experiential learning program that uses customized WEB based learning tools to support edu-cational simulations and simulation-based training. Our ... programs cast students in the role of decision makers tasked with trying to resolve conten-tious political issues of the day. The ICONS project also uses its simulations to support training programs related to conflict resolution, decision making, cross-cultural communication, and crisis management."

More importantly, its development was able to build on the increased recognition, within the field of education, that students learn best when they can construct their own knowledge. As Judith Torney-Purta, one of the earliest evaluators of the ICONS project, notes, it is through active processing of a student's cognitive structures that knowledge takes on new meaning and becomes ingrained as part of the student's consciousness (Torney-Purta 1996). The program was evaluated heavily to ensure that real learning was taking place, which the assessment process confirmed. Not only did students' cognitive skills improve, but students exhibited a more complete understanding of complex issues and their interconnectedness, as well as improved communication skills. In effect, not only did they learn more about the world around them, but they were better able to articulate an understanding of that world.

From that beginning point, ICONS spawned a number of other programs. The INP, based at Whittier College, was created specifically to adapt ICONS for high school students on the West Coast. Created in 1989 with the support of a grant from the United States Institute of Peace (USIP), INP has celebrated twenty years of simulations that reached thousands of high school students. Because this, too, was a grant-funded program, it was evaluated at various points. These evaluations confirmed the results of the earlier assessments of the ICONS program regarding student learning, but they also found another effect that had not been anticipated: faculty members who taught using the simulation noted that the experience altered their approach to teaching other classes as well. No longer reliant on the "sage on the stage" pedagogical approach, the faculty became more comfortable shifting the burden of responsibility onto the students, who became actively engaged with their own instruction.

The ICONS/INP model was further adapted for community colleges to meet the needs of that educational group. With a growing emphasis on internationalization of the curriculum, one of the innovations of the community college model was the simulation's application in various disciplines, including anthropology, economics, English, French, geography, and political science, among others. The underlying theoretical idea was that by participating in the simulation, students in any discipline would start to get a grounding in current international issues while simultaneously using Internet technology as a tool for research and writing as well as for communication. This meant that the issues chosen as the main topics of negotiation in the simulation had to be selected carefully to meet the needs of a range of disciplines—a task that was part of a regular workshop with the participating faculty members.

With funding from FIPSE, the INMP was created and piloted in 1996 for community colleges in California. California was selected because of the community colleges' significant role in that state's higher education structure and because of the active support by California Colleges for International Education, an organization of more than eighty community colleges with a specifically international focus. Thirty interested faculty members applied to participate, and nine were ultimately chosen to become part of the pilot year. Over the next two years of the grant, community colleges from across the United States were invited to participate. One of those was JCC. The experiences of that college follow and represent a case study of the ways that one community college in a rural area was able to take advantage of all that the simulation offered.

Disciplines represented during the fifteen years since the INMP's creation include political science, history, and economics, which are an easy fit for this type of program. However, faculty in "nontraditional" disciplines, including mathematics, French, English composition, anthropology, and sciences such as geology also found the approach effective. One of the things that make the INMP especially impressive is the range of disciplines into which the simulation has been integrated effectively (Raby and Kaufman 2000a, 2000b).

Since INMP's creation, a core group of some eight to ten colleges continues to participate annually (the simulation usually runs in the spring), with additional colleges joining as they hear about the program and it suits their curricular needs. Over the years, the advisers have found that an ideal simulation has anywhere from ten to fifteen participating schools. New schools are always welcome and, indeed, encouraged to participate. Unfortunately, over time, we have also lost some colleges due to faculty retirements and the inability to find other faculty members interested in participating, the costs involved at a time of economic cutbacks, and changes in administrators. Nonetheless, the program continues with a committed group of faculty at its core. Because real costs are involved, community colleges pay a fee to participate. This covers participation in a faculty development workshop, technology and support, and ongoing monitoring of, and feedback on, students' performance.

The INMP has also given birth to other models for the community college. In one case, a Chicago-area group of community colleges, based at the College of DuPage, have their own regional version of the program. The colleges' proximity, as opposed to their coming from all over the United States, makes it possible to end each simulation by bringing all the students together for a final meeting and banquet, during which each team gives a presentation about the country it represented and what it accomplished and learned. This also offers the faculty members another opportunity to meet and to share their own experiences.

In another exciting variant of the INMP, Joliet Junior College, also outside Chicago, used the simulation as part of a Department of Education Title VI grant on international studies and foreign language to create an intramural learning community of faculty and students, with the simulation as the common element. The focus was again interdisciplinary, and classes as varied as veterinary science, physics, and horticulture were participants. The challenge here was to have the faculty agree on a range of issues for negotiation that would be appropriate for all the participating classes. But by identifying elements that all had in common, such as the importance of understanding environmental issues (which could be done from the perspective of many disciplines), it was possible to arrive at three viable issues for discussion for each simulation, at least one of which was relevant for all classes.

Implementing the INMP

The simulation process is parallel to the one developed by ICONS, though adapted for the particular needs of the INMP. Thus, the first step is a meeting of the faculty members involved, which usually takes place in the fall. This workshop is a combination of faculty development, where guest speakers are invited to talk about current issues that have been or could be included in the simulation and planning for the simulation that will take place in the spring.[2] With the wide range of disciplines and classes participating in the simulation, choosing the issues for negotiation becomes especially important, since they must be applicable to a range of curricular areas. Generally, four issues are selected, although not all classes participate in all four issues. Because of the importance of economics in a globalized world, one issue usually pertains to some aspect of economics. But everything is up for discussion, and by the end of the workshop, the faculty members will have agreed on the issues to be the focus for the next simulation, and the country or nonstate actor that their class will represent.

Over the years, we have approached issues in a range of ways. For example, one year the focus of the simulation was the UN Millennium

---

2. Speakers have been invited to talk about a range of issues, including water scarcity and the environment, women and Islam, and globalization and trade. In September 2009, the workshop was held at Whittier College, with participation by USIP. The discussions focused on issues such as using negotiation to resolve conflict and how to prepare for peace. Thanks to David Smith at USIP, a Sudanese former child soldier, George Latio, was also invited to speak about his experiences.

Development Goals, with four goals identified as being especially relevant. Other times, the faculty identified issues that were timely and important, such as global warming or human rights abuses. It is then the responsibility of the simulation director (Joyce Kaufman) to narrow and frame the issues so that students have a focal point for their research and the negotiations that will follow. The director does this in a simulation scenario that includes (a) some background about the negotiation process and how countries use it to further their own policy goals; (b) a general statement about international conditions, with a focus on the various countries/actors in the simulation; and (c) a section that is case-specific on each of the issues to be addressed in the simulation, ending with "questions for consideration" that can help guide the students' research.

During the workshop, the faculty members also identify the countries or nonstate actors that they want their students to represent. By the end of the workshop, the participating faculty members know the issues that will be addressed and all the actors their students will be interacting with during the simulation. This allows them time to prepare their classes so that they are ready for the spring semester.

The introduction of non-governmental organizations or international organizations such as the World Health Organization (WHO) is a significant move away from including only nations as the primary actors and is one of the unique features of this simulation program. This approach seemed to suit the community college faculty quite well. For example, a sociology class that focuses on global health issues could easily represent the WHO, giving the students the opportunity to look at health issues and policy questions from a macrolevel that transcends any state. In one simulation, a journalism class played the role of "press." They issued press releases and interviewed the student policymakers from different countries included in the simulation, printing news articles on the simulation community. This was an excellent experience for them, as well as an exercise in critical reading skills for the other students. And all this could easily be done online, encouraging the student participants to stay in role.

The simulation takes place in roughly three phases, although in reality, one phase merges, to a degree, with the next. The challenge for the faculty member always is how to allocate time to teach the critical materials of the class while still allotting sufficient time for the simulation. This challenge is common to any academic level, whether high school, community college, or university.

Students begin preparing for their participation in the simulation by researching their country/actor and arriving at positions for each of the issue areas *from the perspective of the actor they represent.* This is one of the earliest lessons that the students learn: specifically, that not all countries and actors see the world in the same way. It is in this stage that faculty members determine how to integrate the simulation into the subject of the class. For example, a French-language faculty member had her students represent France and do some of their research using French-language sources. They also had to write parts of their position/policy paper in French. Before the start of the simulation, each group is expected to produce a position paper outlining the team's positions and negotiation strategies. This is often a critical aspect of the student's grade for the class.

After the research period, the actual negotiations begin as students engage in online discussions on the issues under consideration. Negotiations take place in a closed community on a server hosted by the University of Maryland. When the simulation first started, this was a new way of communicating; now, with students accustomed to e-mail, instant messaging, and social networking sites, this community can seem a bit archaic. However, from a pedagogical perspective, it is important because it allows for monitoring of the students' messages and provides an ongoing archived record of their work online. Students communicate only country-to-country (or actor-to-actor), and no personal information is shared. They do not know what colleges are participating. The focus is on the negotiation and on development of positions. We describe this as similar to what takes place before a summit meeting attended by a head of state. Before that meeting, especially if an agreement is going to be signed, there is a lot of behind-the-scenes discussion and hammering-out of positions. That is what this early stage of the negotiations should be about.

The simulation community also has a proposal center, where students can post proposals about each of the issues and then negotiate on the specific proposals on the table. In some simulations, a proposal requires two cosponsors before it can be opened up for general discussion and negotiation. This further requires students to work together and build support for their proposal so that by the time it is posted, at least two actors have a vested interest in seeing it pass. That option is agreed by the faculty.

Toward the end of the period allotted for the simulation (usually about four weeks), the students engage in ninety-minute online real-time summits. One issue is the focus of each summit, which is generally built around a specific proposal. The simulation director, who monitors all messaging and gives the teams feedback, generally designates a team to chair the summit. The chair is usually the team that has put forward the proposal to be discussed. At the conclusion of all the summits, the proposal center is opened so teams can vote on the proposal. Thus, the teams have the opportunity to see whether they were successful in garnering support for passage of their proposal.

For some simulations, such as the ones based at College of DuPage and Joliet Junior College, where the participating teams are in proximity to one another, a banquet and discussion conclude the simulation. For those colleges in the national INMP, the voting that concludes the simulation becomes a way to assess what they accomplished.

The final phase of the simulation is the debriefing, when teams return to their original position papers to determine what was or was not accomplished and why. In many ways, this is the most important aspect of the simulation because it enables students and faculty to reflect on the simulation experience and tie the lessons learned to the subject of their class.

Application of the INMP: Jamestown Community College as a Case Study

In the late 1980s, long before such terms as "active learning" and "student-centered learning" became ubiquitous, JCC became concerned that its students taking courses in world politics for political science credit were too passive and not actively engaged in their learning. JCC was also concerned that many of the more traditional assignments, such as multiple-choice tests and even essay or short-answer tests, were not helping students develop essential writing and critical-thinking skills. Also, many of the students were very similar to each other, coming from a predominantly white, rural county in southwestern New York State, and the college was concerned that they were not being adequately prepared to live and work in an increasingly diverse world. For these and many other reasons, the political science department decided to experiment with simulation-based learning involving external partnerships with other colleges.

External partnerships were the only way to develop complex simulation-based learning opportunities for students. Although such partnerships can be difficult to manage and very time intensive, the benefits to students are worth the effort. Such partnerships also allow small departments (in the case of JCC, one person) to develop collaborations with other colleagues, including professional development opportunities through the United States Institute of Peace, the Fulbright programs, and the National Endowment for the Humanities. Although the primary benefit is for students, there is an important secondary benefit for faculty as well. Simulation-based learning requires a faculty member or members to be willing to take risks and put in the extra time dealing with a great deal of uncertainty in the classroom, since simulations, once they begin, go in many unanticipated directions, requiring both students and teachers to develop a capacity for dealing with ambiguity. During the simulation, the teacher often says, "I don't know" to the students. Many teachers/professors are uncomfortable saying this, and even more students are uncomfortable hearing it.

An important warning is needed at this point: the instructor has to change his/her teaching style to partake in simulation-based learning. But both experience and evaluation have shown that the faculty members (and all their classes) will change in ways never anticipated but all for the good, resulting in better teaching and greater learning, with a more engaged, excited student body.

While adventurous students and risk-taking faculty are essential, a supportive administration is also required. Simulation-based learning is probably not suited to every student, but all students should certainly be encouraged to try. JCC's success in simulation-based learning owes much to the support by the late academic affairs dean, R. Theodore "Ted" Smith, who supported a nontenured faculty member's interest in experimenting with simulation-based learning. Without his support, none of this would have happened.

ICONS/INMP Simulation at JCC

JCC joined the INMP in the third year after we were introduced to Joyce Kaufman's work through the United States Institute of Peace's summer community college seminar in Washington, D.C. It was then that we learned about the community college version of the ICONS simulation: the INMP.

JCC has two campuses fifty miles apart in two different counties. Although the same faculty member works with both groups, students on one campus typically play the role of the Republic of Korea (South Korea), while those on the other campus typically play the Democratic People's Republic of Korea (North Korea). The former has a softer, more conciliatory negotiating posture, and the latter a harder, more aggressive one, especially with the United States. This approach of using the two Koreas as the actors started when JCC was awarded an East Asian Fellowship from Columbia University because of our work in simulation-based learning. JCC uses a textbook, *Global Politics*, supplemented by a simulation scenario and online resources (Kaarbo and Ray 2011). (A sample syllabus is appended to this chapter.) In the class, the students playing the role of South Korea run their delegation like a democracy, with a student playing the role of president, and four students playing the ministers responsible for key ministries. The students representing North Korea run their delegation like an authoritarian, totalitarian, hereditary Communist dictatorship, with one student playing the role of "the Dear Leader," and four others playing the key government ministers. Both groups learn to think, write, and negotiate as Koreans (albeit in English) in this text-based simulation. The head of government (HOG) must prepare a general opening statement, and the ministers must also prepare opening statements for their various issues and ministries. By the time of the summits, each ministry must prepare a proposal for posting in the proposal center.

For purposes of assessment and grading, at the end of the simulation, students prepare a paper comparing the simulation with the real world. This simulation has led students to do the face-to-face European Union simulations (in which JCC also participates), study abroad, and pursue different career options. Because this simulation is all text based, it has the important benefit of helping students write better—and do so quickly, especially during the online real-time summit. When students are chosen to chair the summits they also learn how to chair meetings.

Students can read messages at any time, from anywhere, but can post messages in class only after getting approval from their governments. This is usually the only class where students remain after it is over, interrupt their spring break to participate in the summits, and ask to come and participate in the summits the next year, when they are no longer in the class. Another prediction is warranted at this point: students will become more active learners in all their classes, not just the one with the simulation. They become better learners.

Before and after the simulation, students are asked to do a simple, open-ended anonymous survey, in which they are asked five questions about international negotiations in general and the four issues in particular. The presurvey answers are vague and general, whereas the postsurvey answers are specific and sophisticated. The most frequent general comment is, "Since it was so hard to come to an agreement in the simulation, how does anything ever get done in the real world with real countries?"—a valuable lesson about the difficulties inherent in international negotiations.

Because JCC students do not play the role of the United States and because typically, most of our students have European backgrounds, playing the role of Asians requires them to step out of their "American skins" and learn to think differently. The surveys show that they have learned to think like Koreans. Experience has shown that they enjoy the process, using "we" when talking about themselves as Koreans and "they" when talking about the Americans, which is quite a change. Successful diplomacy requires the diplomat to learn to think like the other side, and the simulation allows students to do just that. The survey responses and the simulation postings were reviewed by the East Asia experts at Columbia University, who reported that JCC students "got it." At one of our discussions and meetings at Columbia, one of the East Asian faculty members briefly left the room and returned amid a conversation about Korean affairs based on the simulation and JCC student messages. She thought the discussion was about the real world and was pleasantly surprised to find that we were talking about the work of first- and second-year community college students.

Summary of the JCC Case

Simulations have changed learning and teaching at JCC for the better. Simulations require extra work by the faculty adviser and the students, but the feedback, both anecdotal and through formal evaluation and assessment, has been overwhelmingly positive. By all accounts, the opportunities for teaching and learning are well worth the effort. While simulations do require institutional support, the real key is passionate, interested faculty members willing to take chances and step outside their comfort zone for the benefit of themselves, their students, the college, the community, and perhaps even the world.

Conclusions

As the case study of JCC illustrates, the INMP has succeeded in meeting the goals identified when the program was created. In addition to integrating technology across the curriculum, the simulation introduces students to the importance of negotiations as a tool for communication across countries and international actors. Evaluations of the program confirm that it has achieved these other objectives as well:

- acquisition of factual knowledge about particular countries
- exposure to issues and perspectives that help students understand the world today and their place in it
- knowledge of interconnections among countries and of the issues they are facing in a globalized world
- development of decision-making skills as students work together within the class, and then as they begin their negotiations with other groups
- enhancement of critical-thinking skills as a result of doing research, communicating, formulating negotiating strategies, and both developing and responding to messages from other countries

- fostering of written communications skills because the students must depend on the written word to get their ideas across
- acquisition of skills that can be used in the workplace, since students must learn how to work together in groups to develop their positions, as well as use technology to support their work
- facility with different forms of technology as tools for research as well as communication
- more global perspective and greater multicultural awareness through honing students' abilities to see the world from multiple perspectives and points of view
- transformation of the way participating faculty members teach.

Taken together, these educational and pedagogical objectives ensure that the students who participate in the INMP will become better and more aware citizens. Indeed, they may someday emerge as policymakers and leaders who can then apply the skills they have learned to ensure a more cooperative and peaceful world.

References

Kaarbo, Juliet, and James Lee Ray. 2011. *Global Politics.* 10th ed. Boston: Cengage Learning.

Kaufman, Joyce P. 1998. "Using Simulation as a Tool to Teach about International Negotiation." *International Negotiation* 3 (1998): 59-75.

Raby, Rosalind Latiner, and Joyce P. Kaufman. 2000a. "The International Negotiation Modules Project: Using Computer-Assisted Simulation to Enhance Teaching and Learning Strategies in the Community College." In *Case Studies on Information Technology in Higher Education: Implications for Policy and Practice,* ed. Lisa Ann Petrides, 168-84. Hershey, PA: Idea Group.

————. 2000b. "Navigating the Digital Divide: Using Technology to Internationalize Community College Curricula." *International Journal of Educational Policy, Research and Practice* 1 (3): 389–404.

Torney-Purta, Judith. 1996. "Conceptual Changes among Adolescents Using Computer Networks and Peer Collaboration in Studying International Political Issues." In *International Perspectives on the Design of Technology-Supported Learning Environments,* ed. Stella Vosniadou, Erik De Corte, Robert Glaser, and Heinz Mandl. Hillsdale, NJ: Erlbaum.

Wilkenfeld, Jonathan, and Joyce P. Kaufman. 1993. "Political Science: Network Simulation in International Politics." *Social Science Computer Review* 11 (4): 464–76.

POL 1520
Gregory P. Rabb
Jamestown Community College

Class Description and Objectives

World Politics is an introduction to the historical, contemporary, and future structure of the world political "system." Since the Cold War ended with the demise of the Soviet empire, the world has become more complicated and dangerous (witness the attack on the World Trade Center and the war in Iraq). The Cold War world was a simple first world (United States and its allies) versus second world (USSR and its allies). The post-Cold War world, to a great extent, is now seen as "rich" versus "poor" (the so-called third world), "north" versus "south," etc., complicated by terrorism (e.g., 9/11) and nuclear and other dangerous weapons of mass destruction in the "wrong" hands (e.g., North Korea's).

Military power is being joined by economic and cultural power. The world is becoming more complex while, at the same time, we are more closely connected than ever before. World Politics is an attempt to try to organize the world political "system" into some coherent whole. In this effort, we examine and use the traditional methods of idealism versus realism. In addition, we examine and analyze the roles of various international "actors," including but not limited to the nation-state, transnational organizations, supranational organizations, and multinational organizations.

World Politics also attempts to introduce the student to the art and science of international negotiation by taking part in electronic simulations (ongoing and real time) online. Students will learn to negotiate over the Internet by taking part in the International Negotiation Modules Project-International Communication and Negotiation Simulations (INMP-ICONS), coordinated through SIMCON at Whittier College in California, using the computer technology available through the University of Maryland at College Park. JCC students will play the role of North Korea (Democratic People's Republic of Korea) and South Korea (Republic of Korea)—and learn to act and think like Koreans—in negotiations with other "countries," played by other colleges from here to Hawaii. Negotiations will take place during a monthlong ongoing simulation (starting in March) and four real-time "summits" in April.

Course Objectives

Students, upon successfully completing this course, will be able to

- analyze the world political system using both the idealism and realism models;
- define and explain the role of the nation-state, as well as the roles of international organizations, in the world political system;
- explain the origins and stresses on the nation-state system from above and below;
- explain the changes in the international system from the balance-of-power model (late 1700s through World War II), through the bipolar period (the Cold War), to the multipolar world of today;
- define power and its uses;

- negotiate conflicts and agreements among international actors;
- describe the European Union as the only true supranational organization; and
- analyze and explain the behavior of international negotiators.

Simulation-Related Activities

Weeks 1–3: Read simulation scenario. Be assigned to country delegations and roles.

Weeks 4–5: Research country positions. Prepare opening statement for the simulation.

Weeks 6–11: Actively participate in ongoing simulation culminating in "real-time summits."

Weeks 12–15: Debrief and prepare paper comparing the real world with the simulated world.

Textbook: James Lee Ray, *Global Politics*

16

Moving Forward

The Engaged Educational Experience

BARBARA THORNGREN AND MICHELLE RONAYNE

If you've come here to help me, you're wasting your time. But if you've come because your liberation is bound up with mine, then let us work together.   —Australian Aboriginal elder Lilla Watson

The notion of collaboration and unity toward a common goal as expressed in the above quote is one that those involved in peace work can easily appreciate. Educators working to shape the next generation recognize that they must be innovative when teaching. The idea of a dynamic, dialogical, and differentiated classroom is not a new one and neither is the term "progressive education," which can help bind many of those ideas together. It has a rich history, starting when John Dewey (1889) recognized that schools were not promoting growth and development and argued in favor of education that, rather than merely promoting rote memorization, actually helps students *learn to think*. Constructivists Jean Piaget (1951) and Lev Vygotsky (1997) agreed that in order to learn, students needed to interact with their environment. Both were at the forefront of educational theory and cognitive development in the mid-twentieth century and, in fact, argued against many of the educational techniques (standardized testing, top-down and teacher-centered strategies) that we use today.

Research indicates that progressive techniques such as teacher-as-facilitator are effective in developing critical and reflective thinking (Mascolo 2009; Harkins and Wells 2009). Our experiences with students indicate that they learn more from experiential exercises than from lecture alone, and that empirically participative learner-centered approaches are successful (Harkins and Wells 2009; Ronayne et al. 2010). Also, as Alfie Kohn notes, progressive classrooms are rare throughout education and even more so at the college level, making it difficult to find fault with learner-centered techniques, because they have not been adequately tested (Kohn 2008).

The twenty-first century demands that we bring new strategies and techniques to the college classroom. The fast-paced society in which most of our students have been raised requires a perspective that takes us out of the classroom and into the world. Students want to have enriching experiences that allow them to do more than merely "hear" about the lives of those they are studying. Educators must be open to dynamic, innovative, and differentiated approaches that challenge traditional "top-down" models of education. We must be brave and challenge the status quo. (After all, that is what we ask of our students.)

Our philosophy and educational techniques at times make us uncomfortable. This is because we worry about what students unaccustomed to nontraditional techniques will think when we do things differently. That is, if most faculty are using traditional top-down methods, learner-centered strategies may feel inappropriate to students. We question our methods, particularly when working in newer areas such as peace and social justice, and wonder whether we are the only ones doing things in a different way. There is also the question of how to measure success—perhaps we don't define it in narrow terms or by quantitative means alone. This is a concept familiar to those in the terrain of progressive education, and some out there question the merits of grading. Kohn (2006) suggests that grading can often have a negative effect on students, so that they tend to think less deeply, avoid taking risks, and lose interest in learning. It may be that a good evaluation involves more than simply defining a set of measurable outcomes.

Programs such as the Peace and Social Justice Program at Nashua Community College, a small school with a fairly homogeneous student population (primarily white and of traditional college age), strive to bridge multiple disciplines, tying together peace studies, conflict resolution, cultural understanding, and micro/macrolevel differences. We can create an environment that strives to empower students to become reflective practitioners of social justice, both by giving them opportunities and by practicing it ourselves through analysis of what it means to truly engage students. Moreover, we can move away from the traditional and tired notions of education as what Paulo Freire (1993) would call "the banking method." We can adjust our techniques so that we do more than treat students as passive receptacles of educational information that they then merely spit back at us. We can treat students like whole individuals and concern ourselves with their growth as individuals as well as in what they learn—an idea that echoes Bell Hooks's idea of a fully engaged student (Hooks 1994).

Social justice requires a willingness to take action and to work with others to promote change in our communities, and peacebuilding is not for the weak. Many factors influence success and failure; some you can control, and some you can't. The whole endeavor takes courage and conviction. Therefore, we must require that our students have experiences doing the actual work in order to understand whether this is something they want for their future.

Noddings (2005) suggests that schools should be centers of caring. In her view, students should learn to care for all around them. This is especially important to a peace and social justice orientation. Models that look not just to the academic outcomes but to the development of morals and values are important. This is in keeping with ideas and attitudes that we want our students to learn, including empathy. It is possible for students to learn and observe empathy (Rogers 1980). Helping students learn to care for others and to enhance their own self-awareness by exploring their own morals and values may facilitate the understanding of a social justice orientation (Webster 2009).

They need to know what it means to work with a community, what it means to change, and that it can be a slow process. Some communities that remain in dialogue about their problems may take much longer to move to deliberate action. We must help students understand that this is a normal path to growth and development. We must remain passionate and committed to the work. We also must work to create an empowering environment for our students so they, in turn, can do so for others in the community. This is why it is critical that we as educators practice our craft mindfully as well as give our students the opportunity to examine their growth through experiences that allow reflection. We must be the mirror.

Building Bridges: Empowerment in the Classroom

What does it mean to empower another? Some feel that a global and universal definition of "empowerment" may not be useful or practical for a variety of reasons. Empowerment likely means different things to different people. How do we know if we are achieving our goals? That is, try as we might to empower students, they may not be ready to take on the responsibility we are handing them. Our role may be better defined as creating an empowering environment where growth can occur because it is safe to do so. Rather than define the change for our students, we can allow them to define change within. Therefore, it is our role to hold a space that lets them do this. The strategies and assessments we use both in and outside the classroom can give students room to grow.

We can't underscore enough the importance of empowerment in our communities. Work from organizational psychology has demonstrated that groups that are successful at learning and growing have self-directed and empowered members. (See, for example, Checkland 1981; Senge 1991.) Within the organizational world, empowerment is typically viewed as a means for improving the organization (Alampay and Beehr 2001). That is, empowerment is seen as increasing participative decision making and delegation of power to those in lower levels of the organization. We can bring these same beliefs and practices to our students. If we give them more responsibility for their own growth and development, many will rise to the challenge. We must do so in a supportive way. That is, we provide the challenge (growth and reflective/critical thinking) and give the necessary interpersonal support to help them achieve their goals. So we can send them to have experiences, work in the community, and reflect on those actions, but we must also remain mindful of our role in steadily supporting their progress.

Progressive Community College Classes: A Suggested Model

So how do we do this? How do we create an empowered environment that is both supportive and challenging? We could begin by asking ourselves what it is we want to accomplish. There is something to be said for first acknowledging our own view of what it means to educate. We need to find a style that allows us to pass on our academic knowledge in a way that is meaningful and engaging, allowing students to develop skills in critical thinking and reflection. This may mean thinking outside our own comfort zones so that we can move students out of theirs. Our intellect alone may not be enough—we may also need to make use of our emotional intelligence. If you are paying attention, you can tell an engaged classroom moment from a disengaged one. The key is the willingness to try and then either fail or succeed. A good educator can take a moment that doesn't work and learn from it.

Creating an environment where students can engage in dialogue (a discussion with both peers and instructor that lets students challenge ideas and discover possible solutions) means providing the tools and space for such experiences to occur. For example, we can incorporate trust-building exercises that create community and ask thought-provoking questions (For an example of a classroom exercise, see the exhibit "Life Beliefs" at the end of this chapter.) We must ground students in theory and then let them challenge it. We must teach them to be critical consumers of all forms of media so that they are active thinkers not just in the classroom but outside it. We can use a variety of methods to achieve our desired goals: we can share our knowledge and theory, provide stimulating reading that prompts debate, invite guest speakers, structure our classroom so that it is designed for discussion, include exercises in critical self-reflection, build a culture of respect so that active participation feels safe, and practice listening exercises and reflect on the experience. We can ask ourselves, as they do at the University for Peace in Costa Rica, "what went well" (WWW) and "even better if" (EBI), so that students and educators alike have opportunities for authentic growth and development. Framing questions in the positive rather than starting with the flaws (e.g., "What do you think went well in your project?" and "What strategies did you have for challenges that were in your way?") makes the critique easier for everyone to hear, thereby making it easier for educators to put into practice.

Kohn (2008) explains that what distinguishes progressive education is that students must construct their own understanding of ideas. What we as educators must do, even when dealing with linear information (courses that dictate some degree of data and memorization), is to find ways for students to understand, analyze, and interpret information through their own lens. We suggest a model that embraces the progressive education movement and makes use of techniques that we as educators have found helpful. Below are four key areas to explore (though not all may happen in every class) in creating a successful, progressive community college class. The specific focus here is on peace and social justice (with ideas from the behavioral sciences included), but this model could be tailored to any discipline.

One: Connection

Dialogue occurs best in an environment of mutual trust and understanding. Educators who wish to create connection in the classroom must be willing to explore various modalities for developing it. In Kohn's assessment of eight key strategies for the progressive classroom (reflecting on primary and secondary education models rather than college), he suggests that educating the whole person (creating good *people*, not just good learners) and creating community (where students and teachers work *with* one another) are essential (Kohn 2008). This is why the first key is connection. Educators can create community and connection in the classroom in a variety of ways. Here are some:

The use of circles within the classroom. Psychological research that looks at the structure of organizational spaces indicates that the design can affect performance. Instructors are well aware of this. If you set the stage appropriately, it is easier for trust to grow and community to emerge. The ability to see each person in the room makes for a more shared experience.

Classroom agreements, starting on the first day of class. Students are encouraged to design their own "rules" for the class. They can do this by brainstorming ways to make a classroom environment feel safe for participation, including a discussion about respect, and then picking five or six items from the brainstormed list to have as rules or guidelines. This will help create an empowered space. It is important that the rules or guidelines come from the students rather than the teacher, to avoid a top-down approach. This is particularly helpful for courses that cover sensitive material, so that students feel safe participating in dialogue around topics that are personal.

Check-ins: an opportunity to share personal information about their lives. Students sit in a circle and are welcome to share how their day is going. No one is forced to participate, but those who want to do so may. This lets everyone know that a complete person (not just a learner) is part of the dialogue. It can be helpful for professors to engage in that process as well, to show that they, too, are part of the community.

Focus questions, generated by the professor or students. Depending on the theme for the day, these questions will vary. For example, students may be focusing on social issues, and the question "What is justice?" might lead to a list of class-generated ideas that they can return to later in the class or semester.

Two: Expressing Voices, Sharing Information

It is critical that students have an opportunity to develop their own ideas. Some students are challenged by this. Therefore, educators must design specific activities to let even those students who hesitate to share with the larger group find their voice. Work here should focus on student development of questions, critiques of material, and possible topics for debate. Kohn (2008) also suggests that active learning is essential because it allows students to construct their own knowledge. We have several suggested techniques:

Pair/share. Students pair up (with a different student each week) and discuss a reading, an assignment, or a project they are developing. They ask each other questions and then share their conversation with the class.

Discussion questions. Students generate the questions, and they can then discuss them in small groups. Each group reviews the questions that others have developed for class, and then selects one for discussion. Then they share their ideas with the whole class.

Exploring pros/cons of social issues in small groups. Each group could be assigned readings that discuss a different element of a social problem. Then, after presenting the pros and cons of each, the class discusses the relative merits of each.

Role-playing. These activities can be helpful in getting students to take perspective. Activities that give students a character or a problem to address allow them to see the situation in a different way. This gives them an alternative view that might not occur to them if they were not asked to think in a different way.

Three: Relevance

It is critical that students be able to take the material from class and apply it to other situations. Generally, they want to find a way to connect to things in their own lives and the world around them. Teaching theory is not sufficient—students must also see that it matters. Kohn (2008) talks about three ideas that seem to be linked to this idea of relevance: the concepts of social justice, intrinsic motivation, and deep understanding. Here are some possible ways to make the material relevant:

Revisiting earlier discussion questions. This can allow students to connect the ideas they first presented about a topic (e.g., "What is justice?") to examine how it might relate to their own lives. Often, students will see things as relevant if they hear fellow students present their views.

Readings that tell stories of real people. These have more salience than texts alone. Many students find they can relate to first-person accounts or to current media pieces on the topics being explored.

Exploring what students would do "if it happened to me." Many students do not react to the intolerance they see in the world around them and being asked what they would want to see happen if they or a friend were in that situation may change their perspective.

Four: Reflection

It is important to give students a chance to process the information they have taken in. All too often with more linear material, the information is presented and then recalled, with little time to think about what it actually *means.* This is an essential step in the educational process from a progressive perspective. Kohn (2008) echoes this when he talks of active learning and taking students seriously. If we want students to be fully engaged, we must involve their voices in every step. Here are some possible ways to do this in class:

Closing circles, to give an ending to the discussion. Students can process what they have heard and talk about what they took from it. They can also share how it affected them emotionally.

Papers asking students to reflect and critically explore the concepts. This promotes deeper understanding. There are times where "hearing" a student's voice in the written form allows professors to see growth more clearly than a test or quiz could ever allow. Students should be encouraged to express their ideas and focus more on content than on form when asked for a reflection. These exercises ask students to reflect on their views of a particular topic, find ways to support those views by critically analyzing a particular reading, and explore whether they agree with the perspective provided in the reading. This can be a challenge for many students because they are so rarely asked to explore what they think.

How Has It Been Working?

Authentic opportunities also allow students to engage with the material and to have healthy debate or dialogue. It is difficult to talk about peace and social justice without doing the work. The psychology program recently decided to make its capstone, or culminating project, more experiential, allowing students to work in the community as well. Rather than merely talking about research and community, "doing" the work enriches student knowledge. Much has been made in recent years about the impact of service learning, and yet, not a lot of research has occurred to demonstrate its success empirically. However, educators know what they see in the classroom. Students' lives are affected when they have opportunities to face their stereotypes, step out of their comfort zone, roll up their sleeves, and participate.

Many peace and social justice programs require ten or more hours of service learning, structured opportunities to reflect critically on the service experience. One student had the opportunity to complete a project that a shelter had always wanted to accomplish but had never had the time. She collected the stories of those who lived in the shelter and left the organization with a written record of the narratives. She also gained a much deeper appreciation for the experiences of those who found themselves homeless.

Field trips also offer an opportunity to experience firsthand something that a student might not otherwise ever encounter. The Peace and Social Justice Program organizes a field trip to a local prison, helping address stereotypes and challenge previously held assumptions about what it means to be a prisoner. This is a trip that takes courage—on the part of both educator and student. Yet it is a powerful learning experience that could never fully be realized in the classroom and is transformative for all involved.

Conferences and field trips provide an opportunity for students to experience a wide array of lectures and workshops. They can learn from others working in the field. Many peace and social justice students attended the Department of Peace Campaign Conference in Washington, D.C. Many of the students who attended were members of the Student Peace Alliance, ranging from high school to college age. They came together as strangers and left as friends. They left renewed and refreshed, knowing they were supported by a network of friends throughout the region, all committed to working for peace. Conferences also provide an opportunity for students to share their work. The psychology program had a similar experience taking students to the 2010 Eastern Psychological Association Conference, and several students were also involved with presentations at the 2011 conference. This led to the creation of an institutional review board on our campus, which promotes this kind of learning activity across disciplines. And we have taken students to visit the United States Institute of Peace to learn about international peace and conflict issues (see box 16.1). The peace and social justice program can now take their community experiences and share them with the larger community through research and participation in the larger community of academics.

Action, both locally and internationally, can show students that they can take an active role in change. It does more than give them an opportunity to experience and reflect; it shows them that every citizen has the opportunity to bring change. Students given the opportunity to understand how government works and how laws are created can be empowered to become

Box 16.1: Global Peacebuilding Center at USIP

The Global Peacebuilding Center extends USIP's long-standing educational work to new audiences through new means, using multimedia exhibits, educational programs, and online resources and activities to introduce a broad public audience to peacebuilding concepts and skills. For community colleges, the Global Peacebuilding Center's Web site (www.buildingpeace.org) is a valuable resource, offering educators the opportunity to infuse a learning environment with global content. The Peacebuilding Toolkit for Educators provides lesson plans and activities on conflict management skills designed for secondary school audiences, and this content can easily be adapted to community college settings. Other online materials include the Witnesses to Peacebuilding series of short videos, profiling individual peacebuilders from around the world. Through on-site educational programs and online engagement, the Global Peacebuilding Center is helping foster the next generation of peacebuilders and supporting the efforts of educators, including those in community colleges, to teach about peace.

agents of change. Students had the opportunity to work with a local New Hampshire state representative to create a New Hampshire house resolution in support of the Youth PROMISE Act. This act puts together policy suggestions from law enforcement, school systems, mental health professionals, and other members of the community to have a coordinated response to youth violence. The students held a public forum to provide information and gain local support. They testified in the state house and state senate, and the measure passed. They were thrilled to see the process through (Scott 2011).

The trip to Costa Rica that students made in the summers of 2010 and 2011 is a clear example, start to finish, of engaged and experiential education. This is a course that takes place at the University for Peace in Costa Rica. A short ten-day, three-credit course teaches students about knowledge, perspectives, and skills for teaching and leading with understanding, cooperation, and sensitivity to global interconnectedness. Many students described it as challenging, demanding, and inspirational. They were required to meet the usual demands of academic rigor as well as conduct service projects and came away feeling inspired and empowered. They thought about their own lives and what they took for granted. Reading their reflections, it is clear that the experience transformed them. For an educator, there is nothing better than that moment when a student realizes that they can be different from how they were before they entered your classroom. A shy student who spent time in a very discussion-based course struggled to speak and worried about what others would think. Yet she routinely challenged herself with the same discussion-type courses. She later explained, after a class where she was the center of discussion, that her father had been very abusive and would hit her if she spoke out of turn. It took three semesters and a lot of support, but slowly she moved from being a shy, frightened woman to one who knew she could use her voice. This is what we want to happen. We know it can work. We just need to stay brave enough in the face of challenges to keep working and moving toward the fully engaged educational experience.

References

Alampay, R. H., and T. A. Beehr. 2001 "Empowerment, Span of Control and Safety Performance in Work Teams after Workforce Reduction." *Journal of Occupational Health Psychology* 6 (4): 275–82.

Checkland, Peter. 1981. *Systems Thinking: Systems Practice*. Chichester, UK: Wiley.

Dewey, John. 1899. *The School and Society: Being Three Lectures by John Dewey, Supplemented by a Statement of the University Elementary School*. Chicago: Univ. of Chicago Press.

Freire, Paulo. 1993. *Pedagogy of the Oppressed*. New York: Continuum.

Harkins, Debra, and Yvonne Wells. 2009. "Critical and Discursive Teaching in Psychology." *Pedagogy and the Human Sciences* 1 (1): 38–49.

Hooks, Bell. 1994. *Teaching to Transgress: Education as the Practice of Freedom*. London: Routledge.

Kohn, Alfie. 2006. "The Trouble with Rubrics." *English Journal* 95 (4): 12–15.

———. 2008. "Progressive Education." *Independent School* (Spring).

Mascolo, Michael. 2009. "Beyond Student-Centered and Teacher-Centered Pedagogy: Teaching and Learning as Guided Participation." *Pedagogy and the Human Sciences* 1 (1): 3–27.

Noddings, Nel. 2005. *The Challenge to Care in Schools: An Alternative Approach to Education*. 2nd ed. New York: Teachers College Press.

Piaget, Jean. 1951. *Play Dreams and Imitation in Childhood*. London: Heinemann.

Rogers, Carl. 1980. *A Way of Being*. New York: Mariner Books.

Ronayne, Michelle, Manila Austin, Debra Harkins, and Carol Sharicz. 2010. "Power and Empowerment in a Non-Profit Organization." *American Journal of Psychological Research,* 1 (6): 59–89.

Scott, Bobby. 2011. "Youth PROMISE Act: Fighting Juvenile Crime vs. "Playing Politics." www.bobbyscott.house.gov/index.php?option=com_content&view=article&id=291&Itemid=111.

Senge, P. M. 1991. *The Fifth Discipline: The Art and Practice of the Learning Organization*. New York: Doubleday.

Vygotsky, Lev. 1997. *Educational Psychology*. Boca Raton, FL: St. Lucie Press.

Webster, Debra. 2009. "Promoting Empathy through a Creative Reflective Teaching Strategy: A Mixed-Method Study." *Journal of Nursing Education* 49 (2): 87–96.

Life Beliefs

Purpose: Community building to develop self-awareness

Time: 30 Minutes

Materials: None

1. Have the group stand and move chairs out of the way. Draw an imaginary line down the middle of the room. Explain that the line is a continuum and that the ends are extreme positions on each of the questions that will be asked: "For example, if you answer 'yes' to a question, you would stand at this end; if you answer 'no,' stand at the other end. If you are in between, place yourself at the spot along the line where you think you are: in the middle, leaning toward 'yes,' or leaning toward 'no.'" (For each question, be certain to indicate which end of the line corresponds to which extreme.")

2. The facilitator will read four or more questions and ask participants to line up according to how they believe they stand on that question. Participants can be at any place along the line, depending on how strongly they feel about the question. After each question, ask a few volunteers to explain why they answered the question the way they did. Don't let it drag on. Move on to the next question.

3. **The Questions**

   1. Do you believe humanity is basically good OR evil?

   2. Do you believe in a higher power (however you define it)— YES OR NO?

   3. Which is more important: who you are OR what you do?

   4. Is your fate or destiny predetermined (decided in advance without instructor's/facilitator's input), OR are you free to make your own choices?

   5. Which is more important: the individual OR the community?

   6. Do you believe that society should help its members who are unable to help themselves? YES OR NO?

   7. Do you believe that some people are entitled to special consideration under the law? YES OR NO?

   8. Do you believe that people should be allowed to make their own choices regardless of potential harm to themselves? YES OR NO?

Processing:

- Were you surprised at the different positions that people took on the line?
- With any of these questions, were you unsure what you believe?
- Do you think you might have answered any of these questions differently at some other time in your life?

Note: Sometimes we break this exercise into two segments and do four topics early in the workshop and four later on.

Some facilitators prefer to simplify this by making all the questions statements, as in "Here is a statement: 'People are basically good.' If you agree, stand at this end of the line; if you disagree, stand at this end."

Source: *Alternatives to Violence Project Manual for Second Level.* 1982. Reprint, Plainfield, VT: Omlet Publications, 2005. This manual is published for the use of volunteers serving as team members and coordinators of workshops conducted under the sponsorship of the Alternatives to Violence Project, USA. Anyone engaged in offering training in conflict resolution is hereby granted the right to reproduce this document in small quantities for their own noncommercial use, without prior permission.

PART FOUR

FUTURE IMPLICATIONS

17

The (Yellow Brick) Road Ahead

DAVID J. SMITH

Peace may sound simple—one beautiful word—but it requires everything we have, every quality, every strength, every dream, every high ideal. —*Yehudi Menuhin*

Having just returned from a faraway land inhabited by munchkins, flying monkeys, and other odd sorts, Dorothy Gale proclaims that the next time she needs to find her heart's desire she will look no farther than her own Kansas backyard. The iconic American film *The Wizard of Oz* is the story of powerless and defenseless inhabitants of various sizes and species, subject to oppression and violence, who are liberated by a courageous heroine from a foreign land. At the story's end, Dorothy emotionally proclaims, "There's no place like home!" During her adventure, she learns much about herself and applies many newly discovered insights. She is tolerant, kind, persistent, brave, a good listener, and a champion for many along her journey. She does not seek vengeance on her foes but rather tries to help her friends as best she can and make sure that promises are kept (particularly by the wizard), without harming others. These are all traits that one would find in a peacebuilder.

Public officials, business leaders, and everyday citizens have lately been finding that "there's no place like a community college!" They view community colleges as versatile institutions that can help solve the most pressing challenges faced in the United States and abroad. As American society continues to be reshaped by immigration influx, economic struggle and opportunity, and social change, community colleges find themselves centers of community life as well as providers of an accessible education. They are places where a laid-off steelworker can get retrained in information technology, where an inner-city youth can learn to swim, or where a senior citizen can experience travel abroad for the first time. Community colleges serve newly arriving immigrants needing to learn English, the homeschooled who are seeking their first formal classroom experience, and, increasingly, local residents interested in exploring issues of global importance that, more and more, carry local implications. Today, Dorothy need not venture to the Land of Oz, for she could learn much about herself and her world at a community college. The same two-year college that produced the real-life Kansan peacebuilder John Paul Lederach can educate a new generation of peacebuilders prepared to use their talents and passion to bring about important global change.

Students in community colleges will inherit a world where conflict and violence continue to undermine political, social, and economic stability; drain natural and financial resources; and, most importantly, take human lives, particularly of the young and vulnerable. Today's community college learners are the educational, business, military, and political leaders of tomorrow. They will be PTA presidents, emergency room nurses, community activists, business owners, military reservists, technological entrepreneurs, classroom teachers, and the cops on the street. They will participate in the greater world through travel abroad, help newly arriving immigrants adjust to life in the United States, and engage in globally connected business activities. They will increasingly live and work overseas as employees of international companies, volunteer as humanitarians in parts of the world in need (often through their faith communities), and learn foreign languages necessary to operate in a globalized world. For them, having an informed understanding of the changes, opportunities, and challenges that originate in the far corners of the planet is vital to keeping global society prosperous and peaceful. Particularly for younger audiences, community colleges must provide the important tools and skills for global engagement. They must pique and sustain students' interest in the greater world that they will inherit. As community college populations continue to grow and campus identities reflect an ever-changing mosaic of cultures, languages, aspirations, and values, community colleges have an important obligation of creating the global peacebuilders of tomorrow.

A Common Vision

We might ask if there is a common framework that community colleges are using to achieve their ends in educating for peace. The range of community college identities in the United States reflects the varying objectives that they are trying to meet and the approaches they are using. While some college efforts focus strongly on liberal arts education and opportunities for students to transfer, others may be looking at their work as a means of improving vocational skills. Still other educators see their role mostly in supporting community education; thus, their efforts may be strongly influenced by local needs and engagement.

In the end, the ideas set forth in this book reflect a variety of individual and institutional visions of what can be taking place to promote global peacebuilding. Some common aspirations are present:

First, approaches should be designed to engage students not only in critical thinking and exploration but also in critical action and engagement. This need is made more relevant when we consider the career and workforce focus that is central to community colleges. Whereas in four-year institutions teaching about peace and conflict, the experiential nature of peacebuilding might be viewed in a supplementary context, at community colleges it is core. Faculty want students to leave their classrooms not only with a greater understanding of the world and its challenges but also knowing ways in which they can make a difference in that world, whether in a local or global context. Practicing the "ways and means" of peace is vital to forming the characteristics consistent with a global builder of peace.

Second, it is essential to make the connections between the world that students experience and the world that is further removed. Unlike graduates of private liberal arts colleges and many state universities, most community college graduates will spend their personal and professional lives in the same communities where they studied. Although study abroad and travel in general is expanding for community college populations, for the most part, these graduates are deeply connected to local environments and will make most of their contributions in these same communities. Therefore, faculty members teaching about peace feel obligated to make their classroom experience as global as possible. Through the myriad of technological (via the Web) and traditional means (such as reading global narratives and listening to accounts from international guests and students), educators want the students leaving their classrooms to have every possible opportunity to experience the larger world and see the challenges and opportunities, as well as the consequences, of their local actions.

Third, the complexity and interdisciplinary nature of conflict demand framing responses and solutions in similarly interdisciplinary ways. Teaching about peace begins with the proposition that violence and war are seeded in many ways. Therefore, the answer to the question "How do we create peace?" must be found in varied human responses and contexts. The nature of community college learning is ideal for applying this interdisciplinary framework (e.g., box 17.1). For one thing, many faculty members teach across various disciplines, thus coming to a topic with an interdisciplinary lens. "Learning community" models are often used to show students new relationships between fields. Also, students often attend community college with undetermined academic or career objectives, and looking at problems

Box 17.1: Global Education through the Child Soldier Issue

For a college that is looking to integrate a major international conflict issue across the curriculum, the global crisis in the use of child soldiers is a good issue. Today there are more than 300,000 young boys and girls forced into military service with insurgent and government armies. While the boys take on combatant roles, the girls are frequently sexually abused. After repatriation, multiple challenges face these young people: from illiteracy to post-traumatic stress disorder (PTSD). These myriad challenges can be readily explored in specific fields. A psychology course can look at PTSD; a global health course (possibly in a nursing program) can examine the medical needs of these victims, including treatment for HIV/AIDS; a criminal justice course can look at the criminal responsibility of insurgent commanders (through international law); courses in the visual or performing arts can examine ways in which artistic outlets can benefit youth coming to terms with their experiences; a literature course can offer biographical works written about and by child soldiers; and business and economics classes can explore rehabilitation approaches that center on teaching ex-combatants to enter into the work environment through the use of microfinance grants. A campuswide effort can help students understand an important issue from multiple perspectives and can further internationalize a college.

from various sides, often in a survey context, is very much in the nature of the learning they experience.

Finally, strategies for teaching peace in the community college context can contribute to solving important social, political, and economic problems that we face as a global society. There is no reason why community colleges and the students they produce cannot engage in tackling our most pressing challenges. As the authors in this book have pointed out, exploring solutions to ecological problems, advancing humanitarian responses to conflict, promoting human rights, and fostering global literacy are all squarely within the capacity of community colleges. While other educational sectors may underestimate the capabilities of community colleges, those working with two-year institutions are coming to realize what gold mines they are today.

Some Critical Imprints

Many community colleges have a long-standing identification with the military. Community colleges are often located near military installations, and they frequently offer classes on base. ROTC chapters on community college campuses are increasingly common. A major Army base was within a short drive from the college where I taught. As a result, our campus had a noticeable military presence: spouses learning occupational skills that they could use wherever their family might be assigned, soldiers taking classes to advance themselves between deployments, and recent retirees taking courses to advance their next career opportunity. Where there is a community college, there will likely be men and women in uniform, and their dependents, taking advantage of the range of coursework and scheduling flexibility that allows them to serve their country and improve themselves at the same time.

In 2004, Abu Ghraib prison in Iraq was the center of controversy when it was discovered that members of the 372nd Military Police Company, a National Guard Unit based in Western Maryland, had engaged in acts of prisoner abuse. The ensuing investigation brought to light the lack of awareness, among low-ranking military personnel, of human rights and humanitarian law. The guardsmen and -women who perpetrated the acts were ultimately dealt with through the military justice system.[1] Some of these soldiers had attended community college before their enlistment, which raises the question of the role that community colleges might play in better preparing military personnel for the roles they will eventually fulfill in times of war. One of the guardsmen at the center of the storm had attended Allegany College of Maryland, based in Cumberland, Maryland. In 2008, United States Institute of Peace (USIP) staff visited the college to consult with faculty about the college's interest in developing a peace and conflict program. This resulted in the establishment of a letter of recognition in peace studies in 2009. Though the effort to develop the program was not directly in response to Abu Ghraib, the faculty initiator was aware of the need to incorporate the understanding of international and human rights law into the program. The efforts of one community college in examining human rights might have only a "drop in the bucket" impact on the awareness of military recruits, but it demonstrates that our men and women in uniform can use the community college classroom to hone skills and awareness that better prepare them to work in conflict situations. A military presence provides an opportunity for a community college to promote international peace, improve national security, and work toward global stability. In short, community colleges can play a role in helping prevent other Abu Ghraibs.

The experiences that military personnel have in conflict zones can result in personal and professional transformation. One colleague shared with me a former student and soldier's words to her: "What I learned in Iraq is that peace will only emerge when people get together at the village level. That's what I want to work on. I'm trying to forge a career path that will put me

---

1. It was another member of the same company who brought the situation to the attention of military criminal investigators. For his actions, he was awarded the John F. Kennedy Profile in Courage Award in 2005.

there so I can help [in conflict environments]." It is becoming ever clearer that community colleges can help our men and women in uniform take the lessons they learn on the battlefield and cast them into important professional peacebuilding objectives (box 17.2).

Community colleges have seen a rise in the numbers of international students, many of whom have fled conflicts in their homelands. This is resulting in large ethnic and diaspora concentrations on a number of campuses. While many communities have rather heterogeneous populations, some community colleges are developing distinct identities because of recent immigration. Many community colleges have strong Latino identities, and other ethnic and cultural groups continue to make a significant mark. Minneapolis Community and Technical College has supported Puntland State University in northern Somalia as a result of the encouragement of a sizable Somali student and community population.

Henry Ford Community College is located in Dearborn, Michigan, a city that is nearly 40 percent Arab-American. Walking down Michigan Avenue and seeing the shopkeepers and grocery signs in Arabic and English leaves the visitor with the impression that this community is straddling multiple cultures. (The local McDonald's offers halal selections.) The college is pursuing a programmatic initiative that examines peace and conflict within an Arab-American context. As we continue to be challenged as a nation by concerns about youth extremism, encouraging the exploration of conflict prevention and resolution approaches in places like Dearborn is more important than ever before. The students in many community college classrooms bring with them powerful, often wrenching experiences. Many

Box 17.2: Jacki Wilson, Global Peacebuilder

Jacki Wilson is a professional peacebuilder and a senior program officer at USIP. She has had a wide-ranging career, starting with the military after college and retiring, after twenty-three years' active service in the Air Force, with the rank of lieutenant colonel. She has lived in remote parts of the world, including Saudi Arabia and Kenya. She has taught high school, holds two master's degrees, and is working on a doctorate. At USIP, she has served as a trainer working extensively in Sudan, Iraq, and Nigeria. Jacki attributes much of her awareness of the world and her interest in peacebuilding to when she was a student at Gulf Coast Community College (now Gulf Coast State College). "What elements of my community college experience led me to believe I could make a contribution to peacebuilding in places like Sudan, Iraq, or the Niger Delta? I believe that the seeds were planted in community college: humility, tolerance, flexibility, courage, patience, persistence. The basic human foibles that face one in community college are similar to the basic issues presenting challenges in zones of conflict around the world."

students are survivors and witnesses to violence and abuse, and still others harbor deeply held frustration and anger. Under the right conditions, these students are willing to share their experiences in the safe environment of a community college classroom. I remember a colleague once sharing with me that she had spent a lecture talking about violence against women in Africa, only to be approached after class by an African student who shared with her that she had, in fact, been abused. It will be up to experienced faculty to create a sensitive and tolerant environment for students to share their experiences if they choose.

Many of the current civic, business, and education leaders in Dearborn started college at Henry Ford Community College and have since become pillars of their community. A colleague at the school shared that recently he was approached by an Arab-American high school administrator, who reminded him that he had been the colleague's student years before. The administrator began quoting from Ralph Ellison's *Invisible Man*, which he said he has never forgotten and that he quotes often to his students. In the work, the African American protagonist rejects violence as a viable solution to social and ethnic conflict and chooses to work to enforce the principle on which the country was founded: "all men are created equal," from the Declaration of Independence. It is from these communities that important role models will come for a generation of youth who are frustrated and angry and, if not exposed to peacebuilding, may engage in destructive behavior. Community colleges both in the United States and elsewhere have a crucial role in fostering peaceful approaches to solving problems brought on by political events and social conditions (see box 17.3).

Hopeful Trends

Patterns are already apparent in the ways that community colleges are putting forth a peacebuilding strategy. Many of them have been explored in this book. One measure of the growth of a field is the number of academic programs that are producing graduates. The Peace and Justice Studies Association estimates that 450 programs worldwide focus on peace and conflict issues or related content such as human rights or global studies, but until recently only a handful were in U.S. community colleges (Peace and Justice Studies Association 2007). In recent years, important efforts have been made by USIP, working with the Global Issues Resource Center at Cuyahoga Community College, to support initiatives to develop sustainable programs offering degrees or concentrations in the field. Recently, faculty members and administrators from community colleges and groups supporting community college efforts have formed a special interest group that sup-

Box 17.3: Peacebuilding in Community Colleges in Canada and Overseas

The U.S. community college model is increasingly being applied in countries around the world. Rosalind Latiner Raby, of California Colleges for International Education, reports that international counterparts of community colleges exist in some ninety countries, where they may be called "community colleges," "colleges of further education," "polytechnics," or "technical colleges." Many of these institutions address peacebuilding in their curricula, including social justice, multicultural understanding, and education for civil society. Raby's recently coedited volume on international community colleges is a useful resource for anyone interested in exploring peacebuilding curricula overseas (Raby and Valeau 2009).

Within Canada's community college and Collège d'enseignement général et professionnel (CEGEP) system, John Abbott College in Quebec and Langara College and Selkirk College in British Columbia have peace studies programs. Most recently, Sault College in Ontario established a peace and conflict studies program in 2009 and graduated its first class of students in 2012. The curriculum includes conflict analysis, human rights, indigenous and aboriginal peoples, and sustainable development.

The strong connection between local challenges and the ways that community colleges can make a difference is also part of the Canadian model. In 2011, after experiencing violence on its campus in 2006, Dawson College in Montreal held a three-day conference cosponsored by the Association of Canadian Community Colleges, examining how education can play a role in promoting solutions to violence, intolerance, and inequality. The conference focused on how educational practices and curriculum can be informed by an understanding of the psychological and cultural roots of violence. Sessions focused on a range of issues such as conflict management, nonviolent approaches, the development of empathy, and dealing with Islamophobia.

ports community college peacebuilding efforts. Much capacity building has also taken place through USIP's seminar for community colleges. As a result of these collective efforts, the number of sustainable peace and conflict-related programs and initiatives has increased considerably to twenty-one programs. (See appendix B.) Programs and courses have been developed to attract high-performing students interested in exploring issues more typically found in a four-year college curriculum. Colleges are attempting to harness the local character of their communities to provide a meaningful experience that can help engage students in the greater community, socially and politically. Some colleges recognize the increasing diversity and globalization of their institutions and see teaching peace as a means to creating a meaningful and well-placed strategy for students to learn about the greater world. Colleges may see the value of advancing aptitudes that are key in peacebuilding education, with students who can then apply those skills in professional and personal situations. This includes seeing the value of teaching about peace in vocational contexts. Teaching peacebuilding and leadership skills and aptitudes can be advanced in a range of occupational programs from nursing to business to homeland security to education.

A noncredit approach is often an intermediate step to establishing a credit program, can supplement a credit program, or can be an end in itself. Noncredit lecture programs, artistic showings, or annual events such as a peace week or fair can be an effective, community-sensitive strategy. These approaches have the potential of allowing the greater community to participate in the initiative and speak to a central premise of community colleges: being of and for the community. Alumni, students, faculty, administrators, and particularly community members often see two-year colleges as venues to promote discrete issues affecting specific communities or local constituencies. Two examples, both in New Jersey, speak to this approach. Brookdale Community College supports a Center for World War II Studies and Conflict Resolution. Though seemingly self-contradictory, the center's mission focuses on exploring U.S. military conflict—in a community with a large number of veterans—but also creating a forum for considering important contemporary issues that can lead to violence. Bergen Community College supports a Center for Peace, Justice and Reconciliation. A major focus of the center is to provide support for educators teaching about the Armenian genocide, which is covered in New Jersey secondary education curriculum. This effort is also in response to the large Armenian population in the region.

A third approach calls for engaging faculty in the global environment, with the objective of promoting peacebuilding. This can involve programmatic partnerships and collaborations using the inherent strengths of community colleges, particularly those related to vocational and professional training and education, such as nursing or teacher education. In chapter 10, the discussion of Richland College's English-language teaching efforts as a peace education strategy in Mozambique is a good example. It can also be a more individualized effort, with faculty pursuing study-abroad efforts, for example, through various federally supported exchange programs. In 2009–10, the peace studies chair at Oregon's Portland Community College was a U.S. Fulbright scholar in India. In the summer of 2008, Oakton Community College, near Chicago, secured a Fulbright-Hays travel grant to India, which permitted faculty from several colleges to launch peace studies efforts. Global engagement efforts call on college leaders to grasp the important nexus between the college's strengths—frequently centered on instruction—and the ways that the school can contribute to preventing conflict and rebuilding societies affected by violence. This often requires institutions to collaborate for purposes of securing funding and building initiatives. Allies are wide ranging, including Community Colleges for International Development, the Midwest Institute for International Intercultural Education, the Center for Global Advancement of Community Colleges, the U.S. Department of State, the U.S. Department of Education, the United Nations, and other groups and agencies.

The fourth emerging strategy centers on promoting innovative pedagogical approaches to teaching about peacebuilding. Experiential learning, particularly where students role-play and engage in simulations, is increasingly being developed as a way of getting students to experience what peacebuilding can look like. Students can play the role of humanitarians (chapter 14) or diplomats (chapter 15) to test whether a professional commitment in this sphere of work is right for them. This encourages peacebuilding by doing and promotes important skills as they are applied in the field. One example is Model UN, a long-standing program that casts students as members of national delegations for purposes of solving global issues. Several community colleges, including Sinclair Community College (OH), participate in Model UN. Experiential learning also can include student participation in activities and efforts that are extracurricular but require engaging in policy discussions. The Student Peace Alliance, established to promote student awareness of policy issues related to peace and violence prevention, is finding footing at a number of community colleges, such as Nashua Community College in New Hampshire.

Work to Be Done

The writers of this volume have demonstrated the potential for community colleges to contribute to global peacebuilding, but the work is far from complete. To be fully actualized, community colleges must negotiate a myriad of challenges and harness opportunities as they continue to meet the needs of ever-changing communities while serving new national and global priorities. Several crucial issues arise in the ongoing effort to bring peacebuilding fully into the community college.

Four-year institutions often hesitate to give value and, more specifically, academic credit for the work that students have pursued in community colleges. Issues of the transferability of a specific course, let alone full academic programs, to both private and public institutions continue to be a significant point of intersection and contention between the various levels of higher education. Already established peace and conflict programs at the four-year college and university level have much to gain by accepting the work of students at the community college level, who may be nontraditional but are no less academically or professionally focused than other students. Incorporating these students' work can help "democratize" the field by giving students with limited means or opportunities comprehensive university experiences important to their professional and personal growth. As more students elect community colleges because of affordability, convenience, and innovative programming and teaching, transfer institutions will want to develop relationships that lead to direct articulation, advancing the overall objectives of the field. Creating a seamless way for students to achieve a bachelor's degree in a peacebuilding-related field, starting at the community college level, is an important objective. This will demand more coordination between community colleges and four-year institutions on curricula, materials, and pedagogical approaches.

Whatever the field, students must be able to determine the career potential of a particular course of study. In looking at peace and conflict studies, the expectation can be challenging. While a student who graduates with a degree in allied health (where course work may include looking at the impact of violence on public health) or law enforcement (where course work may include the application of international law) may not face the challenge of underemployment, a student who pursues a liberal arts-focused degree in peace studies may face the dilemma of graduating with a credential without a well-defined career path. Employers should not dismiss the value of a degree in a field that gets students to challenge current assumptions about the social and political environment, instills critical-thinking skills, raises awareness of global issues, and teaches important skills and aptitudes that will help students function well in a wide array of settings. It will take persistent and innovative career counselors to make effective arguments for why students with a community college degree in peace studies or conflict resolution are competent choices for entry-level positions in business or government. Counselors will need to work with faculty to formulate strategies that show the relevancy of a global peacebuilding-oriented degree in the work world (Smith 2011; Mueller and Overmann 2008; Zelizer 2012). The economic downturn that began in 2008 has made this work even more challenging. It will be important to highlight helpful models, case studies, and examples of students who have thrived in varied employment settings. (See Kroc Institute 2008.)

Ultimately, the issue centers on how to promote a peace and conflict academic effort, particularly one that is skills based in the marketplace. Whereas community colleges are used to placing students with paralegal, dental assisting, or hospitality degrees in employment settings, placing students who have engaged in skills-based conflict resolution programs in employment—where there are few jobs and where even a bachelor's degree in conflict resolution is often insufficient as an entry requirement—is an enormous challenge. However, as Cuyahoga Community College (chapter 6) has shown, a peacebuilding program can emphasize skills and abilities that are essential to employment settings as diverse as education; law enforcement; not-for-profit; business; state, local, and national government; and military. It will be the responsibility of promoters of peacebuilding efforts to lay the groundwork for how to apply learning in ways that justify their programmatic development in the first place.

Closely related to the employment challenge is the increasing need to expand the relevancy of a peacebuilding curriculum beyond the humanities and social sciences. Teaching about peace can focus on vocational and occupational skill sets applicable to career paths that have long been the emphasis of community college efforts. Students pursuing career education should be given the opportunity to learn about global peacebuilding. This integration is critical because students completing vocational education, upon leaving a college, may never be in a classroom setting again. Whereas with transfer students, faculty might argue that the full peacebuilding education experience will include a course of study at the transfer institution, career programs cannot make such a claim. Thus, it will be important for vocational programs to incorporate conflict resolution and other peacebuilding content in their curricula. Possible approaches include a mediation course in a paralegal program, a human rights course in a homeland security program, and a restorative justice course in a law enforcement program. Recently, I traveled to Arizona Western College and learned about a student group called Welders Without Borders/Soldadores Sin Fronteras, whose objectives include using knowledge and skills to "make the world a better place for all mankind to live," through a commitment to volunteer service—a peacebuilding aim through vocational education.

Kent Farnsworth, in chapter 4, addresses the important alignment between peacebuilding and international education approaches. The conversation should be directed to how a peacebuilding approach can better focus a global education strategy. If a case can be made for the relevancy of peace and conflict programs in community colleges, and if more and more community colleges are embracing international education, why not employ peacebuilding as the means to achieving global education objectives? Many colleges struggle to formulate cogent and sustainable campus internationalization efforts. There are compelling reasons to consider global peacebuilding as a relevant and essential strategy for improving international awareness. Because community college graduates will inherit global as well as local challenges, they will need to understand the stresses and obstacles to creating sustainable and peaceful environments, whether they end up living in Bethlehem, Pennsylvania, or Bethlehem, Palestinian Territories. Diffuse, ineffective, and unfocused efforts can be replaced with approaches that are purposeful, with potentially strong career and professional benefits.

Notwithstanding the strong case made by the writers in this book, many administrators and trustees remain dubious about the need for teaching about international issues, to say nothing of global peacebuilding. Community college governing boards are generally locally focused, and it is often difficult to make the case for programmatic efforts that do not provide immediate and tangible benefits to the local economy and community. Those in the field, both faculty and community members, who see the inherent local benefits to a peacebuilding approach need to present trustees with a better case for the overall merits, both long and short term. Many boards may be unaware of the demographic changes that have swept their campuses and communities and of the needs that a college can address in these newer communities. Leaders may not be aware of how global businesses now present in their community can benefit from students who have a worldview encompassing contemporary challenges. The connection between the military and community colleges may not have been made. With the presence of Web-based learning and increasing diaspora and immigrant populations moving into previously homogeneous communities, the notion of what the "community" is that a college serves bears reconsidering.

Much still needs to be done to make teaching global peacebuilding a mainstay in all community colleges. A foothold has been attained, and a willingness is present among a determined cadre of faculty and supporters of community colleges, to make two-year colleges the next frontier for expanding the horizon of peacebuilding awareness, skill enhancement, and education. The next generation of peacebuilders can most certainly be found in today's community colleges. The key will be to provide them with the tools necessary to engage them in solving some of the most pressing problems we face today. Dorothy Gale needed the help of a wizard, a scarecrow, a tin man, a cowardly lion, and a witch or two to realize that she had within herself the power to get back to Kansas. Today, it is within the grasp of every community college to give students the opportunity to become global peacebuilders—a most worthy heart's desire.

References

Kroc Institute. 2008. "Strategic Peacebuilding." http://kroc.nd.edu/alumni/career-resources/strategic-peacebuilding-pathways.

Mueller, Sherry L., and Mark Overmann. 2008. *Working World: Careers in International Education, Exchange, and Development.* Washington, DC: Georgetown Univ. Press.

Peace and Justice Studies Association. 2007. "Global Directory of Peace Studies and Conflict Resolution Programs." www.peacejusticestudies.org/globaldirectory/.

Raby, Rosalind Latiner, and Edward J. Valeau, eds. 2009. *Community College Models: Globalization and Higher Education Reform.* Dordrecht, Netherlands: Springer.

Smith, David J. 2011. "Starting a Career Building Peace." *Career Convergence,* Feb. 1. http://associationdatabase.com/aws/NCDA/pt/sd/news_article/39568/_PARENT/layout_details_cc/false.

Zelizer, Craig. 2012. "Guide to Careers in International Affairs (Including Review of Top Job Sites)." Peace and Collaborative Development Network, Aug. 27. www.internationalpeaceandconflict.org/profiles/blogs/guide-to-careers-in.

Selected Resources for Teaching Peacebuilding and Global Education

Academy for International Conflict Management and Peacebuilding (www.usip.org/education-training)

USIP's program that provides training and education for professionals. Site includes online courses and simulations that USIP offers to the peacebuilding community.

Association for Conflict Resolution, Education Section (www.mediate.com/acreducation)

Education section of the Association for Conflict Resolution, the largest membership association of conflict resolution practitioners. Site provides news, information, and standards for teaching conflict resolution issues in the classroom.

Campus Conflict Resolution Resources (www.campus-adr.org)

Resource designed to increase administrator, faculty, staff, and student awareness of, access to, and use of conflict resolution information, specifically tailored in a higher education context.

Center for Global Advancement of Community Colleges (www.cgacc.org/)

Entity dedicated to increasing global knowledge and understanding about U.S. community colleges and serving as resource in promoting global initiatives.

Community Colleges for International Development (https://programs.ccid.cc/cci/)

Consortium of 160 community colleges focused on promoting the community college model overseas and supporting U.S. community colleges in building capacity for global education.

Compassionate Listening Project (www.compassionatelistening.org)

Nonprofit organization dedicated to empowering individuals and communities to transform conflict.

Conflict Information Consortium (http://conflict.colorado.edu)

Multidisciplinary center for research and teaching about conflict. Hosts Conflict Resolution Information Source (www.CRInfo.org) and Intractable Conflict Knowledge Base Project (www.BeyondIntractability.org)

Conflict Resolution Education Connection (www.creducation.org)

Site promoting conflict resolution education by sharing instructional materials and resources. Includes "Manual for Community Colleges Developing Programs in Peace & Conflict Studies."

Conflict Resolution Education in Teacher Education (www.creducation. org/cre/home/about_us/about_crete)

Program designed to educate teachers in conflict resolution to help them constructively manage conflict and create positive learning environments.

Consortium for Humanitarian Service and Education (http://humanitariantraining.org)

Based at Indian River State College (FL), entity that provides training for students and practitioners of international humanitarian response to learn applicable skills in working in disaster and conflict zones.

Educating For The Global Community: A Framework For Community Colleges (www.stanleyfoundation.org/publications/archive/CC2.pdf)

Stanley Foundation and American Council on International Intercultural Education report based on 1996 Airlie Center conference on global education and community colleges.

Exploring Humanitarian Law (http://ehl.redcross.org/)

Adaptable toolkit developed by the American Red Cross that gives educators easy-to-use materials to expose students to issues of international humanitarian law. Offers educators primary source materials and strategies that reinforce and enrich existing curricula and educational programs.

Global Campaign for Peace Education (www.peace-ed-campaign.org)

Information, resources, and networking site providing broad-based support for peacebuilding activities across sectors.

Global Consortium for Sustainable Peace (http://theglobalconsortium forsustainablepeace.org/)

Based at Cerritos College (CA), a network of partners that focus on raising awareness of global issues to college audiences through webcast programming.

Global Peacebuilding Center (www.buildingpeace.org)

USIP's center for teaching and learning about peacebuilding. Includes USIP's toolkit for educators, discussion forums, information on study abroad, and a range of other resources that can be used in community college environments.

ICONS Project (www.icons.umd.edu/highered/home)

University of Maryland-based project that supports online negotiation-based simulations including the International Negotiations Modules Project.

Midwest Institute for International/ Intercultural Education (www.miiie.org/)

Consortium of two-year colleges with an objective to support curriculum and professional development in international and intercultural education.

National Peace Academy (http://nationalpeaceacademy.us/)

Nonprofit organization providing educational support for academics and training for practitioners and citizens engaged in peacebuilding activities across sectors.

Peace and Collaborative Development Network (www.internationalpeace andconflict.org/)

Professional networking site that fosters dialogue and shares resources in international development, conflict resolution, and related fields.

Peace and Justice Studies Association (www.peacejusticestudies.org)

Nonprofit organization dedicated to bringing together academics, K-12 teachers, and grassroots activists to explore alternatives to violence and share visions and strategies for peacebuilding, social justice, and social change.

Peace Media (http://peacemedia.usip.org/)

A USIP supported site that provides a vast collection of media resources that can be used by educators.

Peace Terms (http://glossary.usip.org)

USIP's glossary on terminology and concepts relevant to the field of conflict management and peacebuilding. Users are invited to post comments.

Student Peace Alliance (www.studentpeacealliance.org)

A youth-centered and -run organization focused on engaging communities and policymakers in building sustainable peace. Sponsors student chapters on college campuses, including community colleges.

Sustained Dialogue Campus Network (www.sdcampusnetwork.org/)

A network of colleges and universities using Sustained Dialogue (developed by Dr. Harold Saunders) as a means of engagement to improve campuses, workplaces, and communities.

U.S. Community Colleges with Global Peace and Conflict Programs and Initiatives

Allegany College of Maryland (2009)
Cumberland, Maryland
Letter of Recognition, Peace and Conflict Studies

Bergen Community College (2009)
Paramus, New Jersey
Center for Peace, Justice and Reconciliation

Berkshire Community College (1982)
Pittsfield, Massachusetts
Associate of Arts, Liberal Arts – Peace and World Order Studies Concentration

Bluegrass Community and Technical College (2004)
Lexington, Kentucky
Focus Area, Peace and Justice Studies

Brookdale Community College (2001)
Lincroft, New Jersey
Center for World War II Studies and Conflict Resolution

Cuyahoga Community College (2010)
Cleveland, Ohio
Certificate, Conflict Resolution and Peace Studies

Delta College (2010)
University Center, Michigan
Associate of Arts and Certificate of Achievement, Global Peace Studies

Golden West College (2007)
Huntington Beach, California
Peace Studies

Greenfield Community College (2006)
Greenfield, Massachusetts
Associate of Arts, Liberal Arts – Peace, Justice and Environmental Studies

Howard Community College (2006)
Columbia, Maryland
Associate of Arts, Conflict Resolution

Lane Community College (2008)
Eugene, Oregon
Peace Center

Linn Benton Community College (1990)
Albany, Oregon
Peace Studies

Montgomery College (2006)
Rockville, Maryland
Peace and Justice Studies Community

Nashua Community College (2009)
Nashua, New Hampshire
Associate of Arts, Liberal Studies – Peace and Social Justice Studies Concentration

Northwest Vista College (2009)
San Antonio, Texas
Peace and Conflict Studies

Oakton Community College (2009)
Des Plaines, Illinois
Scholar of Peace Certificate, Peace and Social Justice

Pasco Hernando Community College (2006)
New Port Richey, Florida
Peace and Social Justice Institute

Portland Community College (1990)
Portland, Oregon
Focus Award, Peace and Conflict Studies

Richland College (2002)
Dallas, Texas
Emphasis Degree in Peace Studies

San Diego City College (2009)
San Diego, California
Associate in Arts and Certificate of Performance, Peace Studies

Valencia College (2008)
Orlando, Florida
Peace and Justice Initiative

Index

Contributors

EDITOR

David J. Smith, formerly the senior manager for educational outreach at the United States Institute of Peace, currently teaches at Georgetown University and George Mason University. He is a national authority on the intersection of peacebuilding and higher education. He has served as an associate professor at Harford Community College in Bel Air, Maryland, and has taught at Goucher College and Towson University. During 2003–04, he was a Fulbright Scholar teaching at the University of Tartu in Estonia. A conflict resolution practitioner, he is chair of the Human Rights Commission of Rockville, Maryland. Smith is the author of *Legal Research and Writing* (Delmar/Cengage Learning, 1996). He has a BA from American University, an MS from George Mason University (School for Conflict Analysis and Resolution), and a JD from the University of Baltimore.

***

Vasiliki "Kiki" Anastasakos is associate professor of political science at Northampton Community College in Bethlehem, Pennsylvania. She currently holds the Robert J. Kopecek Endowed Chair in the Humanities for her work on the theme of educating students for peaceful citizenship. She is a founding member of the Forum on Peace, Justice, and Conflict Resolution. In 2009, she was named Pennsylvania Professor of the Year by the Carnegie Foundation for the Advancement of Teaching and the Council for the Advancement and Support of Education.

Jennifer Batton, director of Global Issues Resource Center at Cuyahoga Community College in Cleveland, Ohio, co-coordinates the certificate program in Conflict Resolution and Peace Studies. Batton is the former director of education programs for the Ohio Commission on Dispute Resolution and Conflict Management and serves on advisory committees for the Organization of American States and the Global Partnership for the Prevention of Armed Conflict.

Scott Branks del Llano coordinates the Institute for Peace at Richland College in Dallas, Texas. He provides leadership in global and cultural studies and intercultural competence. His publication "The Faces of Peace" tells student stories within a teacher-formation monograph of the League for Innovation and the Fetzer Institute. Scott is a poet who creates community through teaching and learning.

John Brenner is a sociology professor and global education coordinator for Southwest Virginia Community College in Richlands, Viginia. He has a BA in social science education, an MA in Asian studies (Chinese), and a doctorate in educational leadership. He teaches the courses Principles of Sociology, Social Problems, and Sociology of the Family from a global perspective based on educational trips to India, West Africa, Japan, England, Scotland, Russia, Tunisia, Brazil, and China.

Isabelle Daoust has worked for the Red Cross in Canada, overseas, and in the United States, where she managed the International Humanitarian Law (IHL) program reaching schools, universities, and key stakeholders. As regional legal adviser with the International Committee of the Red Cross in Côte d'Ivoire, she visited political prisoners and advised governments on IHL treaty implementation and (in Switzerland) on mine/disarmament treaty issues. In Canada, she headed efforts to promote IHL with the government, armed forces, media, and academia. Daoust holds a business degree from the University of Montreal and law degrees from McGill University.

Karen Davis is an associate professor of English at Pasco-Hernando Community College in New Port Richey, Florida. She is the chair of Pasco-Hernando Community College's Peace and Social Justice Institute and sponsor of Peace Week. As an instructor in the Peace and Social Justice Institute, Davis teaches two peace courses. She has a BA in English from St. John's University and an MA in English from Rutgers University.

Jeff Dykhuizen served in the Peace Corps in Nepal after completing his BA and received his PhD from Kent State University in 1996. He lived, trained, and taught in Japan before coming to Delta College (MI) in 2002. In addition to teaching courses in psychology, world religions, and education, Dykhuizen is cofounder and current chair of Delta's Global Peace Studies program.

Cindy Epperson is professor of sociology at St. Louis Community College. She teaches Sociology, Criminology, Evil in the Human Condition, and Universal Human Rights. She serves as board secretary of the Midwest Institute for International Intercultural Education, is an international humanitarian law teaching fellow for the American Red Cross, and serves on the Global Council of the Center for the Global Advancement of Community Colleges. She is coauthor of *Evil: Satan, Sin, and Psychology* (2008) and author of *An Analysis of the Community College Concept in the Socialist Republic of Viet Nam* (2010).

Kent Farnsworth is president emeritus of Crowder College (MO) and retired Endowed Professor for Education Leadership at the University of Missouri St. Louis (UMSL). He also directed UMSL's Center for International Community College Education and Leadership. Farnsworth is a recipient of the National Community College CEO Leadership Award and the Werner Kubsch Award for Outstanding Achievement in International Education. His most recent book is *Grassroots School Reform: A Community Guide to Developing Globally Competitive Students* (2010).

Paul Forage received his PhD from the Department of East Asian Studies at the University of Toronto. At Indian River State College in Ft. Pierce, Florida, he oversees degree programs in emergency management and homeland security and develops full-scale training exercises in Florida, Macedonia, and Haiti. His interests include emergency management practice, complex emergencies, and peace and stability operations.

Jennifer Haydel is an assistant professor of political science at Montgomery College in Germantown, Maryland. She serves as the director of the Renaissance Scholars Honors Program on the Germantown campus. This program provides an intensive interdisciplinary honors curriculum to traditional and nontraditional students on the Germantown and Takoma Park campuses. She previously taught political science at Darton College in Albany, Georgia. She has a BA in integrated international studies from Knox College in Illinois and an MA in political science from the University of Minnesota.

Abbie Jenks, a faculty member at Greenfield Community College (GCC), created a Liberal Arts Option in Peace, Justice and Environmental Studies in 2006. She is adviser to the Peace, Justice, and Environmental Action Alliance and a member of the Green Campus Committee and chairs the Peace Education Center Advisory Committee at GCC. A board member of Traprock Center for Peace and Justice, she collaborates on the Roots of Peace Speaker Series. Her leadership in the New England Peace Studies Association and the national Peace and Justice Studies Association has brought national attention to the program at GCC.

Joyce P. Kaufman is professor of political science and director of the International Negotiation Project and the International Negotiations Modules Project, computer-assisted simulations of international negotiations for high school and community college students respectively, at Whittier College. She is the author of a number of books, articles, and papers on U.S. foreign and security policy and international negotiations. She received her BA and MA from New York University and her PhD from the University of Maryland.

John Paul Lederach, widely known for his pioneering work on conflict transformation, has engaged in conciliation work in twenty-five countries. He has published twenty books, including *The Moral Imagination: The Art and Soul of Building Peace* (Oxford Univ. Press, 2005). His most recent work, cowritten with his daughter Angela, is *When Blood and Bones Cry Out* (Oxford Univ. Press, 2011). Currently teaching at the Kroc Institute, University of Notre Dame, he has a PhD in sociology from the University of Colorado and is a graduate of Hesston College in Hesston, Kansas.

Susan W. Lohwater is associate professor of English as a second language at Cuyahoga Community College in Cleveland, Ohio. She co-coordinates the Certificate in Conflict Resolution and Peace Studies, coordinates the ESL department at the western campus, and is the faculty adviser for the International Club, Conversation Connection, Sustained Dialogue, and the Student Peace Alliance. She also served on the board of trustees for the International Services Center in Cleveland. She earned BAs in psychology and Russian, MAs in Russian and TESOL, and a PhD in Russian literature.

George A. Lopez holds the Reverend Theodore M. Hesburgh, C.S.C., Chair of Peace Studies at the University of Notre Dame's Joan Kroc Institute for International Peace Studies. In 2009-10, Lopez served as a Jennings Randolph Senior Fellow at the United States Institute of Peace in Washington, D.C., where a number of ideas contained in his essay were originally developed.

Kara Paige is an associate professor of sociology and the former coordinator of the Peace and Conflict Studies program at Northwest Vista College in San Antonio, TX. She has lived in Nepal, India, Thailand, and Egypt. Through her international experiences, she developed an interest in looking at the world through the lens of sociology. In an attempt to gather information about the Israeli-Palestinian conflict, she has traveled extensively in the region and has received grants to develop units of study on the subject.

Gregory P. Rabb is professor of political science and coordinator of global education at Jamestown Community College. He is also president of the Jamestown, New York, City Council. He holds a BA in political science from Canisius College, a master's in urban planning from the University of Illinois, and a JD from the State University of New York at Buffalo. In 2011, he received the SUNY Chancellor's Award for Excellence in Teaching.

Michelle Ronayne is currently teaching psychology courses at Southern New Hampshire University, New England College, and Newbury College. She also works at Nova Psychiatric Services in Quincy, Massachusetts. She has a wide range of research interests, with a specific focus on issues such as empowerment, empathy, and power and is currently exploring the role of media in our perceptions of these important issues. She received her BA from Connecticut College and her MA and PhD from Suffolk University in Boston.

Jane Rosecrans is a professor of English at J. Sargeant Reynolds Community College in Richmond, Virginia, where she also teaches courses in religion. She is currently working toward a master's degree in theological studies at Union Presbyterian Seminary. She teaches numerous literature and religion courses and is especially interested in incorporating critical thinking and creativity into all her courses and encouraging citizenship among her students. She has incorporated the study of peace into several courses, including American Literature, Religions in America, and World Religions.

Barbara Thorngren, former chair of the Education Department at Nashua Community College (NH), developed a Peace and Social Justice Studies concentration within the liberal arts degree program. She also developed an international study-abroad course, Peace Education Leadership and Sustainability, at the University for Peace, Costa Rica. In 2010, Thorngren received the President's Good Steward Award, presented by Campus Compact of New Hampshire, for her commitment to service learning and peace education. She holds a BA from Vermont College and an MEd from Antioch New England Graduate School in Keene, New Hampshire.

Tu Van Trieu is a conflict resolution coach with the Justice Institute of British Columbia. She is also a registered professional counselor. She was the founding director of the Mediation and Conflict Resolution Center at Howard Community College in Columbia, Maryland. She has an MS in conflict resolution from Portland State University and a BA in criminology from Simon Fraser University.

Sarah Zale teaches at Shoreline Community College in Seattle. Her publications include "Poetry as Metaphor: A Tool to Shape Social Change," in *Educating for a Civilization of Peace: Proceedings of the 2007 International Education for Peace Conference.* Her travels to Israel and Palestine inspired *The Art of Folding: Poems.* Her work also appears in the anthology *Come Together, Imagine Peace. Sometimes You Do Things: Poems* will be published in March 2013 (Aquarius Press, Living Detroit Series). She has an MEd, an MA in English literature, and an MFA in poetry.

United States Institute of Peace Press

Since its inception, the United States Institute of Peace Press has published over 175 books on the prevention, management, and peaceful resolution of international conflicts—among them such venerable titles as Raymond Cohen's *Negotiating Across Cultures*; John Paul Lederach's *Building Peace*; *Leashing the Dogs of War* by Chester A. Crocker, Fen Osler Hampson, and Pamela Aall; and *The Iran Primer*, edited by Robin Wright. All our books arise from research and fieldwork sponsored by the Institute's many programs, and the Press is committed to extending the reach of the Institute's work by continuing to publish significant and sustainable works for practitioners, scholars, diplomats, and students. In keeping with the best traditions of scholarly publishing, each volume undergoes thorough internal review and blind peer review by external subject experts to ensure that the research and conclusions are balanced, relevant, and sound.

Valerie Norville
Director